Kindergarten Architecture

Mark Dudek

Kindergarten Architecture: Space for the imagination

Second Edition

SPON PRESS
· Taylor & Francis Group ·

This edition published 2000
by Spon Press
11 New Fetter Lane, London EC4P 4EE

Simultaneously published in the USA and Canada
by Spon Press
29 West 35th Street, New York, NY 10001

Spon Press is an imprint of the Taylor & Francis Group
First edition 1996 (Chapman & Hall)

© 2000 Mark Dudek

Typeset in 10/12pt Gill Sans Light by Fox Design, Godalming, Surrey
Printed in Great Britain by Bell & Bain Ltd, Glasgow

British Library Cataloguing in Publication Data
A catalogue record for this book is available from the British Library

Libary of Congress Cataloging in Publication Data

Dudek, Mark,
    Kindergarten architecture / Mark Dudek.--2nd ed.
    p. cm.
    Includes bibliographical referenecs and index.
    ISBN 0-419-24520-(pb)
    1. Kindergarten facilities. 2. Schools--Furniture, equipment, etc. 3.
    Architecture--Designs and plans. I. Title

LB3325 .K5 D83 2000
727'.1--dc21

                                        00-025594

ISBN 0-419-24520-0

Contents

Contents

Foreword

Mark Dudek is an architect committed to the well-being of young children. Drawing on his own experience as a father as well as on his professional work, he has sought to counterbalance what he sees as a prevailing view that children's needs are unnoticed and their voices unheard. The author takes the view that visual discrimination is learnt alongside language and that the understanding of, and pleasure in, the use of shape, colour, texture, light, space and functionality – the ingredients of great architecture – are not acquired by accident. In his judgement, nurseries need to be as well designed as any other building. This is not necessarily an extravagant view. In many countries appropriate high quality buildings for young children have been thus designed, and are fully illustrated and explained in the contemporary case study section of *Kindergarten Architecture*. They show the potential longer term value of well designed nursery schools in the nurturing and development of young children, and in the support of their parents.

This book also charts the attempts made by educationalists and architects over the last 100 years to provide purpose made environments for young children. From the earliest utilitarian examples through to more recent attempts to humanize modernist housing projects by including nursery schools, this far ranging text proves the close affinity between architecture and childhood. Dudek explains particular styles and trends in kindergarten architecture and relates them to changing concepts of childhood, child care and education. At different historical periods educators have held strong views about where young children should be, what kind of education they should be receiving who should be delivering what. In 1900 in the United Kingdom, for instance, half of all the three- and four-year-olds were in some education in regular infant schools serving, in effect, as a care system for much needed factory workers. Opposition to herding of very young children into ordinary classes led to demands for separate and distinctive nursery schools and to Margaret McMillan's open air nurseries.

In the 1950s and 1960s there was a strongly held view that whenever possible young children should be at home with their mothers, leading to a decline in the provision of high quality kindergartens and nursery schools. At the end of the twentieth century the pendulum is now swinging as more women enter the workforce and there are increasing demands for full-time provision. In the United Kingdom and

the United States much of this provision is in the private sector and this has frequently led to an emphasis on cost-effective, functional and sometimes pre-fabricated buildings. Such designs meet health and safety regulations but are repetitive, unadventurous and unambitious. By comparison, in many European countries architects and educators are combining care and education to create nurseries of the highest architectural quality. By providing environments which are uplifting and exciting for young children, they show the importance of young children to the future well-being of society at large.

Peter Mortimore
Director of the Institute of Education
University of London, UK

Peter Blundell-Jones adds...

Some say a poorly designed house can break a marriage, and it is easy enough to imagine the tensions and conflicts resulting from insufficient privacy, or even an insufficient supply of hot water. But after the divorce, how could one prove that the house was to blame and was not merely an incidental factor? There is no sure way of recording everything that happened, and even if one could, there would still be room for a range of interpretations. The parallel question of whether a poorly designed school damages a child's education – or a good one enhances it – is yet more difficult because so many people are involved. Probably more influential than a good building are a committed staff and a sympathetic Head, not to mention the political background and social context of the pupils. Even in the rare case of the same staff and pupils being moved from one building to another, there will be so many other incidental changes that it is impossible to isolate the effects of the building. Also, the features most noticed by the inhabitants will simply be those that have changed most, for good or ill. Building science can provide accurate records of physical parameters such as illumination or temperature, but relating these to people's expectations is difficult. Even defining what constitutes comfort is a thorny problem.

If objective measurement of architectural performance is therefore impossible, reflection on practical experience convinces one that buildings must none the less have a considerable social effect. Perhaps only prisons are directly coercive, but by their organization buildings of all kinds facilitate or frustrate activities. They bring people together or keep them apart, and the identification of institutions with their buildings – house, school, court, kindergarten – is a telling symptom of their role. Buildings provide the spatial framework for institutions, the background order under which they operate. This is usually completely taken for granted by users, who may never reflect that things could be otherwise, but who act in complicity with the building. They do this by carrying around in their heads a mental map of the institution, and this 'mental map', this interpretation of what the order of the building means, meshes with the physical spaces provided. Thus years one to four in a school may be assigned classrooms along a corridor, as a result of which the corridor represents the age hierarchy. The rooms may later be re-assigned, and the meaning of the corridor changes. The point here is that the building does not in itself dictate how people use it; it merely offers them a framework for interpretation. In evaluating a building's success or failure, it is therefore important to consider not only the physical fabric and the intentions of the designer, but also the way it is understood and exploited by users.

While building science has proved a disappointing tool because it focuses too narrowly on the physically quantifiable, architectural criticism in the press is too frequently superficial and ill-informed, being required too fast and given too little space to allow real research. Architectural history, with its greater depth and range, tended until relatively recently to concentrate excessively on forms and styles, neglecting the relation between use and meaning. Nikolaus Pevsner's famous *Outline of European Architecture*, for example, deals mainly with religious buildings but never discusses how Mass was held. In his later years, Pevsner recognized the gap and began to fill it with his *History of Building Types*, which set out to trace the way various institutions crystallized out in building forms, but it is hardly more than a sketch, pointing the way to fields of research some of which remain uncharted even today. We lack systematic comparative histories of many building types from earlier centuries, let alone studies of those evolving today. All solid and well-founded work in this direction is therefore welcome and a book such as this will give direction to many creative architects as well as informing historians.

Peter Blundell-Jones
Professor of Architecture
Sheffield University, UK

Preface and acknowledgements

A civilised society is one which struggles to make the world better for its children.[1]

Stephen Kline

Preface

This project grew out of my conviction of the need for a reappraisal of pre-school care and education facilities, following my own child's experiences in London. As Stephen Kline states, raising children can be a radicalizing experience at the best of times. When an irrevocable breakdown of parental relations occurs at an early stage, the child may be reasonably oblivious to the pain and difficulty of his parents. However, when a father is communicating with his child's mother through the kindergarten teacher, the onus upon the institution to show care of the highest quality is amplified and is of greater significance than might normally be the case.

The various forms of pre-school experiences of Benjamin have been mostly beneficial. It was our good luck that professional individuals gave him shelter during what might otherwise have been a difficult time; for this we will be eternally grateful to all those who helped. However, many children are less fortunate. Even when parents are together, modern lifestyles can be stressful for children, but this can be significantly relieved by good kindergarten provision. Simply to adapt an existing building such as a church hall fails to recognize the rights of young children to their own space, and the need to support and reassure parents in every way possible. Equally, it demeans our view of the role of architecture as a power for good in society.

Acknowledgements

I would like to thank all those who assisted me during the preparation of this text, especially Jean Middleton and her Learning Resources colleagues in the University of Brighton.

I would also like to acknowledge the support and encouragement of Professor Jeremy Till, Head of the School of Architecture, University of Sheffield, where this second edition has been prepared. Thanks to Paul Crawley, Nick Davies and James Galpin who redrew many of the plans, and to all diploma students on the the architecture courses at Sheffield University and Brighton University who provided ideas, inspiration and constructive criticism during the course of this study. Finally, I would like to express my gratitude to Ken Macdonald, whose knowledge, experience and humour were essential throughout.

For assistance during my work 'in the field' I particularly wish to thank Luis Cantallops in Barcelona; Claus Jensen and Anette Riber at the Institute of Political Science, University of Aarhuis, Denmark; Vibeke Bidstrub in Copenhagen, Denmark; Patricia Guedini and Maura Vecchietti in Bologna, Italy; David Lloyd and Elisabeth Mayo in Hertfordshire, England; Klaus Zillich, Thomas Robakowski and Thomas Woolf in Berlin; Monica Bergman of Falun Borlange University College, Sweden; Marjanna Berg at the University of Lund, Sweden; Stephan Emhjellan, Oslo, Norway; Roland Burgard at the Planning Department of the City of Frankfurt, Germany; David Linford in Lucerne, Switzerland; June Sale and Kris Weishaar in Los Angeles, California, USA, and Jane Read of the Early Childhood Collection, Froebel Institute College, Roehampton Institute, London.

For reading parts of the text and offering useful insights I wish to thank Helen Penn at the Department of Education, University of East London; Prof. Hugh Cunningham at Kent University; Prof. Douglas Clelland at the School of Architecture, Liverpool John Moores University; Nora Grainger at the Education Department, University of Brighton; Sue Barker Wolff at the Environmental Design Research Unit, School of Architecture and Interior Design, University of Brighton.

Mark Dudek
London, January 2000

Reference and note

1. Kline, Stephen (1993), *Out of the Garden – Toys and Children's Culture in the Age of TV Marketing*, London and New York, Verso, p. vii.

A note on methodology

Chapter 1 is an attempt to explain the different complex forms of pre-school facilities which are illustrated as architectural precedents. Section 1, 'Definitions', explains the terminology in detail. Section 2, 'Playing within a secure world', gives a generalized picture of this diverse background and explains further the use of the term 'kindergarten' in its widest sense to describe all types of pre-school.

Chapter 2, a historical background, does not try to cover exhaustively all precedents and influences in relation to kindergarten architecture, but rather to show how early radical ideas were demonstrated. As such, it comprises a collection of essays on converging architectural, artistic and educational themes, relating particularly to the debates of the 19th and early 20th centuries.

Chapter 2 includes references to a number of 20th-century educational impulses, but its scope does not cover in great detail the most influential advances in pre-school educational theory, such as the work of Susan Isaacs at her Malting House School, or the research findings of child psychologist Jean Piaget. Their work is well documented and accessible elsewhere.

The case studies and theoretical essays are largely based on first-hand consultations with architects, educationalists and kindergarten teachers over a period of six years up to March 1999. A range of diverse opinions canvassed during this time form the framework for our recommendations, contained particularly in Chapter 1, section 9, on the curriculum and Chapter 4, section 1, on 'Symbolic meanings' within the kindergarten environment. Although they have held their own opinions, those from whom we have taken advice have always been confirmed specialists in this field – educationalists, kindergarten teachers or architects who have designed and built for children. Any quotations not referenced in the notes are from conversations between the author and various experts consulted.

The framework for these consultations has always taken the form of site visits to recommended buildings and facilities, accompanied by the architect or a relevant client representative. Approaching 100 facilities have been visited in many countries, but this is not a controlled research project. Each visit has concentrated on the study of a number of representative facilities, in a single city or region. For example, our trip to California took in the UCLA Child Care Center and the Jardin de Niños la Esperanza, Tijuana, both included as case studies; the Pacific Oaks children's centre, discussed in terms of its art studio, and the Dolores Mission in downtown Los Angeles (which is not featured).

Many other site visits were made to kindergartens which are not referred to in this study. Nevertheless, as with the Dolores Mission, these too have almost invariably contributed valuable insights. We are grateful to all those who spent time showing us round and discussing aspects of pre-school environments. I am aware that many excellent facilities, which should rightly have been included, may have been overlooked. Nevertheless, I hope that the 'state of the art' kindergartens and nursery schools illustrated here help to guide and inspire future designers.

Although I may appear critical in part about the support given by educationalists in the furtherance of *architecture* for pre-school children, particularly in my perceptions of a separation between the two disciplines, I am nevertheless in awe of the depth of much research work that has been carried out over the past 25 years into many aspects of the history and contemporary needs of pre-school children. I am painfully aware of the scholastic 'minefield' into which I am now dipping a tentative, but well-intentioned, toe.

This, then, is a study that attempts to combine aspects of pre-school educational theory with complementary architectural responses. Inevitably, any architect–critic tends to interlace his or her own intrinsic values and delusions. This work is no exception, as the author's own attitudes and personal experiences contribute to the form and content of the ideas discussed. However, an attempt has been made to present the diverse approaches to kindergarten architecture in a balanced way. Clearly, the philosophies that have informed both the architectural and educational agenda in relation to children's architecture in the 20th century are open to interpretation. The architecture of the kindergarten is uneven and incomplete; it cannot be approached either from a purely sociological or a psychological viewpoint. To discuss kindergartens exclusively on the level of architectural style would be equally meaningless. It will become clear that, despite the international nature of kindergarten developments, in this study the British viewpoint is the predominant concern.

Introduction

The kindergarten has been in existence as a recognized institution for over a century. However, it has been identified only relatively recently as a distinct architectural type.[1] Its gestation can be traced from the original idealistic educational theories of the 18th and 19th centuries to the present sophisticated architectural and educational synthesis seen in many of the best contemporary examples. One is tempted therefore to carry out research in the hope that there is an intimate relationship between the theory and philosophy of pre-school education and its manifestation in built form.

However, research studies relating the quality of early childhood education to the physical environment are inconclusive, tending to concentrate on largely utilitarian aspects such as space standards or functional layouts. Educationalists frequently make reference to the environment and its importance to pre-school educational curricula, but seldom touch upon the architectural agenda in any significant detail. There are very few studies which relate spatial quality to the educational curricula and the more precise needs of young children in relation to their surroundings.[2]

When assessing many of the built or adapted examples of pre-school facilities it is evident that the architects and educationalists involved in these projects have failed to communicate regarding certain fundamental issues. Frequently, there has been an inadequate match between the design process and the imaginative spatial needs of the young child. Of equal concern is the failure of the architect to comprehend and work with the pre-school educational curricula where appropriate. These concerns, together with the increasing social importance of the kindergarten, have been the catalyst for this study.

While the social nature of kindergarten architecture ties it inextricably into pedagogic theories, this study is primarily an architectural enquiry. The premise we make is that the needs and requirements of babies and children up to the age of six or at most seven are particular; their right (as individuals) to high-quality educational environments that care for them and rigorously support their social development is as crucial in the modern world as is the provision of specific buildings for any section of the population, whether banks, churches, theatres or houses.[3] We accept that this is by no means a broadly agreed view. In Chapter 1 we will therefore set out some of the most important socio-cultural arguments which are informing the contemporary debate.

Through a combination of historical and contemporary analyses, we will explore a diverse range of approaches to the design of kindergartens assessed on the basis of practical and theoretical criteria. We explain simply the educational roots that support various types of kindergarten architecture today, and illustrate their use through a series of case studies of selected buildings which are representative of a particular architectural approach. In addition, each of the case studies has some aspect of what we would describe as 'a pedagogical convergence', where the architecture goes some way towards meeting the educational and social needs of the children. This, we believe, is a significant and defining aspect of kindergarten architecture. We explore other related aspects, including appropriate theoretical strategies adopted in the design of some of the best contemporary examples.

Statutory child care regulations and existing technical guides, usually compiled by experienced educationalists rather than architects, provide precise (often minimal) space and programmatic standards for designers. These tend to share common roots and principles across national boundaries; they are summarized at the beginning of Chapter 4. It would be inappropriate for us to attempt a single prescribed definition for the design of kindergartens, given different national, regional and local conditions. Therefore we do not set out to produce a 'design guide', but rather illustrate and explore the practical and aesthetic concerns of those architects and nursery school leaders who have, in our view, gone some way towards the design of 'high-quality' educational environments for young children.

Our criteria for the selection of the key examples to be discussed and illustrated in detail will include not just architectural quality per se; it will also take into account those examples that have advanced interior qualities, that are technically or ecologically experimental, or that are overtly economical within this overall framework of excellence. We feature predominantly contemporary examples, designed over the last ten years. Some older kindergarten buildings are included on the basis of their continuing relevance to the debate. We do not feature projects from developing countries or those from the former eastern European bloc.[4] The issues we explore relate particularly to the post-industrial societies of the west and the specific socio-economic pressures which have brought about the need for a reevaluation of the kindergarten as a significant urban institution.

This publication does not set out to deal with landscaping strategies relating to nursery schools, important though we believe these to be; external space is discussed only as an integral part of the kindergarten environment. Nor do we enquire in any detail into children's parks, gardens or adventure playgrounds, crèches or other part-time children's care facilities (although a few pertinent examples will be included). We concentrate mainly on kindergartens, nursery schools and child care centres and the pedagogic systems which, when successfully integrated, create an authentic architecture for pre-school care and education. This, in our view, can be the only form of positive and lasting benefit to children, staff, parents and the wider community.

Partly by way of validation, we look at some of the broader cultural aspects of childhood and architecture. In the development of the most influential architectural theories of the 20th century, the effect of kindergartens on those who attended them, particularly in the early part of the century, will be explored. Froebel (1782–1852), the educational pioneer who invented the term 'kindergarten', was initially trained as an architect. Therefore we will include a section on the important historical relationship between architecture and the kindergarten movement. There is an almost mystical connection between pre-school experiences and architectural theory, which we will attempt to disentangle. The transforming effects of the kindergarten and related educational reforms will be explored both through their influence on some of those who attended, and through their cultural role reflecting profound changes in society.

Coherent pre-school educational systems have developed broadly in Japan and most European countries over the past 30 years, bringing very many good nursery school buildings and a number of excellent 'state of the art' examples. Over the last decade, Frankfurt has completed a programme of 32 children's day care centres throughout the city, conceived with architectural quality as a priority (with architects rather than educationalists dictating the environmental priorities). Similar high-quality kindergarten buildings have been completed or are currently under way in Berlin, Barcelona, Copenhagen and Bologna.

This quality has not emerged in Britain and the USA to the same degree. For a number of reasons, the UK and USA preschool systems have tended to blur and confuse the original kindergarten ideal. This has brought about an incoherent range of pre-school care/education buildings, which vary in scope from two-hour play-groups held in church halls to full-day nurseries run by welfare or social services departments. Some private day care centres run on educational lines are of an architecturally high quality.[5] As we write, the UK government's Early Excellence Centre initiative is beginning, with some significant investment in capital works planned. However, the view that children do not require decent architecture remains the prevailing view.

Functional issues are of profound importance, particularly in relation to safety and security. However, in our view, it is not enough merely to adopt prescribed technical standards and then expect an authentic kindergarten architecture to emerge. The case studies illustrated in the final section of this volume have been selected with an emphasis on what we believe are the highest contemporary architectural values. These are international in scope, pluralistic and responsive to a broad range of cultural influences. Invariably, they incorporate aspects of the 'pedagogical convergence' already mentioned. Most importantly, they disclose the imaginative potential open to architects and educationalists, when planning, designing and creating buildings for young children.

References and notes

1. 'The word "typology" means the study of types; it is concerned with those aspects of human production that can be grouped because of some inherent characteristics which make them similar. The theory of typology is thus that of conceptualizing those categories.' Bandini, M. (1994), 'Typological Theories in Architectural Design', in Farmer and Louw (eds), *Companion to Contemporary Architectural Though*t, London, Routledge, p. 387.

2. Moss, P. (1993), 'Environment', *Quality in Services for Young Children – A Discussion Paper*, European Commission Child Care Network, Thomas Coram Research Unit, 27–28 Woburn Square, London WC1H 0AA, p. 11. Educationalist Marjanna de Jong of the Malmö School of Education, Lund University, in conversation with the author, made the point that, despite a great concern with environment and settings for pre-school, educationalists tended not to engage architects in their debates. In her paper at the Fourth European Con-

ference on the Quality of Early Childhood Education, Gothenburg, Sweden, 13 September 1994, 'Settings in Interaction: Research and Implications', de Jong uses 'space syntax analysis' in a study of five Swedish day care centres. This pseudoscientific invention uses a checklist of attributes such as the functional proximity of rooms as the only indication of quality in the environment. De Jong also refers to other Swedish studies by Kärrby (1992), Lidholm and Lidholt (1992) and international research by Laevers (1994) and Pascal and Bertram (1991).

3. The functional, spatial and psychological needs of babies and young children are very different.

4. An exception is James Hubbell's Jardin de Niños la Esperanza in Tijuana on the US/Mexican border. This could be considered to be located in a developing country, but we justify its inclusion on the grounds that it was funded and designed by individuals and groups from the USA, and its curriculum is well established and coherent.

5. The distinction between care and education should be borne in mind when comparing individual projects from different countries. This area is analyzed in more detail in Chapter 1, particularly in relation to the current condition of a British debate that is considering how best to catch up with most of the rest of Europe in pre-school child education facilities.

The Japanese nursery school system is supported by a mixed range of state, religious and privately funded facilities which provide pre-school kindergartens for 85% of children over the age of three. The competitiveness of Japanese society is renowned, and kindergarten is considered an important first step on the social ladder, providing lifelong advantages to children who attend. Approximately 25% of pre-school facilities are state-maintained. Private kindergartens charge fees of up to one-third of the parents' income; the remainder is made up of government subsidies and funding from endowments and loans. Since space is at a premium, standards allow only 1.98m² per child as interior space and 3.3m² as external space. The schools themselves are characterized by highly organized planning which makes optimum use of this minimal space.

In the USA, kindergartens are usually pre-school classes associated with the main school. There are so-called 'nursery schools', which are privately run, often funded by corporations and located close to the parents' workplace. Other part-time 'play group' facilities fill in some of the gaps. Community day care centres offer full-time care for the children of working mothers for a small fee; these are funded by central government or through charitable or religious trusts. The facilities are licensed and controlled at state level, and must provide 35ft² (3.25m²) per child as interior space (not including ancillary space such as storage and washrooms) and 75ft² (6.97m²) per child as external play space. Child development centres support children from poor communities and are organized under the well-known Head Start pre-school programme. Briefly, this is a long-term initiative which seeks to engage the whole community in the life of the institution. It is considered to include both child and parents in educare, and parents offer time within the projects as part of their financial commitment.[3] In 1992 President Bush called a conference on a vision for the future of child care and drew attention to a report written by Ernest Boyer which called for spending on Head Start to be increased from $2 billion to $8 billion by 1995. Head Start funding has since increased by 46% to almost $4 billion in 1994.[4]

In France, state-run nursery schools are usually called écoles maternelles, while privately run nursery schools are known as jardins d'enfants. The state sector, which has grown gradually during a 90-year history, now serves over 95% of children aged three to five. Local authorities are required by law to provide pre-primary education if it is requested. France also operates other day care provision, such as crèches collectives which cater for under threes, and some centres de petit enfance (children's centres) which deliver combined age-integrated services. The term 'crèche' is widely used internationally, either as a term to describe baby care, or to denote a part-time care facility (usually attached to a place of work or leisure such as a shopping centre) where children are cared for, for periods of less than two hours.[5]

Spain's Educational Reform Law of 1990 was established in response to the 'existence of strong social pressure to create nursery and infants' schools'.[6] The law recognized the state's responsibility in this area: it is currently exploring the possibility of providing this service free of charge. While still under way, the implementation of pre-school education for all children from three to five (and for 15% of under threes) will become a reality in the next five years, on a non-compulsory basis.[7] The structure of the Spanish system is broadly in three parts: babies have their own centres attached to, but physically separate from, the kindergarten; the 'kindergarten' caters for the two- and three-year-olds, and the infants' school for four- and five-year-olds.

In Italy, pre-school education is provided in both public and private nursery schools. Since the creation of the *Scuola Materna Statale* in 1969, attendance has risen steadily; at present 90% of children aged three to five attend full-time, sometimes six days per week. Although quality varies from region to region, there are examples of advanced nursery school provision, centrally funded but regionally administered. For example, in the Emilia Romagna region, the Communist Party has been in democratic government for many years. Patrizia Guedini, Director of Child Care Services in the region, believes that it attracts a large number of women's votes, and that its regime has brought about a 'culture of emancipation'. Partnerships between public and private companies maintain a good standard of living for the region's 4 million people. Emilia Romagna supports a high proportion of working women, with 95% of pre-school children in some form of 'educare'.

The most common form of pre-school care is the nursery or children's school, which caters for children from three to six. These are usually run by the regions, although some facilities are privately maintained by religious groups. The day nursery (*asol-ida*) for babies up to the age of three are always run by the municipality, although some are managed by cooperatives. Few very small babies attend since maternal leave is available in varying forms for a year after the baby's birth. However, an integrated range of play or 'drop-in' centres (*stregatti*) which cater for children up to six ensures that young mothers can have some free time and maintain social links; they require a parent or carer to be in attendance at all times. It is important to note that the Italian term for 'classroom', which would never be used in the context of pre-school, does not readily translate; however, *sezione* implies a dual function, combining security with activity and exploration. We will generally use the term 'activity area' when referring to the class base.

The constitution to protect young children has been national law in Italy since 1973. However, its general principles are more precisely defined by the regional administrators and the system is regularly updated as a result. Emilia Romagna is, for example, in the process of updating its current 18 articles of regulations, to reflect more clearly the needs of the new millemium. One particularly important aspect of this 'child's constitution' is the requirement that all new facilities are developed by a multidisciplinary group comprising local councillors, architects and pedagogic experts. Interestingly, the stipulated area for new buildings – originally specified as 2400m^2 for facilities for 41 to 60, and 1800m^2 for 25–40 – is now being reduced, to reflect more financially straitened circumstances. However, the revised recommendations for space per child are still high, giving 7. 5m^2 per child for three- to six-year-olds and 10m^2 for the under threes. These areas are still generous when compared to Denmark (2m^2 per child absolute minimum) and Britain (2.3m^2).[8]

Due perhaps to its German derivation and the somewhat mystical, Froebelian connotations of the term, 'kindergarten' is used less frequently in Britain and then usually in the context of Waldorf schools (except in Scotland where it is in general use). In England, due to the confusing state of early years provision, terminological inexactitude by unknowing architects can be a source of considerable concern to educationalists.[9] Social services provision, so-called day nurseries for under-privileged children, and nursery schools essentially run by local authority education departments formed the basis of the system up to the election of a new reforming Labour government in 1997. These state-funded institutions were supplemented by a perplexing range of alternative provisions which dealt with the care (but not necessarily the education) of groups of pre-school children. These ranged from pre-school play groups held in church halls or often at the homes of child minders, to private nurseries, and reception classes in existing infants' schools for the so-called 'rising fours'. The imperfect nature of the British system was succinctly and evocatively described by Helen Penn:

> We have a crazy system which offers 25% of children nursery education in shifts, shoves four-year-olds into school before they can cope with it, segregates depressed and forlorn children into a different and temporary system in social services . . . and considers children of working parents best catered for in the private pay-as-(or if)-you-earn sector.[10]

While British politicians explained this in a positive light, by describing it as various and diverse, Penn concluded that this was far from a provision of choice, but in fact one which was 'very nearly pointless'. It has frequently been pointed out that the British government encouraged crèches and nursery schools during the war when women were needed to work in factories;[11] it was perhaps no coincidence that at a time when unemployment was high, during the 1980s, the availability of public nursery school places fell sharply. The virtues of a close family life were accentuated and mothers were urged to stay at home and look after their children. Similarly, the post-war ideas of William Beveridge created a social welfare system which positively benefited the homemaker–breadwinner family model. Thus the liberal British political system supported what Anette Borchorst describes as 'political motherhood'.[12]

In Britain during the Cold War period the political climate favoured less state intervention in family life, so that when the Plowden Report was published in 1967 only 7% of all children under five in England were receiving some form of education in a nursery school or class. Despite Margaret Thatcher's pledge to expand nursery education massively when she was Education Minister in 1972, 'political motherhood' became even more entrenched throughout her years as Prime Minister. However, in Sweden there was a massive explosion in nursery school provision during the 1970s, when manufacturing industry was expanding, causing labour shortages. In some quarters it was anticipated that, as the UK skills shortage bit towards the end of the 1990s, the government would once again recognize the economic value of pre-school care and education.[13]

Sure enough, as the British economy massively expands in the south of England, all sorts of new initiatives are developing in both the public and the private sectors to enhance provision for working parents. For example, all local authorities are now required by central government to produce an early years development plan, with precise information about existing and proposed facilities. Competitive bids from local authorities have been required for the limited number of new Early Excellence Centres, which are intended to act as paradigms to which other day care centres in the region will relate. The Sure Start initiative directed towards existing communities in deprived areas will benefit from £250 million of new capital funding. Private operators such as Jigsaw and Kids Unlimited have established chains of new day care centres usually located at corporate headquarters sites.

However, as we write, the debate as to the form and quality of a more integrated, better quality system is just beginning.[14] For social and political reasons, one must sound a warning note as the preferred approach would appear to be based purely on economic criteria. For example, rather than supporting a fully fledged nursery school programme comprising special kindergarten buildings for three- to five-year-olds (which could be built over a number of years), the strategy which is more likely to be adopted is to create 'nursery units'. These would be housed predominantly in adapted classrooms in existing primary schools, aimed at the three- to five-year-old population.

One of the distinctions between Britain and the USA, and most of the rest of Europe, is the compulsory school starting age of five. To provide places for four-year-olds in inadequate and inappropriate environments may satisfy politicians who wish to play the numbers game. In our view, this strategy will merely reinforce the inadequacies of the existing system. 'High quality' must be the objective in how the services are delivered and be integral to the environments within which these services take place. We believe fundamentally in the need for a state-funded full-time system of optional nursery school education, delivered in purpose-designed buildings.

By comparison to Britain, the system currently in Denmark is both coherent and diverse, having developed from a fundamental sympathy and understanding of liberal, cooperative socialism. Crèches provide full-day care for babies up to three. Public kindergartens provide care with informal educational activities for children from three to six, when compulsory school commences. New age-integrated institutions are also being developed which attempt to cater for the needs of children from birth up to 14, but these are relatively few in number. There are also age-integrated nursery schools for children up to six. In addition, there are so-called *fritid shjem* or centres for school-age children, which are often part of the kindergarten itself. These cater for the needs of schoolchildren in an elementary school system which terminates at 1pm or 2pm, a common model throughout much of Europe.

Although there are some private kindergartens in Denmark, 65% of children attend state-funded crèches and 76% of the three-year-old population attend publicly funded institutions. By comparison, in Britain only 41% of three-year-olds attend institutions, which are almost totally of a part-time nature.[15] In Denmark as in the UK, it is important to stress that attendance is optional, depending on the parents' circumstances, and that parents must contribute something to the cost. Denmark spends approximately £1.1 billion per year on child care, with a population of 5 million.

There are important differences between the essential nature of the Scandinavian pre-school systems, and the Anglo-French–American model, which is rooted in a more educational philosophy. When Danish educationalists refer to the term 'social pedagogy' (loosely translated), they are not alluding to a political idea as such; in this context, the term 'social' refers to the primary goal of the kindergarten which is to introduce the child to social interaction, particularly with other children, and to recognize that the child has rights which must be respected. 'Education', as distinct from socialization, is perceived in Denmark as something aimed at older children, above compulsory school age. It is clear, therefore, that the practical way in which Scandinavian thinking can be realized is to allow children to construct their own activity patterns and games, rather than having adults dictate to them. Adults may be catalysts to activity but, beyond that, are merely role models and enablers. Therefore the Danes do not refer to 'nursery school teachers', but 'pedagogues'.

Generally we identify two types of pre-school kindergarten system, the British–American model, and the Scandinavian–European model.[16] The Japanese system is largely funded by private corporations, and is an integral part of the economic success of Japan,

1.3

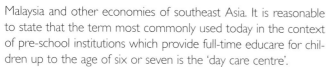

1.3 The 'wilderness': the gardens at Pacific Oaks Children's School, Pasadena, California.

Malaysia and other economies of southeast Asia. It is reasonable to state that the term most commonly used today in the context of pre-school institutions which provide full-time educare for children up to the age of six or seven is the 'day care centre'.

Children's day care centres hold at their core an essential concern for the family, and often have rooms or spaces which can be used by parent groups in the evenings. Although parents do not become involved with teaching, the more advanced systems recognize the need to be relaxed about young children having contact with their parents during the long days. This freedom of movement is encouraged when related facilities such as family centres and clinics are included on the same site, to form a related group of functions. For example, the recently completed Frankfurt programme of children's day care centres (Kindertagesstäte, or 'Kita', for short) includes afternoon study spaces for older children, in addition to the kindergarten accommodation. The Makoto kindergarten at MuRo Machi in Japan includes a chapel within such a framework. Additional activities that complement the basic childcare function can create a more significant focus for the local community.

In the context of this publication, the terms kindergarten, nursery school and 'pre-school institution' are used to define a great range of differing child care buildings which cater for the physical, social and emotional needs of pre-school children. These environments should have a liberal approach to pre-school education, stressing the importance of learning through play as opposed to formal education. However learning or education, as opposed to straightforward care devoid of pedagogic intentions, is the key defining aspect of the contemporary kindergarten.

1.2 Playing within a secure world

Do young children have basic needs which can - and should - be fulfilled through design and architecture? For some psychologists the essence of childhood is playfulness and exploration, but these must take place in a secure setting. The contradictions inherent in a child's being secure and yet free to be adventurous were neatly summed up by the American psychoanalyst Bruno Bettelheim when he stated that 'the child's environment has to be organized in such a way that it not only transmits to him, on both a conscious and unconscious level, the assurance

of being secure there and now, but it also has to transmit to him the sensation that venturing into the outside world does not constitute a risk, whilst the future, though difficult, holds success in store for him and not failure.'[17]

Playful self-direction and exploration are not expected from children in formal education where instructional methods often prevail, and children are viewed more as passive recipients of knowledge than as active constructors of their own learning. What distinguishes the kindergarten school environment from that of the first or primary school is the idea – vividly articulated by Rousseau and inspiring generations of educationalists thereafter – of a young child as a unique individual with few if any social preconceptions. If the mainstream educational system could, and still can, be characterized by large teaching groups and conformity – educational factories, so to speak – nursery schools have long aimed to develop the natural, innocent 'free spirit' of the child.

Although these ideas have evolved over the years, and pedagogy has been through many shifts of view – from the semi-mysticism of Froebel, the pragmatism of Margaret McMillan, the behaviourism of Watson and Skinner, the epistemology of Piaget, and the current 'scaffolding' theories post-Vygotsky – the essential distinction remains. In nursery education, young children are granted a freedom of being and expression which does not exist elsewhere in the education system.

It is the challenge of the nursery school architect to 'celebrate' early childhood by creating safe, reassuring and stimulating play environments: 'if a child is not allowed to be a child he will remain a child'.[18] The contemporary kindergarten designer should get used to the contradictions and confrontations which are implicit in these statements and, in some respects, central to an understanding of children's architecture.

In the UK the earliest nursery was that of Robert Owen in New Lanark, founded in 1816. Owen certainly saw children as vital innocents: 'children, if left to their own impulses, fill the air with perpetual questionings. Every new thing being a mystery to them . . . rational children should not be stinted, rebuked, dispirited . . . [but allowed to develop] a continuous elastic spirit, ever enquiring, and ever extending to others the fulness of its own aspirations'.[19] His nursery, amazingly innovative in his factory workplace, was light and airy, with a small gallery where musicians could sit and play to the children, so that they could sing and dance.

Margaret McMillan, one of the pioneers of nursery education in the UK, argued that young children, particularly those from the slums where she worked, needed outside space above all to liberate them from their cramped, depressing environment. Her nursery took the form of a rudimentary building with a garden, within which young children could move and play freely, engage in individual or group play activities, and learn to appreciate the beauty of nature otherwise denied to them. Her view that children growing up in the chaotic conditions of the newly industrialized cities were emotionally fragile, physically impoverished and badly needed a compensatory environment, was widely shared. This was a strong thread in discussions about early kindergarten design during the 19th century.

This indoor – outdoor dimension became a theme in kindergarten design. The belief was that children would feel secure within the safety of their own semi-private space inside the building, whereas the garden representing the 'wilderness' would enable them to free themselves when feeling more adventurous. Early kindergarten theorists, such as Robert Owen, Froebel and Montessori, recognized how much children learned from direct experience. (Robert Owen's kindergarten teacher was even authorized to buy a small crocodile to illustrate some fundamental principles about handling live objects, and to engage children directly with the animal world.) The realization that young children perceive real objects as opposed to reasoned ideas, that they grasp by experience how to catch a ball as opposed to 'being taught in the classroom the second order differential equation of the angle of gaze $(d^2 \tan \alpha)$' was a fundamental truth from the outset.[20] This was understood by the earliest educational theorists; Froebel and Montessori developed special toys to encourage pre-reasoning perceptions.

John Dewey attempted to cast these ideas in a more sophisticated form when he published *Democracy and Education* in 1915. He engagingly defines the unique way in which children conduct themselves during pre-school education when he states:

Before the child goes to school, he learns with his hand, eye, and ear, because they are organs of the process of doing something from which meaning results. The boy flying a kite has to keep his eye on the kite, and has to note the various pressures of the string on his hand. His senses are avenues of knowledge not because external facts are somehow 'conveyed' to the brain, but because they are used in doing something with a purpose.[21]

Whereas adults control the world largely through verbal and written communication, children do not have the verbal skills to express themselves. They need to explore and test a variety of means of self-expression – physical, emotional and aesthetic. Children learn to interpret and draw out meanings from the people and places around them; they learn through bodily experiences and sensations, as well as trying to make sense of words and emotional currents.

The context or the environment within which this learning takes place, and the way in which adults structure and define it for children, acts as a 'scaffold' or framework on which children build their own theory of time and space. An environment of sensual variety with texture, sound, light and colour which challenged and inspired children, rich enough to provide cosy quiet spaces for withdrawal and security, as well as more open communal and social places for group activities; and an exciting outdoor space, for freedom of movement and physical daring – all these were regarded as fulfilling the needs of children in a kindergarten setting. The qualities of the seen, touched and experienced were considered to be the main conduits of learning for the pre-school child. They still are, although romantic ideas about the innocent awakening of children in a kindergarten setting have given way to much more complex theories about their learning and development.

There is an ongoing debate – discussed in the subsequent pages – regarding what age children should attend kindergartens, how long for and what they should do in them. Undoubtedly briefs have been sharpened: in today's kindergartens the functional programme is specific and usually set out in statutory planning guides. Class-based activity areas for groups of between 14 and 25 children form the main focus; toilet and washing facilities, storage, cloakroom areas, and an external play space are complementary requirements. The size of the buildings which respect the original kindergarten ideals can vary from 14-place facilities to large and complex 'children's centres' comprising a diverse range of facilities for as many as 150 to 200 children up to the age of six or seven.[22]

Space standards are usually defined by local or regional educational or welfare authorities, and vary hugely between coun-

1.4 Peter Wilson's Blackburn House, London (1990): the step detail.

tries. Having more space is preferable, but architects can produce a satisfactory environment within the framework of lower space standards. The success of any kindergarten generally depends upon the way in which space is divided up and the form in which it is then offered to the children. We will explore the implications of this in more detail in Chapter 4, particularly the value of adding purpose-made spaces such as art studios.

Beyond functional criteria, kindergarten architecture relates to a complex set of practical and psychological needs. It should support and be reflective of the diverse range of spatial experiences which might appeal to the playful enquiry of a young child, and maximize children's creative potential. It must also aim to encourage the child's awareness of a social world. The needs of the adults who care for and teach the children should not be overlooked because their views of the kindergarten environment and satisfaction with it in turn influence those of the children. Architecturally it is not easy to rationalize a building type which is multifunctional and from which teachers and children need and expect a great deal. The best kindergartens synthesize faultless functional criteria with an almost mystical sense of wonder for the children using them.

1.3 An architecture for the imagination

While visiting kindergartens throughout the world and speaking to many teachers during the course of this research, I heard frequent complaints about the fitness of the architecture, even in the case of recently designed buildings. Architects and those who work in kindergartens do not always see eye to eye. Teachers often complain that, in practice, their buildings do not reflect clearly enough the very particular needs of young children in an authentic learning environment.

This suggests that the dovetailing between the building and the educational programme should be carefully thought out. Not only should the general atmosphere of a building for young children be spatially and functionally reassuring, but the architecture should go a long way towards the practical support of a planned programme of daily activities. It can also be seen as having therapeutic or educative qualities in the precise way in which it is designed. For example, one of the defining criteria set out by the city of Frankfurt for its programme of recently completed children's day care centres was for the quality of the architecture to

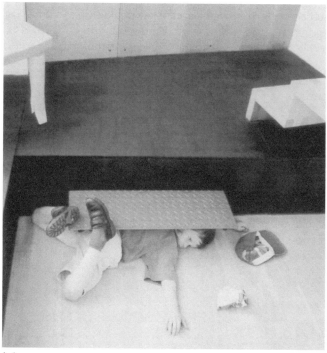

1.4

be directed towards the needs of the children: 'The structural space should support the children in their social learning as well as in their sensory learning. By adapting the premises to the powers of sensory perception, a sense of spatial awareness should be transmitted . . . the contemporary kindergarten architect risks taking up the challenge of play. His spatial play should harmonise with the children's play.'[23]

Implicit in this enlightened statement is the challenge for the architect not just to design functionally appropriate spaces to support the children's activities, but also to engage their imaginative powers in a radical way – to put themselves into the state of mind of their clients (the children) and come to terms with their potential for fantasy and play.

When Swiss child psychologist Jean Piaget described the age up to six years as a period of intuitive learning, he identified the challenge not just to consider practical issues but to shed preconceptions and enter the illusory or dream-like state of childhood. Although many child developmentalists have subsequently challenged Piaget's view of the child as a dreaming egocentric, it is nevertheless a powerful image.[24] For some architects, it seems that this challenge is not difficult. Peter Wilson, who codesigned one of the Frankfurt 'Kita' projects, states: 'my own thinking is sometimes quite naive, so one relates quite well to children'.[25]

Indeed, child-like perceptions have held a particular fascination for artists, architects and designers throughout the 20th century. In the work of creative pioneers such as Paul Klee and Frank Lloyd Wright, there appears to be a fundamental link between childhood and the impulse to 'create' on a number of different levels. Being able to recall the images and intensities of childhood may be important in understanding an appropriate architecture for children. Many influential architects, particularly during the 1930s and 1940s, designed kindergartens or incorporated children's spaces into their projects. Erno Goldfinger Maxwell Fry, Leslie Martin and Le Corbusier showed how a radical approach to children's space could provide an important focus for their own wider architectural preoccupations.

Why have some architects found designing for children so creatively fulfilling? Perhaps the most important factor is the profound significance that the first learning experience can have on individual creative development. Many writers claim that the experiences and images of early childhood are the most deeply scored and enduring.

One of the characteristics of contemporary industrialized society is a fragmented family life, and a focus on the post-nuclear family. This concept is vividly described by Ulrich Beck, when he talks of children as the focus of stability, the 'port in the storm' which the stresses of life sometimes call out for:

Doting on children, pushing them on to the centre of the stage – the poor over-pampered creatures – and fighting for custody during and after divorce are all symptoms of this. The child becomes the final alternative to loneliness, a bastion against the vanishing chances of loving and being loved. It is a private way of 'putting the magic back' into life to make up for general disenchantment. The birth rate may be declining but children have never been more important.[26]

Where the extended family has disappeared, kindergarten is usually the child's first experience away from home and from the familiarity and attachment to mothers or other primary carers. Arnold Gesell stated in 1923 that because kindergarten is likely to be the first experience outside the home, its influence will be a powerful one: 'coming first in a dynamic sequence, it inevitably influences all subsequent development. These years determine character much as the foundation and frame determine a structure'.[27] While Gesell is probably overstating the case, the kindergarten is nevertheless a context for initiation into more complex social relationships with both adults and peers.

The affinity that designers may have with their own childhood, echoed in bringing up their own children (which makes almost every parent a concerned expert), is of particular relevance to architects who are parents and who may have to leave their children in inadequate environments. This relationship between architectural practice and parenthood is illustrated on a practical level, when Peter Wilson talks about the step detail in one of his early projects (his own London apartment repeated in his Frankfurt kindergarten project). Here, he is responding directly to the experience of preventing his own three-year-old from climbing the stairs and falling. Thus, in a single architectural gesture, Wilson resolves a functional problem and at the same time celebrates his own paternal feelings. Is this the ultimate architecture of the imagination?[28]

Frank Lloyd Wright had a more cerebral view of the significance of his pre-school experiences, and kindergarten education in general. Froebel, the important 19th-century educational theorist, believed that a child should not be allowed to draw from nature until he or she had mastered rudimentary forms and elements, which he identified as the square, the circle and the triangle. Wright felt that Froebel's thinking had a fundamental effect on the physical embodiment of his own architecture:

Here is the square – symbol of integrity, the triangle – symbol of aspiration, the sphere or the circle - infinity: all forms in one dimension, the flat dimension. Then the forms go into the third dimension. Out of the circle you get the sphere; out of the square you get the cube; out of the triangle comes the tetrahedron. Well, that significance is merely a little indication of their importance in creation. We haven't time to talk much about this thing, but I've touched upon it to show how the elemental basis of thought in creative architecture goes back to these primary things, primarily. As a result, when I learned these things thoroughly, I didn't care to draw from nature, or to boondoggle with the surface effects of anything at all. I wanted to combine, construct, to build, to create with these simple elements, and I believe that's where creation must begin in education.[29]

The obvious similarity between the primary forms used in Froebel's pre-school structured play system ('the gifts', see Chapter 2, section 4) and much of Frank Lloyd Wright's architecture illustrates the importance of kindergarten play in the architect's development. Not only was his rejection of the 'imitation of nature' as a valid architectural tool a principle learned largely in kindergarten play, it was also a conscious rejection of the arts and crafts tradition. It helped to bridge the gap between De Stijl and the Bauhaus in the development of abstraction. In the light of this statement it is perhaps paradoxical that one of the most distinctive aspects of kindergarten architecture (when viewed as a 20th-century building typology) is its almost unique sustenance of a mystical organic tradition which continued to develop as a significant architectural impulse alongside radical modernist forms. Indeed, this philosophical dialogue between radical modernism and organic spirituality remains at the centre of the contemporary debate.

Common to both the organic and the modernist tendency in kindergarten architecture is the notion of creativity, imagination and fantasy. These are ideas inextricably linked to early childhood and are largely at odds with conventional views of education. The world of the child after the age of six, after pre-school, seems to place its emphasis on logic, reason and the need for discipline. Scientific certainty, stressed above artistic or spiritual values, exemplified by the philosophy of logical positivism, is at the heart of school education, replacing the spirit of freedom and naturalism so close to the heart of the kindergarten idea.[30] It is the sense that designing a kindergarten is a philosophy of the imagination which makes this building type so intriguing to the contemporary designer.

Valid contemporary approaches to the design of architecture for children are no longer sustainable by the simple technofunctionalist approach common to many of the kindergartens built in the 'first major wave' of nursery schools during the 1960s and 1970s. The perception of the kindergarten as a sort of 'hospital' with toys' is no longer valid, and much recent work by kinder-garten architects and designers shows the possibility of an architecture which is a reflection of the enigmatic notion of education through play. As Peter Davey points out, the best contemporary kindergartens 'show how the principles of Modernism can be enriched by a deeper understanding of the real needs of users, and how a humane hierarchy of spaces can be evolved which encourages the immensely subtle and complex process of education'.[31]

Architecture with any humane purpose cannot be approached from a solely utilitarian stance. While practical issues such as safety, ergonomics (the small child sees the world at a different scale to the adult) and optimum levels of light, space and air are important and will be discussed at some length, notions of childhood and how best children flourish are of equal importance. Architects feel a keen responsibility to create appropriate environments which will support and nurture young children in a holistic way. The kindergarten should be structured as a total environment, much in the way an adventure playground appeals to the fantasy of the child as well as serving the more practical aspects of physical play.

Throughout Europe, and especially in Germany, Spain and Japan, high priority is put on pre-school education and care. The requirement to provide a nursery place for every child is a statutory one. In Germany, it is now every child's democratic right to have a kindergarten place. It is possible to see superb purpose-designed kindergartens or day care centres which relate directly to the needs of small children. Imaginative details such as sheltered gardens, low level windows, integrated wet play areas – in short, an architecture which specifically supports a play-based education – are becoming increasingly common. The fully developed kindergarten environment considers detail design to be as important as the so-called 'space standards' – the limited and limiting criteria which inform design in regulatory legislation such as the UK Children Act.

Peter Moss of the Thomas Coram Research Unit, Institute of Education at London University, believes that children are not just embryonic adults, but people in their own right: 'it is therefore axiomatic that particular age groups have specific needs in relation to their environments which are not just based on square footage criteria'.[2] The need to form architectural space which is not just functional but supports young children's learning, and their sense of psychological well-being, and develops their spatial and bodily awareness, is fundamental.

Is this view about the contribution of architecture and design to kindergarten environments widely shared by educationalists and architects? In Italy, Denmark, Germany and Spain, it is. In others, it has yet to appear on the agenda. The notion of 'high quality' education is frequently mentioned by educationalists and behavioural psychologists, but high quality does not include architectural high quality. For instance, in a recent report published by the Royal Society of Arts on the importance of early learning, 'Start Right', the following statement was one of the six requirements defining 'good practice':

The fifth requirement is a well planned, stimulating, secure and healthy environment. The learning environment should provide a variety of learning experiences indoors and out, space for movement and small, intimate areas for rest and quiet; it should provide equipment and resources to reflect the children's range of development and to promote early learning through purposeful play. While the environment should provide a place for the personal belongings of each child and adult (and an area for adults to have to themselves), it should as a whole be 'owned' by the children and organized so as to be accessible to them in such a way as to promote their growing independence and autonomy.[33]

While this is a clear educational statement, any understanding that it has architectural implications is ignored. It seems that what constitutes 'quality care' in an architectural sense is so subjective, and therefore difficult to clarify, that it is simply excluded from the educational agenda. Architects, town planners and urbanists are rarely involved in debates which might be concerned with defining a vision for the future.

The only implicit architectural theory on 'the quality of space' is based on economic functionalism. We will argue that metaphor and analogy, the relationship of architecture to concepts of childhood, should be part of the discussion. If functionalism is the only defining characteristic in the design of the kindergarten, if adults ignore the possibilities of fantasy, imagination, space, form, light, colour and texture – all qualities that make an enriching environment – then the children they teach and care for will almost inevitably absorb the view that the environment is of little or no consequence.[34] If architects continue to be sidelined and excluded from these debates, then

kindergartens will be the poorer for it. The importance of purpose-designed kindergartens of the highest spatial quality needs to be sold to sceptical politicians. Until an architecture for the imagination is included on the kindergarten agenda, then the earliest goals of the kindergarten movement will not be realized.

1.4 Benefits of the recent growth of pre-school facilities

The important socializing role of the kindergarten experience is increasingly reflected in the public domain. In 1991 the European Parliament recognized that equality of opportunity for women in the labour market would be possible only if young children were properly provided for; and defining quality in services to young children was an important contribution to the equality debate. The Council for Ministers accepted that the Commission should encourage the development of publicly funded, widely available high-quality child care services for children because 'it is essential to promote the wellbeing of children and families'.[35]

Many advanced industrialized societies are going through a period of immense economic adjustment, partly due to the transforming effects of globalized trade. While it is important to state that this is a period of adjustment rather than social disintegration, it is nevertheless a time when young children appear to be particularly vulnerable. Family life is more fragmented, relatives are less available to share caring, crime rates have risen, and traffic is dangerous. As a result, children live much more restricted lives. Education attainment suffers in this less socially cohesive world. These factors suggest that kindergartens will become increasingly important in the new millenium.

One of the barriers to providing nurseries in the 1950s and 1960s, at least in some countries, was the commonly held belief, articulated by the psychiatrist John Bowlby, that it was damaging for young children to spend time away from their mothers or primary carers. Working mothers were particularly discouraged. Extensive research carried out over the past decade has disproved Bowlby's theory of attachment, provided that the alternative nursery care is of good quality. As long as the very young child experiences stable relationships, being cared for by others in a group setting is not harmful, and is often more enriching: 'It is not so much the quantity as the quality of the interaction with the child [and its mother] that matters, and attention should therefore focus on improving quality.'[36]

The ability of children to develop social skills and sensibilities through interaction with their peers rather than with adults is one of the primary benefits of kindergarten. There is some evidence, mostly from American studies, that good kindergarten experience confers long-term benefits on children.[37] The most frequently cited evidence is the research programme carried out over 20 years in the USA by Schweinhart and Weikart (1993). This claims that children undertaking the High/Scope curriculum gain more self-respect and have a view of themselves as more competent persons: 'for every dollar invested in the pre-school programme the return to society is fourfold'.[38] In the sample of children tested over a 19-year-period, of the group participating in structured curriculum-based nursery school education, 20% fewer than the national average were classified as being mentally retarded, 18% more held on to jobs, 20% fewer were arrested for criminal acts, 14% fewer were arrested for crimes involving property or violence, and far fewer were on public assistance (18% as opposed to 32%). However this research was carried out using part-time nursery programmes, with very disadvantaged, mainly black, populations: there is therefore some question about whether the findings can be lifted out of this very specific American context.

A kindergarten or nursery environment can act as a protection against growing up in very disadvantaged circumstances. Educated parents increasingly see kindergarten provision as a significant educational opportunity for their young children, as well as a caring environment for them while they are at work.

1.5 Gender issues

Beyond their attachment to work and their rejection of old forms of family and community, something deeper is also happening. Young women are exhibiting what have typically been seen as male attributes – they are less emotional than older women, more willing to take risks and seek excitement in such things as foreign travel, parachuting and rock climbing.[39]

This somewhat risible stereotyping is all too typical of the way in which the populist media portrays 'the new woman'.

However, it is clear that not only have domestic labour-saving devices enabled homes to be run relatively easily, but household tasks are now more equally shared than in earlier times. Feminist views which would have been considered radical 20 or so years ago have today become part of mainstream culture. These changing perceptions have brought about aspirations for autonomy and equality among men and women, which are one of the most fundamental factors in the recent growth in the demand for kindergartens.

Many young women (and young men) are not prepared to commit themselves to parenthood today until their thirties, if at all.[40] Often they have children outside stable relationships. Of equal significance is the fact that many professional women demand to continue their careers after childbirth, sometimes wishing to take only a few weeks off work to deliver and settle their babies. Men also search for a more equitable role in bringing up children, one that can create a fulfilling and more balanced relationship. Peter Blundell Jones states the case even more forcefully:

the kindergarten is taken increasingly seriously as an educational institution, while it also becomes a vital instrument in the liberation of women. If their tendency to minimise the length of career breaks to have children continues, the experience of kindergarten or creche may end up being more important in a child's life than that of the family home. For better or worse, therefore, the kindergarten is becoming a social institution of considerable importance.[41]

What could be described as the modern desire for social autonomy among men and women in society immediately poses the question of who looks after the children. In the USA and UK it has been left to market forces: private provision, of variable quality, is available to those who can afford it; others must make shift arrangements, as in the USA, or live on benefits, as in the UK. Other European countries accept that the state-funded system of kindergartens must be extended, in either a welfare or an education context, to provide care as well as education.

Historically, kindergarten movements came about as a humanistic, if Utopian, response to industrialization and its effects on city-dwellers. The need for a fresh impetus in this area has never been greater than it is today. In the modern developed world, family lifestyles are evolving at great speed. Parents increasingly choose to share the task of looking after their children, adapting to the demise of the extended family structures which in former times played an important role in the care and socialization of young children. Urban life has become more hectic and impersonal, placing undue stress on even the most organized family groups.

The failure to provide adequate child support in modern urban environments can damage the well-being of children and affect the longer-term cohesion of society. The strain on women who go out to work without access to good-quality kindergarten care in turn affects their children. In his important study of parent–child relations, 'Making Decisions about Children', H.R. Schaffer states: 'The provision of good quality nursery and day care facilities in particular ought therefore to be regarded as an [economic] priority: for policy makers, in the interest of public economy'. To fail to recognize this, Schaffer concludes, will ultimately result in a far greater cost, 'financial as well as emotional'.[42]

Perhaps we are now paying the cost of this neglect. Within the UK and USA it is widely recognized that there are behavioural and learning difficulties being experienced by a wide generation of young boys. When boys and girls commence their education in pre-school classes, they are generally at the same emotional and social level. Gradually they move apart until by the age of ten, there is considerable tension between the two groups. Boys develop at a slower rate than girls. Their inability to 'keep up' academically, in a crowded classroom, will often result in low self-esteem exemplified by bad disruptive behaviour or sullen indifference. This can dramatically influence the quality of education the whole class receives as well as those children experiencing these feelings. Boys are suffering most as a result of this perceived gender gap.

For example Alan finds it very difficult to fit into the class group without disrupting it … 'whatever sophisticated planning has gone into curriculum design at Alan's school, the distinction between a good class and a bad class, from his point of view, has a lot to do with the freedom it offers to stand up and walk around'.[43] In his weary review of life, this ten-year-old described the nature of the problem many boys have. In essence, they sit all morning in the classroom, they have to keep track of their books, remember not to drop their pencils on the floor, and most importantly, to pay attention. Unfortunately, if they can't

move around they feel trapped and turned off to anything the teacher might have to offer.

Studies tracking children's development through the school years suggest that by the age of eight, a child has established a pattern of learning that shapes the course of his or her entire school career.[44] We use the word 'pattern' deliberately. Post-occupancy evaluation studies show that given the space, boys make much wider patterns within the pre-school setting than girls. They will tend to use the area available to them in a more physical way, within the framework of a structured pre-school curriculum.

These findings probably come as no great surprise to most of us; what they tend to support is the view that the environment is vitally important in developing healthy attitudes to school, and to learning, and a key criteria in this is 'space'. Furthermore, the notion of 'confinement' would appear to be a dangerous concept to establish in the minds of young children, particularly in boys. The idea of a classroom is one which reminds us of regimentation and discipline precisely because of the restrictive nature of most classrooms currently in use. Given less restrictive environments throughout their school years, our future citizens will feel valued and perceive education in a more positive light. The environment should offer Alan the freedom to 'stand up and walk around' at the very least.

1.6 Unemployment, social deprivation and the television as pacifier

Kindergartens benefit children and they are an essential service for working parents, but there is a further argument for them: they compensate children for their increasingly restricted lives in urban environments. The freedom to play outdoors relatively unsupervised, enjoyed by the majority of children who grew up before or during the 1960s, is no longer possible in most cities. Dangers of the motor car and heightened fears of crime often make children prisoners in their own homes. The economic and social pressures which take mothers out of the home often place great power in the hands of the television, to the point where it acts as a surrogate baby-sitter

Concerns about the all-powerful and pervasive effects of television are considerable; it has been estimated that by the age of eighteen American children have seen 350 000 com-

Kindergarten Architecture

1.5 Ground floor plan of the Windham Early Excellence Centre, Richmond upon Thames, UK designed by the Education Design Group. The new centre provides a range of services for families including drop-in facilities for parents and carers with babies, part-time and full-time care/education for children aged two to four years, a special needs centre for children aged one to sixteen years and community training spaces.

Key:
A New combined entrance area
B New community space (connecting two existing buildings on the site)
  1 reception desk
  2 interview room
  3 kitchen area
  4 external play courtyard
  5 toy library
  6 meetings room
C Existing Croft Centre atrium
  7 sensory room

8 autistic development space
9 parents' meeting room
10 meeting and assessment
11 therapy
12 social workers
13 access to community park
D Sensory garden
E Existing upgraded nursery, the activity area
  14 waiting area and office
  15 computer corner
  16 home corner
  17 language and literacy
  18 maths and construction

19 science and exploration
20 display and woodwork
21 art and modelling
22 open access kitchen
F New day care house
  23 story corner
  24 wet play
  25 quiet space
G Cloakroom area
H Outside classroom
  26 covered external play
  27 climbing frame
  28 sand pit and slide
  29 sinks and water feature

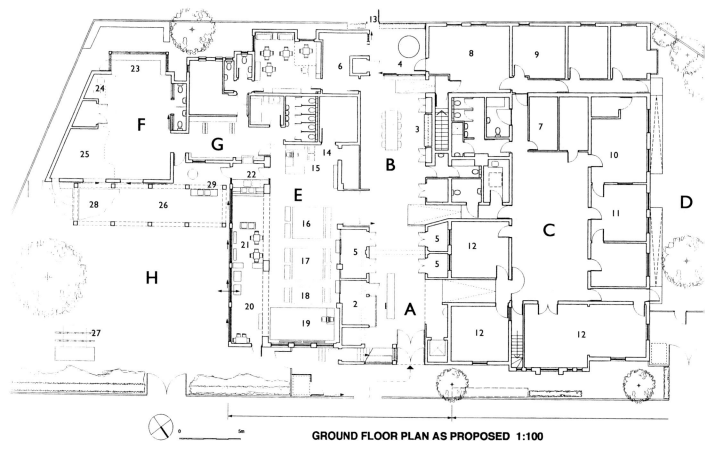

GROUND FLOOR PLAN AS PROPOSED 1:100

1.5

mercials. The toy industry in the USA has an approximate turnover of $100 billion annually, and children are exposed to 18 000 to 21 000 commercial 'messages' per year.[45] This, believes social commentator Melanie Philips, is 'a culture which sets out to exploit children cynically'.[46] Not only is television creating passive spectators, it is also telling those who do not have money how to spend it. In this sense, it is marketing dreams and aspirations that are often portrayed in violent or avaricious images.

There are, of course, some positive benefits of interactive technology, such as computer-aided learning for the young child.

Moreover, not to recognize the cultural significance of the technological shift that has taken place over the past decade would be a rejection of the real world.[47] However, anxieties are widespread that the development possibilities available to many young children are adversely affected by an overtly commercialized and passive urban environment. The notion that children's culture is changing at a faster rate than at any other time in history causes great concern to parents; paradoxically, at the same time as their children are exposed to this powerful commercial culture, parents lose control in another way – to the professionals who look after and educate their children.

1.6

1.6 The inner courtyard of the Folet's Forschulle provides an intimate space for storytelling on sunny days. The style of the building is modest and unassuming, if somewhat overstructured by the regularity of the grid. This was originally intended to give flexibility by the design of movable partitions; in fact, they are rarely altered.

While there are still conflicting views in some quarters as to the benefits of kindergartens, it is generally recognized that they are a fundamental element in a successful urban structure. If they can help to bind children and adults together, by developing environments in which parents feel comfortable when they deliver or collect their children, then some of the conflicts are at least being addressed. In the face of widespread social fragmentation, it can be argued that kindergartens should be viewed as being no less important for the well-being of the community than churches, police stations or town halls.

The following two views on the socializing qualities of kindergartens perhaps define the essential differences between 19th- and 20th-century attitudes. They nevertheless both have equal contemporary relevance:

an establishment that lays the ax [sic] to the root of all evil by fixing a solid foundation to the future superstructure of men's moral and physical comforts.[48]

Each child lives in a defined micro-space: his house, his habitat, where he grows up. At the child care services, the child discovers and establishes relations, plays with other children like himself, inaugurates his own socialising experience and his incorporation into group life. These first areas of his life occur within a larger context, the macro-space of the town or city.[49]

Children who come from vulnerable or abusive home environments face many problems of adaptation to ordinary life. In some circumstances where criminality and drug abuse are widespread, children have little chance of emerging unscathed from these experiences. This problem is particularly evident in parts of Britain and the USA where the decline of traditional heavy industries such as shipbuilding and the motor car industry have left employment vacuums. Without employment prospects, youngsters are poorly motivated and lack clear role models for both work and family life. Their depressed environment can be compounded by a lack of kindergarten provision –the numbers of poorly motivated, disorientated children who begin school in areas of deprivation has been increasingly reflected in the number of truancies and school refusals.[50]

In some inner-city environments, social structures have completely broken down, society has become fragmented, and people live more transient lives. Margaret McMillan argued at the turn of the century that urban blight affected the health and aspirations of generations, and that kindergartens provided some hope in otherwise hopeless circumstances. It has long been understood how important is 'the potential of pre-school education to overcome the harmful effects on the development of unhygienic living conditions, a restricted environment, family poverty and other hardships'.[51]

The wheel has turned full circle. In the late 20th century, the requirement to stimulate and socialize young children may be as important as it was in the late 19th century in ameliorating the effects of poverty.

1.7 Demographic transformations: needs and benefits

The other aspect of this argument in favour of an expansion of kindergartens reflects the social transformations affecting the industrialized nations, in particular areas of Britain and the USA. The birthrate is dropping significantly and, in some countries, it is less than required to replace the population. It is anticipated that by the end of the 20th-century women will be needed to make up over half of the country's workforce. In France the creation of kindergartens is associated with pro-natalist policies – support for family life which will enable women to combine work and domestic responsibilities.

In other countries, economic expansion has caused significant labour shortages, which must be made up by an immigrant workforce, or by encouraging women to stay in work, or both. In Japan and the Pacific rim countries, attitudes towards women workers have changed considerably, and are reminiscent of the shift in Sweden during the 1960s and 1970s when kindergarten policies were explicitly directed towards the needs of industry: 'Even right-wing parties which regretted the necessity for housewives to work outside their homes supported the reforms'.[52]

It is anticipated that the educated and skilled members of the workforce who will be needed in the new technology-led industries of the 21st century will in many cases be women. Today, evidence suggests that schoolgirls outshine their male peers academically; they appear to be more ambitious and more likely to get jobs on leaving university (8.2% of women in Britain are unemployed a year after graduation, compared to 12.25% of men). It was predicted that by the end of the 1990s more than 80% of new jobs would be taken by women.[53]

In the free market, fluctuating employment patterns are the norm, and men's and women's work patterns are more erratic. Demographic predictions are complex, and individuals need to be flexible in order to cope with rapid change. Kindergartens are a stabilizing factor, and, like the rest of the education system, they need to support individuals who are resilient and creative. The early pioneers claimed that kindergartens did precisely that.

Today, the global economy increasingly means a global culture. Societies vying for economic prosperity seek to acquire factors which add competitive advantage. The kindergarten is one important element in a social support structure which is recognized as giving such competitive advantage. If the culture of regional particularity is to be maintained and is to thrive, then it is a lifelong process starting with early childhood. Well-designed and aesthetically pleasing buildings are an integral part of this process.

Radicalism is inherent to kindergartens, both from an architectural and an educational perspective. Social trends and analysis can be used to support arguments in favour of more nursery school provision. Detailed analyses can help (albeit in a limited way) to define practical criteria such as space standards and to aid discussions on functional issues, but these analyses do not recognize the benefits of *architecture*. Yet the notion of an architecture driven by radical social concerns is as pertinent today as it was in the 1940s, when Le Corbusier chose to locate a kindergarten on the roof of his Marseilles Unité modernist housing project.

Our own anecdotal evidence on visiting a Head Start project – the Dolores Mission Women's Cooperative in Gless Street, Los Angeles, California – confirms the success of these programmes and the importance of pre-school, particularly where environmentally deprived home circumstances prevail. We were told how the behaviour of a seemingly bright and well-balanced four-year-old boy changed when he spent weekends at his parents' crowded apartment. There, three people were forced to share a room, he had no garden and no personal space. On returning to school on Monday mornings, he was listless, uncommunicative and aggressive. Within three to four hours of being in the caring kindergarten environment, he reverted back to his naturally happy and positive personality.

1.8 The wider role of kindergartens and children in the city

In many European countries, the concept of child-friendly cities has been gathering strength over the past five years. In 1992 Edinburgh decided to become the first child-friendly city in the UK, identifying three main areas of concern: safety in public play areas, a reversal of the fear of 'nasty people', and cars. These ideals were summarized as: 'children [being] valued as customers and citizens . . . and listened to with respect . . . and where every public space should be designed to take account of children's needs as well as adults".[54]

Nurseries located for the convenience of the parents' work-place, away from the home environment, are becoming increasingly popular. However the notion that kindergartens are best located within walking distance of the home is a plausible one. An awareness of the community within which the child lives is accentuated, and social networks between parents can develop more readily.

The notion that the nursery school is the focus of community development is becoming more widely recognized. In Britain, in particular, there are many services for young children, mainly in the voluntary sector but sometimes also in the state sector which emphasize the nursery as a meeting-place for parents and a route for mothers back into the wider world after being confined at home with very young children. For example, the Greenhill Jenner Patmore Centre in south London, commissioned by Save the Children, includes a training centre for local adults, a creche and community resource united under one roof.

In a similar vein, the Folets Forschulle in Malmö, Sweden, is a full-time nursery school which provides space for mothers to meet each other and their children in the afternoons. The building offers a separate entrance for the afternoon children, with their own coat-hooks and lockers, to replicate the experience of being part of the larger kindergarten community. The service, free of charge, is often the first contact with the wider community for children who are not attending the full-day service, as well as for their mothers. Many similar projects exist, which include community-enhancing spaces such as par-

1.7 A week in a Belgian nursery school, translated from Delvaux-Furnière and Malisoux-Gillet (1985), Ministry of Education, Research and Training guide (ERT), p. 25. Advice given in the curriculum document defines a range of activities that relate to sensory experiences. For example, making faces in the mirror is among activities described as *activités psychomotrices* (scientific); playing with puppets is good for language development and hand–eye coordination. This curriculum encourages the imaginative use of space and the involvement of teachers with different skills to provide a varied range of child-centred learning.

	Monday	Tuesday	Wednesday	Thursday	Friday
8.45–9.15	WELCOME	Books, writing materials, games, play etc.			
9.15–9.45	REGROUP on the carpet		Calendar, surprise, day's plans, project discussion etc.		
9.45–10.25	Activities – eldest group have PE; younger children choice of activity		Workshops (rotate groups)	Activities – eldest group have PE; younger children choice of activity	
11.00–11.45	Cognitive activities			Cognitive activities	
	Younger children – sensory activities, emergent literacy and mathematics, etc.				
1.30–3.00	Craft/ creative workshops techniques	Craft/ creative workshops (rotate groups)		Craft/ creative workshops (rotate groups)	Free play
3.30–3.55	Dancing, singing, poems, directed games etc.			Dancing, singing, poems, directed games etc.	

1.7

ents' rooms, on-site training centres for women and spaces for parent–teacher forums.

The Emilia Romagna region of northern Italy provides a real inspiration, an appropriate vision for the 21st century. Tiziana Filippini, coordinator of the Diane nursery school in Reggio Emilia, has at the heart of her school a 'central square'. This terminology is a deliberate reminder of the urban spaces in Italian cities whose primary benefit is to encourage social interaction. So the central enclosed space is analogous to the public meeting place; here, parents, teachers and children make contact with each other, thus fulfilling one of the primary functions of kindergarten life.

Modena distinguishes its child-friendly planning strategies by making them friendly for both boys and girls. The view that the city is a male-orientated space, predominantly given over to the convenience of the car, is at the heart of this philosophy. A multi-disciplinary commission – involving teachers, architects, engineers, solicitors, social workers, psychologists and police representatives – has been established to influence the layout of the city and send reminders to adults of the desire for a child-orientated culture. One of these projects, for example, introduced street signs which could be read and understood by young children.

This initiative begins in Modena's kindergartens, which extend their activities to adults to become a focus for that community. Parents are given responsibility and encouraged to organize events within the kindergarten building at the weekends, even engaging those who do not have young children themselves. Parent classes and pre-natal groups meet in the kindergarten rather than in the hospital or at the home, so that insecure parents are supported discreetly during this life-changing event. It is recognized that whereas mothers and grandmothers might have provided support, knowledge and reassurance in former times, there is now a knowledge gap which is increasingly being addressed through child care services.

The main idea of this and other city-wide initiatives is to bring the life and culture of child care into the broader public view. If a city is friendly for children, then it is friendly for everyone. In Modena it is felt that good kindergarten environments should be offered to all children. However, unless there is a vision which generates a wider public interest, it is impossible, for political reasons, to secure the necessary public investment. Taking children as quality criteria to transform the nature of city space illustrates how important kindergartens may become to the functioning of the city in the future.

The city of Bologna, capital of the region, developed architecturally during the 18th century as the university expanded. The architectural results of this social transformation were the colonnades, which were constructed throughout the city to provide additional accommodation for the increasing numbers of students. The width of the colonnades on most of the main streets was specified: they had to be wide enough to enable three people to walk side by side. This device had a humanizing effect on the social and architectural fabric of the city, giving an underlying structure and cohesion which remains intact to this day.

One might draw a similar analogy with today's city-wide kindergarten facilities: their quality and extent create as galvanizing an impact, both architecturally and socially, as the colonnades did on the 18th-century city. The 20th-century architectural representation is less obvious to the casual visitor, but it is as important to the physical and social cohesion of the contemporary city.

To reiterate, the most commonly agreed contemporary kindergarten model in Europe, the USA and Japan is a building which provides full-day educare for children from the age of three to six or seven. The accommodation can include playrooms or activity areas which act as secure bases or classrooms for predefined groups, a dining-room space and an area for younger children to sleep, although both eating and sleeping may take place within the activity rooms. Where possible, a communal assembly space should be provided which may double as a gymnastics or music space. Most importantly, a garden or secure outside space should be provided which encourages an easy interchange between inside and outside. We will explore and illustrate the nature of some of these spaces in more detail in Chapter 4.

Generally, the contemporary kindergarten is best contained in a single building, usually relating to its residential context; it encourages involvement by parents where appropriate, but not in the educational process as such. Baby units can be included, but should be distinct and separate from the kindergarten accommodation. Initially, the building must be something of a 'home from home', but with scope for more challenging, autonomous spaces as babies and toddlers grow. However, approaches to the design of kindergartens, particularly over the last ten years of architectural pluralism, show that the interpretation of children's needs is broad and diverse and, as a result, architecturally rich.

1.9 Pre-school educational curricula

Often on visiting today's kindergartens it can appear that chaos reigns, and that children are simply playing as they like in order to fill in the time between their delivery and collection. While this may be the case in some part-time (non-educational) facilities, it is not the case with kindergartens or nursery schools. Modern kindergartens support activities that encourage the children's development through their own discoveries. If the nature of these activities is known and understood by the architect, it may assist in the construction of a more precise architectural programme. The following accounts are the result of discussions with a variety of educationalists in different countries. They define a broadly agreed framework for what we hesitantly describe as the 'pre-school educational curriculum'.

Marita Overbeck, who runs a children's day care centre in Neukölln, Berlin, describes the daily routine as follows. The centre is open from 6am. By 8am all the full-day care children have arrived, and they have breakfast together (not all the children come in the mornings; activities take place in groups of 15. They then go to their own activity rooms and commence individual or group activity programmes. These activities might include painting, collage or modelmaking, based on a particular theme such as 'the earth or 'autumn'. Halfway through the morning, external staff come in and offer optional activities such as sport, or music and movement. These classes can be held indoors in one of three large double-height group activity areas. At midday they all have lunch together. After lunch they sleep in the activity rooms – those who do not wish to sleep can use the galleries in the group activity areas for individual or small group play. At 2pm they will all have coffee or soft drinks and most of the children are collected by 3pm.

Frau Overbeck chooses her staff personally and together they carefully design a new programme of activities every month. The staff meeting room is important in this planning process, as all staff members need to gather as a single group. As well as providing closed, fairly conventional classroom or activity areas which allow a degree of privacy and intimacy, the architects Deutbzer and König have created an open, split-level galley which links three larger-scale group rooms. The organization allows long vistas with views up, down and through to the garden outside. The design enables different age groups to mix, giving a sense of both openness and privacy. The diversity of the spaces within the building means that a relatively free curriculum structure can be adopted which allows the children to pick and choose what they do. And the architecture, says Frau Overbeck, 'fascinates' the children. The previous building they used was two-thirds the size of the

1.8 Toyo Ito, Frankfurt
Eckenheim, children's day care
centre: view of the garden.

1.8

present building (which is 2234m² in total, giving approximately 12.6m² per child). The benefits of this additional space are felt to be considerable.

The Tranan nursery school in the centre of Malmö, Sweden, has 48 children who attend at times similar to the Berlin school. Director Rita Theander also tries to adopt a 'free' approach to activities, stressing the importance of the child's individuality. She has 11 full-time staff, of whom half are trained teachers, including one cook. The school is located in an apartment block, which provides a great many different-sized linked rooms for various activities. Two separate entrances are identified with the symbols of a frog and a penguin.

When we visited, at least six different activities were taking place – some supervised, some largely 'private' comprising small groups of children. Four little boys were having a discussion as they played on climbing frames arranged around a soft space; two girls were listening to music alone in a lounge room; two others were listening to a story; and three were painting, supervised, in a crafts room. A pastry class was taking place in a children's kitchen space, directly adjacent to a large kitchen in which lunch was being prepared in full view of the children, with all the fresh ingredients on display – fruit, vegetables, meat and pasta. A group of children was in the garden, which they may use regularly and whenever they wish in all weathers. Rita Theander

1.9 Children enjoying their own reflections at the Diane nursery school, Reggio Emilia.

1.9

would like an additional large space for assembly and singing; however, apart from this she thinks that the range of spaces works well, provided that current staffing levels are maintained.[55]

One of the most positive aspects of this urban school with its high staffing levels is that teachers can regularly take groups of children for outings to the junior school or the local park and, perhaps most importantly, to the local art gallery which runs creative art workshops for local nursery schools. This enables the children to experience a variety of activities which change almost daily. There is no defined programme, as the children are largely encouraged to make choices, becoming gradually more independent as they grow. It is crucially important that activities can be carried over from one day to the next, and the generous space and the range of different-sized rooms with nooks and niches encourages the children to leave a game or model out overnight if desired.

It is difficult to offer this variety and pace of curriculum in state nursery schools in the UK, because of the combination of restricted space, low staff–child ratios and, above all, so few places which must be shared between morning and afternoon shifts. The Tarner Land Nursery School in Brighton, for example, is an open-plan building with a total floor area of approximately 160m^2. There are two daily sessions with 50 children per session (9–11.30am and 12.45–3.00pm), giving a floor area of approximately 3.2m^2 per child per session.[56] The school also provides lunch for 20 children from each session.

Head Teacher Cherry Richmond has four staff, of whom two are fully trained teachers and two are nursery nurses (these are the minimum recommended levels in Britain of one member of staff to 13 children). In addition, a special needs ancillary teacher visits for 20 hours per week. The space of the school comprises a separate soft reading area, an L-shaped open-plan activity area, a block of toilets, a small parents' room and, perhaps best of all, a large, secure garden with a recently constructed animal shelter. Activities are laid out and discussed by the staff prior to the arrival of the children. There are four basic activity centres or 'bases': a creative arts and crafts area comprising water play, painting, modelling, woodworking and sand; a story base and puzzles or games room; a 'home base' where the children have their drinks and fruit, and a music and movement space. 'The basic principle is that we expect the children to be reasonable and responsible people, and so they

are encouraged to realize the implications of their actions,' states Cherry Richmond. 'However, you can't be dogmatic about events you expect to happen'.

1.10 High/Scope

Elizabeth Mayo, Head Teacher at the Birchwood Nursery School in Hatfield, Hertfordshire, uses a similar but more prescribed nursery school curriculum, originally developed in the USA, called High/Scope. 'High/Scope is a way of working with young chil-

1.10

1.10 Sketch of the internal courtyard of the Diane nursery school, Reggio Emilia.

dren derived from Piaget's theory of child development. Based on the idea that children learn best from activities which they plan and carry out themselves, High/Scope offers a framework which allows staff to work with children while enabling them to do the discovering.'[57]

High/Scope defines a set of 'key experiences' designed to encourage active learning. This precise system is worth describing in more detail, as its methods and values are broadly applied, to a greater or lesser extent, in many contemporary British and American nursery schools. The 'key experiences' are grouped under the following broad categories: using language; representing experiences and ideas, developing logical reasoning (classification, seriation and number concepts), and understanding time and space. The implications of this system for design and architecture are considerable.

In the High/Scope kindergarten, the activity areas are the most important part of the school. Each one of these spaces, which cater for approximately 30 children per half-day session, must form the context for the following four types of activity: sand and water play; physical play (with a rumpus areas for particularly boisterous children); construction and manipulation (maths and science activities), and creative representation (art and craft activities). In addition, a quiet space should be available for reading and storytelling.

This is a system that expects the children to make their own decisions and plan how they intend to spend their days. To be able to find their own materials is an important function, therefore cupboards and storage areas must be accessible to the children.

Since a fundamental principle is that children freely choose activities, all materials and equipment should be made available and accessible to children. A High/Scope classroom would have these displayed on low open shelves and hanging from hooks and so on so that everything is within children's reach. A classroom would not be 'set out' before the children come in, which may limit children's choices, but they should be able to select from a wide range of materials they need to carry out their ideas.[58]

For instance, in the art area paint would be available for mixing by children, along with a wide range of papers of different sizes, shapes and textures. If the teacher and children have decided to make collages, the teacher may automatically put out glue,

scissors and so on. If the children have to decide which of several materials will best suit their purpose, they will individually have to test out various options and will learn more about the properties of various materials in the process.

The classroom should be divided into sections, such as the brick area, art area, sand and water area, quiet area, home area and so on. The children need to be introduced to the materials and areas when they first come into the classroom so that they become familiar with the choices available. As new materials are added throughout the year and areas change, children should be involved in these decisions as much as possible.

'Having access to everything in the classroom may feel overwhelming to a chid. Even adults can feel unsafe and unsure when "anything goes". So the High/Scope curriculum offers a structure to the day which provides a predictable routine within which the child can feel secure.'[59] The materials and toys cannot therefore be hidden away in cupboards with doors, or in store rooms. There must be an order to the classroom spaces, but the means by which the children explore their interests must be open and accessible to them. As children attend only for half-day sessions, the morning routine might be repeated in the afternoons.

Elizabeth Mayo supports 80 children in a building which is now over 50 years old. The building has been adapted and patched up over the years but remains essentially unchanged, complete with wartime air-raid shelter (currently used as a storeroom). She is a strong advocate of the High/Scope system and makes the point that 'the environment is crucial because it is how the children access their learning'.

Her typical programme is centred around the High/Scope notion of 'plan, do and review'. The children must all arrive by 9am (disciplined, but sensible when you think that the sessions last only until lunchtime). The day commences with a 'welcome and planning session' which lasts for approximately 20 minutes. In pastoral groups of ten, the children, led by one teacher or care worker, are encouraged to talk about what they intend to do. This could be a painting or a construction, carried out independently or with a friend. The intended activity is recorded by the adult in charge, to establish the importance of the plan in the child's mind, and also to open meaningful patterns of negotiation as well as channels of communication to parents.

The children then go and find a place to commence their

task, in one of the activity corners located around different parts of the classroom. There may be a construction corner where play bricks, lego and other toys are stored in open shelves. If children wish to go to a particular corner they must first check that it is free. The 'doing' activities last for one and a quarter hours. This is followed by a recall time, when children explain their activity and discuss any problems or ways in which it may have been carried out more effectively. Here the older children (four-year olds) will naturally lead the younger ones in the dialogue. If any children are halfway through an activity at the end of the allotted 'doing' session, they can negotiate to have extra time or to continue the activity on the following day.

After recall time, there is a short time for group activity to develop concepts and to practise skills. This is adult-initiated and takes place in what are called the home bases. The children then have a period of free play time when they may go outside in the garden. Again, the outside space is part of the structured activities — High/Scope concerns itself with the whole child, which is why the outside space is so integral to the inside play spaces. After 20 minutes of free play, there is a 20-minute period of 'circle time', when children sit in a large group and talk, sing or read stories.

On a functional level, the environment is crucial in the support of these activities. It defines the spaces within which the children may feel safe and secure in order to develop their games with adult support. The effectiveness of the curriculum may be affected by the physical limitations of the old Birchwood nursery school building. The teaching system centres on the 'activity areas' and their connection with the external spaces. As such, they must be purpose-designed to support the highly structured nature of the system.

This 'structure' appeared less rigid when we visited the recently designed Frankfurt Eckenheim children's day care centre, which does not use the High/Scope system. Here, the children seemed to be occupied with different autonomous activities throughout the whole area of the building (including the internal garden). The system in use was certainly less disciplined, without any visible loss of control evidenced in the behaviour of the children. Indeed, it was difficult to discern exactly what type of curriculum was in use. However, when it was explained, it seemed that the spatial diversity afforded by the building was central to this feeling of freedom. The parents themselves were

to a degree responsible for suggesting the crescent-shaped form of the Frankfurt building. Not only does it make a refreshing contrast to the orthogonal high-rise housing blocks surrounding the site, but it combines a seemingly effortless security with an elegance which is hard to fault.

The children commence their time in kindergarten together in their own classrooms. Afterwards they can roam around the building, engaging in different activities in a free way. The craft and kiln room sits within the garden, and is articulated as an octagonal freestanding tower Like Aladdin's cave, it contains all kinds of tools, paint pots and modelling materials, and the young children may use the space at any time it is available, often with the older children assisting. The positioning of this room actively integrates the outside areas into the daily life of the school. When we visited, at around lunchtime, this openness extended to the parents' popping in to speak to their children, without any great restrictions as would be the case in the (admittedly different) British High/Scope system.[60]

The inherently secure shape of the building, focusing on the internal garden, together with the general openness of the design, enables adult observation to take place in a discreet way. The connecting spaces are not conventional corridors, as they are articulated by interesting spatial incidents which take on the form of rooms in their own right at certain points along the length. The activity rooms are punctuated by child-height panels, both glazed and solid, window seats and other child-scaled niches, which help to create an architecture that encourages movement rather than stasis. The Frankfurt building actively induces social interaction between different ages, rather than solidifying two distinct groups, which tends to be the case in the High/Scope example. The sense of space, tranquillity and fluidity is almost certainly sustained by the form of the Eckenheim building. Added to this is an exuberant and fragmented sort of architecture which makes this kindergarten a paradigm of its type.

When we visited the kindergarten at Viborg Seminariet, Denmark, the garden appeared to be a hive of busy activities, an extension of the interior space of the building. We saw mostly small groups of children building sand castles around a bonfire, climbing trees and tricycling. Loni Miers, the Head Teacher, explained that they used the garden all year round and in most weathers. Inside the building, two little girls were acting out their own fashion show – a rail of dresses and uniforms was clearly important to this drama, as was a curtained niche behind which they changed. A little den was being used by two boys who played peek-a-boo with us as we took photographs. In a large dry sunken bath, filled with cushions and soft toys, a boy and a girl of about six were simply talking. In stark contrast to this behaviour my own five-year-old boy, attending the first class of a London infants' school, was advised that his reading was not progressing and 'he was guessing too many words'.

I took up my anxieties with Loni Miers about the boy lying in the bath simply having a conversation with his friends. She recounted a similar experience, that of a young boy who initially spent all day lying on his back beneath a table seemingly staring into space. This behaviour went on for days. His father was very worried at his lack of activity, but Loni reassured him that in her view it was perfectly acceptable:

If you see children as individual personalities from an early stage, and give them room to play on their own and as they like (particularly boys), they will find their own natural way to behave within the kindergarten society. Socialism has broken down and society is more individual – we must reflect this in the kindergarten. If you respect the children and believe that they are inherently social, but individual, you will create a balanced secure group of individuals capable of growing within a modern society.

The boy had gradually ceased his inactive behaviour and developed his own thoughtful, contemplative personality without any problems. 'In the kindergarten we have almost no rules, just simple goals', said Loni. Her point was essentially a liberal reinforcement of the positive role of the kindergarten space to enable individual development. For Loni, the fact that the kindergarten allowed the boy to behave as he wished, provided it was not aggressively anti-social behaviour, was something to be celebrated. If she was to design a new kindergarten, Loni would provide more small rooms within which children could play largely unsupervised. Again, boys required the opportunity to develop games which could continue for days – perhaps for weeks – on end without disturbance. The young child's desire to 'take space over' is important and must be supported by an appropriate form of the kindergarten environment.

During our visits we have been wary both of the subjective nature of personal observation and also of the possibly false atmosphere that visitors can create and the effect they may have on the behaviour of the children. Most children are notorious 'performers'. The following story was told by Mary Field, who produced a film in the 1930s of Susan Isaacs' influential Malting House School. On visiting the school for the first day of filming, she got the impression that

some of the activities had been laid on specially for us. For example, the children were dissecting Susan Isaacs' cat which had just died, when normally they worked with frogs or dogfish. They all seemed to be enjoying themselves immensely, digging away at the carcass . . . Then there was the bonfire. It was supposed to be an exercise in free play, but it got a bit out of hand. The fire spread and spread and reached the apple trees, and then destroyed a very nice boat. Even Geoffrey Pyke was a little upset about that, and he seemed a very calm man.[61]

However it is reasonable to state that all our observations in many different nursery schools confirm the need for coherent pedagogical systems which are understood by children and staff alike: 'The way in which the educational philosophy is put into practice should be stated and explicit.'[62] The extent to which systems and structures are applied to pre-school varies, and is very much dependent on the culture and the context.

Nursery school in the UK differs from other forms of pre-school 'care' facilities such as playgroups, crèches or workplace nurseries in that it emphasizes the educational development of the children, and insists that only fully trained teachers can deliver the curriculum. The daily routine can be as free and varied as possible within that basic tenet. But the balance between structured, adult-led diversions and adequate physical space which enables children to be autonomous is a crucial one, whichever way the educational philosophy is articulated.

Gaye MacDonald, Head Teacher at the newly built nursery on campus at UCLA in California describes the significance of the kindergarten environment to the children: 'The whole site says something to children: that we think they are important.' She believes they will carry the physical memories of freedom and space around with them; however, the environment on its

1.11a

1.11b

own is not enough to support young children without curriculum structures, suggesting that the architectural form can be one which is quite neutral. 'There are some wonderful programmes in poor space – sometimes it forces teachers to try harder.'

She believes that the development stages of children are quite predictable: four-year-old boys are interested in power and who makes the rules; girls of the same age are still interested in creativity, and setting up possibilities to explore. All children of four want to categorize things, because that is an emerging skill. It is important that teachers know what is normal for children at different ages. This can help in the planning of imaginative activities, which stimulate the children in exciting ways, rather than, for example, the ubiquitous displays of autumnal images which tend to appear in October: 'It's nice to know the seasons change, but that is not the main issue for young children.'

1.11 Mature systems

The High/Scope curriculum has great value, particularly in the context of a British system where services are fragmented and the environment of the provision is often of poor quality, imposing restrictions on teacher–carers and children. If the kindergarten spaces are well staffed, spacious and architecturally diverse, a more relaxed approach may produce benefits over the highly structured High/Scope system. There are many different value systems which inform pre-school provision; it is inappropriate to adopt a single model because nurseries are set up to fulfil different aims and objectives, and they operate in different contexts.

There is another important issue: the culture and maturity of each of the kindergarten systems we viewed. Claus Jensen, a social scientist from Aarhuis, Denmark, makes the point that in order to allow more relaxed kindergarten systems to emerge, not only must the environment and the space support free learning activities, but the staff and, to a degree, the children's parents, must understand kindergarten culture and be in tune with its traditions. When the staff are secure and mature as a profession (and the kindergarten environment is fully supportive), they are more open to the authentic needs of modern children's culture. Instead of having to focus on what the children have to learn, they can concentrate on the children's competencies, exploiting and enjoying aspects they themselves bring

to the kindergarten society. An example of how this might work in relation to a building's function is in an open kitchen/dining area at the heart, which always hosts a pot of fresh coffee. Parents are encouraged to linger, without any fear of overstaying their welcome. Everybody understands the boundaries and is confident within the framework, especially if they attended the same kindergarten themselves when children.

Pre-school children need to explore and appropriate their environment as far as possible. The contradictory requirements – to protect growing children, yet encourage autonomy among them – is a subtle dialogue between the educational curricula and architectural space. Consequently, the architect should almost always develop a close relationship with the school staff and its particular methods and philosophies when developing a design. Perhaps the most successful and sophisticated example of this 'partnership' can be found in the Diane nursery school in Reggio Emilia, Italy.

Here, the child-centred activities of the day are very clearly structured by the functional and physical qualities of the school space. The notion of openness is an important aspect of the way in which the teachers believe children perceive space; they need to understand the space and orientate themselves quickly. The interior of Diane, in particular, fulfils these aims, both functionally and architecturally. On entering the building, a large L-shaped atrium (the central square) provides views across and through to every other part of the accommodation. The space is generally well lit, enhanced by the use of white ceramic tiles on the floors. A rich and well-maintained selection of indoor plants cascades down the sides of the interior walls, gaining light and ventilation from two small courtyards. Imaginatively designed children's sculptures provide important focal points within this communal space.

However, the activity areas themselves also support the overall pedagogical ideals, providing a series of semi-private or niche spaces which can easily be appropriated by small groups or individual children. These are located beyond the square, almost visible through some areas of glass panelling. A spatial transparency is created, while at the same time a degree of privacy is maintained within the activity rooms. It is almost as if there is a second layer of distinct spaces or little self-contained houses wrapping around the inner public court

1.11a+b Activities in day-care centres in Denmark and the UK which may have been viewed as gender stereotyping during the 1980's are now seen in a more relaxed light.

The nature of the activities offered – indeed, the ways in which they are structured – has a superficial resemblance to the High/Scope example. However, the crucial difference lies in the way these activities are presented. They take place over a full day and are developed over a longer period of a child's pre-school life. There is a fundamentally strong, self-motivating philosophy rather than, as in High/Scope, a way of working which children have to acquire in a relatively short time. The school caters for 75 children in three age-related groups of 25. The day begins in the central square when children decide what they intend to do. There is a special art room or atelier which has a wide range of different materials available, from paint, clay and collage, to fancy dress and musical instruments to encourage aural experimentation.

There is a genuine view of children as artists with an almost scientific drive to test their own theories of life. So the activity would start with what the teachers call a 'theoretical discussion'. Children are stimulated into asking questions about seemingly minor aspects of the way in which the world works. It is the teacher's role to treat these questions seriously, and support the children in exploring the meaning of the question. So a child may ask, 'Why does the tree die?' The theoretical answer would perhaps be based on analogies to the human body, or some concept understood by the child, such as the roots being like the brain of the tree. Therefore it follows that they need water and will die from lack of it.

The children might then make clay models of trees, where the forms develop out of their own life experiences. Their trees would not just be copies or imaginative interpretations, but expressive of some life force that trees *feel*, such as dying or being in a thunder storm. Similarly, if a child wants to find out about shadows, first the teacher will test if the shadows can be covered by a mat or by stones. Then a light will be introduced, so the child is made aware of the concept and the different ways in which the sun makes shadows and the light moves them.

For primitive peoples, the image of a shadow or shadows has been the source of legends, stories of spirits, rituals, ghosts, great respect and fear. And nowadays, you just need to want it, shadows can become part of the repertoire of children's games. Some games end quickly – even a mosquito flying by can distract a child – but others go

on and on because they give children the chance to utilize their curiosity and intelligence.[63]

The learning environment is further enhanced as a social experience by the activity of gathering for lunch. For example, whether the child sits on a bench, a small chair or at an adult sized table is important. All experiences are available to the child to choose and negotiate. 'We must help to encourage their identity', states Tiziana Filippini, and develop their awareness of an 'individual enterprise within a social process'. Although adults are not encouraged to participate actively in the daily life of the school, their points of contact such as the children's relationship with their teachers are as important as their peer group relations.

1.12 Summary

What do all these observations mean in terms of kindergarten systems? They certainly point towards a need for architects to understand the educational context for which they may be designing. This may be dictated quite precisely by the teachers, or it may be more relaxed, depending on the teachers' confidence, particularly in the safety and spatial quality of their environment. The educational context, then, would appear to be an essential prerequisite of the contemporary kindergarten. The featured case studies discussed in this section provide openness within a secure yet challenging framework. Striking this balance is the fundamental requirement of the designer. The architect is given the power to interpret the curriculum needs described by the teachers: this interpretation can accommodate imaginative possibilities which may not be immediately obvious to the client. One of the primary requirements of the architect, then, is to disclose these imaginative possibilities through his or her own interpretations.

On a general educational level, our view is that we should guard against the implementation of systems that are foreign to a particular situation, in terms of both the physical context and the experience and abilities of the personalities expected to run it. Filippini describes her system as one where the focus is the school, but the subject of the school is parents, staff and children: 'every system has to try to optimize the quality of these relationships'.

The contribution made by the teachers' commitment and by the environment towards these ideals is always within an overall framework of liberalism, and in a conscious effort to dissolve the children's perception that systems are too rigid. It follows, therefore, that careful consideration must be given to the provision of an environment which nurtures the children's imaginative activities. The kindergarten is, to a certain extent, supporting a utopian ideal. As such, the building should subtly reflect this philosophy and it can engender relaxing, open curriculum systems if it can be made to support the requirements of safety and security,

The imposition of adult-orientated systems for the control of children is not in the spirit of the true kindergarten environment. Childhood culture should develop out of the beliefs and values of the present day, grounded upon the experience of the past. Adults should not attempt to pass on their own childhood culture to children of today through over-systematized structures. Adults should not play at being children, and kindergarten architecture should not pretend to be something it is not. What defines the natural environment is a system that supports and protects, but encourages freedom – a paradox indeed:

> I am talking about some form of protection of the environment, which is about the screening of some unorganised open spaces, some places to meet. I want you to make it possible for children to create their relationships. This might result in us having to protect children from being structured by adults. This is political/children's stuff of the highest explosive potential. And it should be possible to hear the explosion from a distance: I mean deep within the corridors of planners and engineers of the communities . . . We should not fill up the leisure time of children in school, or at home, with structures.[64]

References and notes

1. From Markus, Thomas A. (1993), *Buildings and Power*, London, Routledge, p. 78; also Chapter 4, and the section on. 'The Natural World'. This is an infants' school not a kindergarten, and Stow's understanding of the way in which the kindergarten philosophy evolved is apposite.
2. Margaret McMillan, quoted in Penn, Helen (1994), 'Nursery Education: What Should it Look Like?', text by visiting research fellow at the Education Department at the University of London, Early Years Unit, accompanying an exhibition of contemporary kindergartens held at the RIBA, London, April 1994.
3. The UK government instigated its Sure Start programme in March 1999. This will be based on Head Start, combining child care with other community facilities.
4. Boyer, Ernest L. (1991), 'Ready to Learn: A Mandate for the Nation', Carnegie Foundation for the Advancement of Teaching, Princeton, NJ. Boyer was president of the foundation. In an article by Lucy Hodges entitled 'A Private Matter for Families', Dr Willer asserts that very few nursery places are funded by the taxpayer in the USA and explains this as a cultural phenomenon: '. . . attitudes developed over decades of American history . . . first Americans are hostile to government. Many do not believe it is the government's job to take care of young children'. *Times Educational Supplement*, 30 June 1995, p. 16.
5. In Britain, the crèche enables developers to avoid registration and inspection, yet still show community benefits within new developments. The Children Act 1989 requires that day care facilities must be registered and inspected: 'A person provides day care on non-domestic premises if he or she looks after one or more children under eight years of age for six days or more in any year and for a period or total period of two hours in any day. (The term "premises" also includes vehicles - e.g. a play bus). From 'Registration Standards for Providers of Day Care and Childminding Services for Under 8s', East Sussex County Council, April 1993, p. 5.
6. David, Tricia (ed.) (1993), *Educational Provision for Our Youngest Children: European Perspectives*, Paul Chapman Publishing, pp. 93–4.
7. All systems of pre-school education for the under-fives is optional depending on the wishes of the parents. However, when parents have no choice in their need to go out to work, it is only fair that those children should be provided with high-quality provision.
8. All space standards are given as nett usable space, including ancillary areas such as staff rooms, and for the whole building.
9. In response to a letter criticizing the framework of the RIBA exhibition 'Spatial Play' curated by the author a letter was published in the *RSA Journal* explaining the stance taken by the organizers: 'For the moment, architects designing children's facilities [in Britain] should in my view hold on to and understand the idea of the "school" as the fundamental and defining characteristic of these buildings, whether they are designing to social services or local authority parameters . . . The exhibition was an architectural exhibition and set out with a positive view to show that despite this underfunded and fragmented state, British architects working closely with their clients can produce work of great quality, buildings which can be compared with the best kindergartens in Europe.' Dudek, Mark, *RSA Journal*, August–September 1994.

10. Penn, Helen, *Caravan*, University of Brighton School of Architecture and Interior Design, special issue on nursery education, *Building Futures*, coedited by Mark Dudek, no. 2, April 1995, p. 4.

11. For example, the Birchwood Nursery School was originally bequeathed and funded by Lord Salisbury in 1943, to support mothers who worked in the De Haviland Aircraft Factory. British Aerospace, the descendant company, closed in 1993, precipitating the need to provide a new nursery school, which is now open.

12. Borchorst, Anette (1992), 'Political Motherhood and Child Care Policies, a Comparative Approach to Britain and Scandinavia': quoted in Ungerson, Clare (ed.), *Gender and Caring - Work and Welfare in Britain and Scandinavia*, London and New York, Harvester–Wheatsheaf.

13. As I write, the UK Prime Minister talks with increasing desperation about ways to counter the nation's 'yob culture'. The media diagnosis fails to recognize the important civilizing effect of pre-school education, and the British system finds it difficult to distinguish between good- and bad-quality pre-school care/education. The so-called 'rising fours' are placed in reception classes, often containing 30 children, which are usually housed in conventional elementary school classrooms, a practice that will tend to breed a group mentality which may find it difficult to value and nurture individuality. Meanwhile, in Sweden, young children are encouraged to be independent, working in small groups from the earliest age, in nursery schools which provide spatial diversity so that they can choose to be private if they wish.

14. Ball, Sir Christopher, 'Start Right', The Royal Society for the Encouragement of Arts, Manufacturers and Commerce, March 1994.

15. 'Start Right', *op. cit.*, p. 25.

16. Putting the three Scandinavian systems in the same category is, however somewhat misleading. Anette Borchorst feels that conditions in Norway have many similarities to those in Britain: 'In neither Britain nor Norway has there been a comparable commitment to the employment of women and to the development of public child care. Nevertheless, married women have become increasingly integrated in the labour force, although there appears to be a time-lag of ten to twenty years compared to the other countries, and the increase has taken place in spite of child care policies rather than because of them.' This, she believes, was partly due to the fact that the Norwegian Social Democratic Party was out of office from 1965 to 1971.

17. Bettelheim, Bruno, quoted by Galardini, Annalia (1992), 'The Organization of Space in Services for Children', paper given at European Seminar on 'Space and Quality of Life for Children', Madrid, 27–28 November 1992: trans. Peter Moss of the Thomas Coram Pre-schools Education Institute, University of London.

18. Selmer-Olsen, Ivar (1993), 'Children's Culture and Adult Presentation of this Culture', *International Play Journal*, London, E. and F.N. Spon, vol. I, no.3, September 1993, p. 201. The author is attached to Queen Maud's College of Early Childhood Education, Oslo, Norway.

19. Owen, Robert (1844), *Book of the New Moral World*, Parts IV-VII, quoted in Taylor, B. (1983), *Eve and the New Jerusalem*, London, Virago, p. 51.

20. Schmitt, Peter (1995), 'A Prolegomenon to Designing a Learning Environment', *Caravan, op. cit.*, p. 9.

21. Dewey, John (1916), *Democracy and Education*, London, Macmillan: repr. 1967, p. 142.

22. In many European children's centres, rooms are provided for school-age children.

23. Frankfurt Municipal Building Department specification for architects designing new day care centres: quoted by Münster, Nikolaus (1992), 'Archigrad I - Planning and Building on the 50th Parallel', p. 2.

24. Jean Piaget related the intellectual development of the young infant to the gradual discovery of how the environment can be altered. This comes about through imitation and play. For several years he observed his own children very closely, and was the first to suggest that the newborn baby's world is a confusion of meaningless images. At the age of four months, the baby becomes aware of an outside world distinct from his or her own body. However, what is missing is an awareness that when something disappears from view, it still exists: to an infant, anything not visible is nonexistent. As children develop, they learn to retain an impression of things that have gone from view, and are then ready for a more elaborate form of play, to represent people, things and events in their own way.

25. Wilson, Peter (1995), interviewed by Mark Dudek, *Caravan*, February 1995, p. 26.

26. Beck, Ulrich and Beck-Gernsheim, Elizabeth (1995), *The Normal Chaos of Love*, Cambridge, Polity Press, p. 37.

27. Gesell, Arnold (1923), *The Pre-School Child: from the Standpoint of Public Hygiene and Education*, Boston, Houghton Mifflin: quoted by Maris A. Vinovskis of the Dept of History and Center for Political Studies, Institute for Social Research, Univ. of Michigan, in 'Changing Perceptions and Treatment of Young Children in the United States', paper presented to conference 'Images of Childhood', Satra Bruk, Sweden, 9-11 September 1992.

28. Peter Wilson developed a removable step, which prevented a young child from climbing without assistance, and used it in a non-child environment in Blackburn House, Hampstead, London. Eventually, the detail was used in the 'Kita' project in Frankfurt by Bolles Wilson. There, the step is no longer removable, but the idea persists even though the original functional reasoning for it has gone (author's interpretation).

29. Lloyd Wright, Frank, quoted in Meehan, Patrick J. (1992), *Truth Against the World – Frank Lloyd Wright Speaks for an Organic Architecture*, The Preservation Press, pp. 240–1.

30. Logical positivism was a 19th-century philosophy developed by Auguste Comte, which recognized only facts and observable phenomena.

31. Davey, Peter (1991), 'Schooling', *Architectural Review*, no. 1135, September 1991, p. 27. Davey's reference is actually to schooling in general rather than to kindergartens in particular: however his statement has, we believe, been used in this context without undue distortion.

32. Peter Moss in conversation with the author, June 1994.

33. From 'Start Right', *op. cit.*, pp.54–5. As an architect, I found it a matter of concern that of the 25 members of the influential panel responsible for putting this report together, not a single one was an architect, town planner or interior designer.

34. The connection between architectural quality within the pre-school environment and its development value to children is unproven; however, the author is at present engaged in a long-term research study.

35. European Commission Network on Childcare (1994), 'Quality Targets in Services for Young Children – Proposals for a Ten Year Action Programme', p. 1.

36. Schaffer, H. Rudolph (1990), *Making Decisions about Children*, Oxford, Basil Blackwell, p. 139.

37. Research carried out by McKey *et al.* (1985) into the impact of the long-term American project Head Start concluded that although it had immediate positive effects on the cognitive ability of young children, and short-term benefits on children's social behaviour, motivation and self-esteem, these benefits tended to disappear by the end of the third year after pre-school; from 'Start Right', *op. cit.*, pp. 84–5.

38. Schweinhart and Weikart's cost–benefit analysis suggested that, after adjustment for inflation, for every $1000 invested in the High/Scope pre-school programme, the return to society was $7160. From the Ypsilante Perry Pre-school project in support of early childhood education, research project by David P. Weikart for High/Scope Educational Research Foundation; quoted in 'Start Right', *op. cit.*, pp. 86–7.

39. Wilkinson, Helen (1994), *No Turning Back: Generations and the Genderquake*, London, Demos.

40. See, for example, Eisenstein (1984) and Borchorst, A. and Siim, B. (1987), 'Women and the Advanced Welfare State – A New Kind of Patriarchal Power', in Sassoon, Showstack (ed.) (1993), *Women and the State*, London, Hutchinson.

41. Blundell Jones, Peter, quoted in 'Kindergarten Contrasts', *Architectural Review*, September 1991, p. 48.

42. Schaffer, H.R., quoted in 'Kindergarten Contrasts', *op. cit.*

43. Kindlon, Dan and Thompson, Michael (1999), *Raising Cain – Protecting the Emotional Life of Boys*, London, Michael Joseph, p. 22.

44. For example, Huttenlocher, J., Haight, W., Bryk, A., Seltzer, M. *et al.* (1991) 'Early Vocabulary Growth: Relation to Language Input and Gender', *Development Psychology*, vol 27: pp. 236–48; and Shaywitz, S. E., Shaywitz, B. A., Fletcher J. M., and Escobar, M. D. (1990) 'Prevalence of Reading Disability in Boys and Girls: Results of the Connecticut Longitudinal Study', *Journal of the American Medical Association*, vol 264, pp. 998–1002.

45. 'Design to Grow With: a Response to the 40th International Design Conference in Aspen', *Design Quarterly*, vol 149, April–May 1990. See also Kline, Stephen (1993), *Out of the Garden*, London and New York, Verso.

46. 'The Late Show Special', BBC 2 television, 5 December 1994, with Melanie Philips of the *Observer*; Hugh Cunningham, historian, University of Kent; Carolyn Steedman, historian, Warwick University, and Michael Rosen, editor of *The Penguin Book of Childhood*, London, Viking, 1994.

47. A project initiated by Robin Mudge of the BBC Education Department is to televize the activities of a nursery school for the benefit of children and mothers who do not have access to the real thing. Called the 'School Without Walls', it stresses the importance of a real and imaginatively designed environment within which television technology can be used in a positive way.

48. J.P Greaves (1777–1842), educational pioneer; quoted in Silber, Kate (1973), *Pestalozzi: The Man and His Work*, 3rd edn, London, Routledge & Kegan Paul, p. 310.

49. From European Seminar 'Space and Quality of Life for Children', Madrid, 27–8 November 1992: introduction Peter Moss, p. 1.

50. Operation Head Start began as an experiment 25 years ago in a number of deprived cities of the USA. Its success is considerable and the curriculum is widely used in the USA and Britain.

51. Silber, Kate, *op. cit.*, p.46.

52. Borchorst, Anette, Chapter 8 in Ungerson, Clare (ed.), *Gender and Caring, op. cit.*, p. 172.

53. Wilkinson, Helen, *op. cit.*

54. Willshaw, Isobel (1992), European Seminar 'Space and Quality of Life for Children', Madrid, 27-8 November 1992, plenary session 1: '*The Urban Context*', p. 4.

55. Half of the staff are trained as teachers, with three years of general training and one year's practical training. For the one- to three-year-olds, two fully trained teachers are required per nine children.

56. All space standards are given as nett usable space, including ancillary areas such as staff rooms which may not be used by the children.

57. 'The High/Scope Institute (UK) – an Introduction to the High/Scope Approach to Working with Young Children', High/Scope Institute UK, 190–192 Maple Road, London SE20.

58. *Ibid.*

59. Tomlinson, Caro (1987), 'Play with a Purpose', *Child Education,* November 1987.

60. See note 11.

61. Van der Eyleen, W. and Turner, Barry (1969), *Adventures in Education,* Harmondsworth, Penguin, p. 55.

62. European Commission Network on Childcare (1994), 'Quality Targets in Services for Young Children – Proposals for a Ten Year Action Programme', p. 21.

63. Petter, Guido (1987), 'Shadow Games', in *The Hundred Languages of Children,* trans. from the exhibition catalogue *I Cento Linguaggi dei Bambini,* Dept of Education, City of Reggio Emilia, Region of Emilia Romagna, September 1987, p. 70.

64. Selmer-Olsen, *op. cit.,* p. 193.

CHAPTER 2

A selective history: aspects of children's culture and architecture for children

2.1 History and concepts

The Modern Movement connection

The history of childhood and early childhood education is long and complex. It is argued about up to the present time with important educationalists claiming their doctrines to have been the first or the most significant. If radical thought is at the very root of innovatory ideas in education, then pre-school systems or ideas like 'child-centred learning' or 'open teaching' may be viewed as influential prototypes for many developments in general education during the 20th century. A number of these ideas were reflected in early examples of nursery school architecture.

Although opinions differ, the kindergarten idea is generally considered to have been initiated as early as the 17th century, when small groups of people in a number of European countries became interested in the moral reform of society. Churchmen, lawyers and scholars recognized the importance of education in bringing this about. At this time, Comenius talked about organized child care.[1] In the 18th century, Rousseau rebelled against the pervasive moral atmosphere of pre-revolutionary Paris, asserting the beneficial effects on children of an outdoor life. However, these early prognoses for urban problems were not expressed in any built form which could be described as 'architecture' until the 1920s and 1930s. Even then, kindergarten architecture was seen only in a relatively few 'iconic' buildings.

Despite one-off attempts to come up with high-quality nursery schools during the 1930s and a number of notable Modern Movement examples, these prototypes were not built in significant enough numbers for the kindergarten to be described as a 'building type' in its own right. For reasons of economy, by far the majority of early facilities were located in readymade accommodation of negligible architectural quality. However, the early kindergarten ideal, which related environmental needs to pedagogical needs, did bring about a number of important architectural impulses, both in modernistic and organic forms.

These ideas, illustrated by a few noteworthy projects of this early period (built and unbuilt), can be said to have been signifiers of subsequent developments, not just in later nursery school projects, but in educational buildings in general. In this

2.1 Axonometric of the original scheme of the nursery building for Oak Lane Country Day School, Pennsylvania, by Howe and Lescaze (designer Lescaze), 1929.

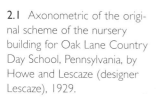

2.2 Site plan.
Key:
1 entrance hall
2 classroom
3 wc/bathroom
4 head teacher
5 platform
6 classroom
7 kitchen
8 larder
9 stairs to roof and canopy
10 stairs to roof
11 playground
12 service yard

2.1

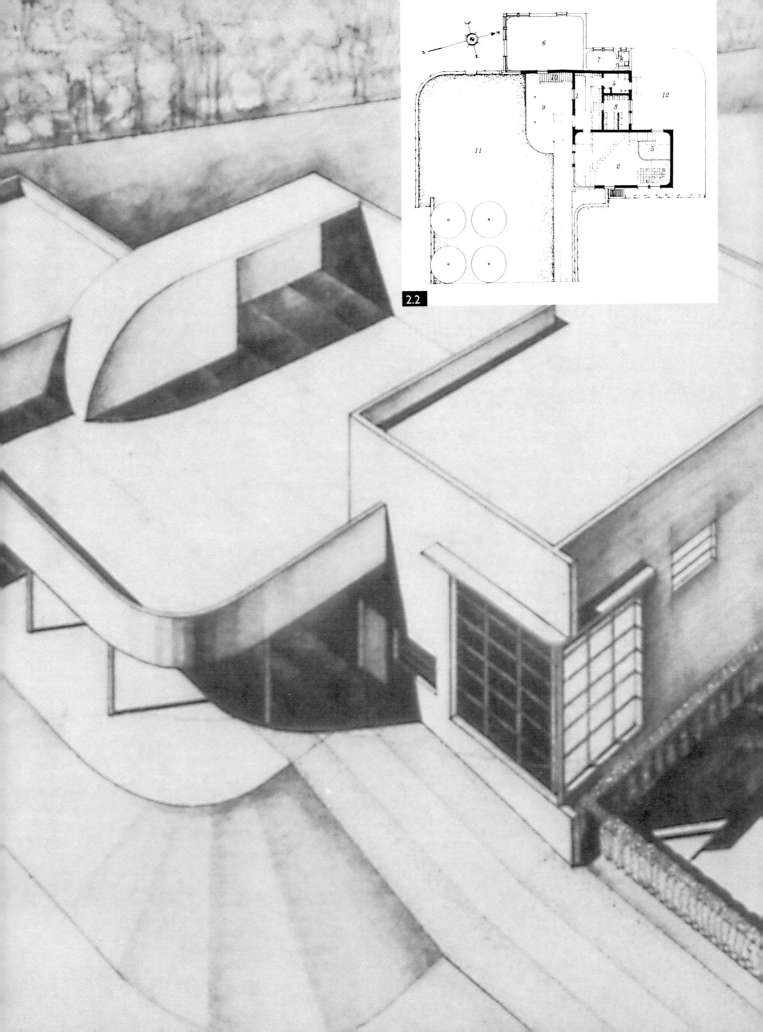

2.2

section, some of the strands of this early educational/architectural convergence will be explored to provide pointers to the current debate.

Middle-class–working-class divisions

Johann Heinrich Pestalozzi founded the first child-centred institution, at Yverdon in 1805. Although not specifically for younger children, it was based on what became the essential kindergarten principles. Ten years later, following a visit to Yverdon, philanthropist Robert Owen established a child care institution in his ideal industrial community, New Lanark, Scotland. Since most children over the age of six worked alongside their parents in the cotton mills, Owen's building sheltered younger children and could therefore be termed a nursery school. It was staffed by nurses in a purpose-made structure which provided a pleasant, healthy, if somewhat scaleless, environment. However, its pedagogical philosophy was unsophisticated.

Educational facilities can be seen as a phenomenon that developed across national boundaries during the latter part of the 19th century and the first third of the 20th century. Instigated primarily through the pioneering and vaguely mystical teachings of Friedrich Froebel, one-off private kindergartens were established in Germany, Britain, Japan and North America initially for middle-class children whose parents were able to pay the fees. This first impulse to pre-school child care and education came from liberal, educated individuals, who had come into contact with the Froebelian philosophy. The influence of Froebel's child-centred view was originated by early 19th-century German philosophers who opposed the empirical approach. Their new philosophy, known as Naturphilosophie, attempted to place scientific progress in the context of a more spiritual world. It stressed the need to comprehend the unity and harmony of nature among the phenomena. Hitherto, child care facilities had been seen as the exclusive domain of the working classes through their need for moral reform. Froebel's philosophy established the kindergarten as being complementary to home life, rather than a replacement for it; this balanced, holistic approach was in opposition to the scientific rationalism associated with the French revolutionary philosophers.

The first kindergarten in the north of England was founded in Salford in 1871 by Sir William Mather, a leading figure in the

British Froebel Movement. A year later he established a so-called 'free kindergarten' for the underprivileged in a working-class district, intended to be for children between the ages of three and six. Although financial problems beset these early kindergartens, they are considered to be the forerunners of the nursery school movement (for underprivileged children) in Britain and the USA.

Kindergartens were first established in the USA largely as a result of the dissemination of the teachings of Froebel. The Ronge sisters, who had been responsible for the first Froebelian Kindergarten in Tavistock Place, London, in 1851, then influenced the formation of one of the first kindergartens in the USA. This was established in 1856, in Watertown, Wisconsin. Mme Kraus Boelte's Boston kindergarten, started in 1872, and Susan Elizabeth Blow's at St Louis, Missouri, of 1873 were both early examples based on Froebelian principles. It is important to state that we are talking here about the kindergarten as an educational institution, devoid of any architectural form or intent.

As a result of research into child behaviour by theorists such as Granville Stanley Hall and John Dewey, a less pedagogic approach to child care developed in the USA in the following years, parallel to the more middle-class Froebelian establishments. The employment of young women in industry at the turn of the century resulted in some neglect of young children; the Association of Day Nurseries was established in New York City in 1897 to help remedy this problem. By 1914 there were 96 day nurseries in the city, largely funded by socially minded philanthropists. Similar developments took place in other large industrial centres.

In Germany, in the wake of Froebel's revolutionary ideas, kindergartens were established in many centres after 1840. In 1848 the possibility that the kindergarten would form the first stage of a coherent educational system was discussed at a large teachers' conference. These ideas were lost in the restoration policies of Prussia from 1851 onwards, but reemerged again around the turn of the century in a number of open-air kindergartens – for example, in Charlottenburg near Berlin in 1904.

In response to a Board of Education report of 1908, a number of nursery schools were set up in London. They came about as the result of cooperation between community groups, mainly in slum areas, and local infant welfare clinics. The first large-scale facility for underprivileged children in Britain of any note was an open-air nursery school in Deptford, south London. Partly inspired by foreign examples such as the open-air schools in Prussia, it was founded by Rachel and Margaret McMillan in 1913. The sisters endeavoured to move away from the faintly metaphysical Froebelian theories towards a more pragmatic approach, concentrating on the basic needs of children for fresh air and physical games. When Margaret met Rudolf Steiner she was highly taken by his personal charm, but rather less impressed by his pre-school philosophy.

It was the origins of the kindergarten idea which define certain attitudes to pre-school education that are still prevalent to this day; in the intellectual, romantic philosophy propagated by Froebel, middle-class libertarians found the perfect articulation of their children's needs for educational development, socialization and stimulation within the framework of his holistic Naturphilosophie. As a response to the oppressive urban environment of the newly industrialized cities (initially in England), more pragmatic health concerns were considered to be the primary need of young children from poor working-class areas – the kindergarten as a form of orphanage/hospital.

Although these middle-class pioneers wanted to assist working-class children, lack of financial support for the pre-school system prevented it. Kindergartens for the working classes were later built to higher densities and located in ramshackle or readymade buildings for financial reasons. It was left to individuals such as Margaret McMillan and Maria Montessori in Rome to bring kindergartens to the poor during the early years of the 20th century. Class prejudice is still evident in a number of pre-school systems today, particularly in Britain. There was, and one suspects still is, a characteristically Anglo-Saxon scepticism for fanciful intellectual ideas such as the early European kindergarten ideal.

Mysticism versus rationalism

Another important intellectual theorist who has influenced kindergarten thinking throughout the 20th century is Rudolf Steiner (1861–1925). He founded a spiritual movement based on the notion that there is a world comprehensible to pure thought but accessible only to the highest faculties of mental knowledge. He believed these faculties could be cultivated through the total harmony of the senses, which could be partly brought about by the use of an expressive, organic architectural form. His early years in Vienna at the Technische Hochschule saw the beginnings of his fascination with Goethe and Naturphilosophie. He established an ideal community which focused on the Goethanium building, which encapsulated many of his architectural ideals. After this first timber structure was destroyed by fire it was replaced by a moulded concrete building, which prefaced many of the later architectural themes of plasticity and growth.

As a result of Steiner's experiments, the Waldorf School Movement was founded in Germany in 1919. By 1969 there were 80 schools attended by 25 000 children in Europe and the USA, many of which were nursery schools in themselves or which included kindergarten classes. The highly metaphysical nature of the Steiner philosophy, however, worked against its being adopted by mainstream state or local education authorities. They adopted a more scientific approach in the 1930s, much more in tune with the rationalist thinking of the time. In 1928, when Hannes Meyer, the newly elected Head of Architecture at the Bauhaus, proposed the universal design formula 'Function × Economy = Building', it was intended to be a rejection of certain Bauhaus ideals that Meyer believed still retained some of the pseudo-mystical influences of Steiner.[2] In the debate between the organicism of Steiner and the romantic faith in positivistic progress through science, the latter was to prevail.

Similar views were being articulated in some influential educational circles. In 1929, Henry Morris, Secretary for Education at Cambridge County Council, asserted that only by becoming free of all concepts stemming from 'the magical view of man and the universe' could education be discussed in contemporary terms. 'A scientific, logical and relevant manner in relation to human problems' defined the architectural aspirations of the new nursery school builders, not just in Britain but in Europe and the USA. However, Morris's patronizing reference to the inability of professional educators in training colleges to make any original contribution to contemporary thought reinforced the separation between pre-school architectural and educational theory.[3]

This somewhat élitist view of the professions as separate entities continues to prevail in some areas. It is a modernist view, which arguably has hindered the possibility of any form of the architectural/educational 'convergence' that was the implied aim

Kindergarten Architecture

2.3

2.3 The former Michael House School, Ilkeston, Derbyshire, designed by a Steiner architect, Georg Nemes, and established in September 1934. In 1925, following visits to a Froebel school and the first Steiner school in England, Miss E.B. Lewis petitioned the Board of Education for permission to establish a Steiner elementary school in Ilkeston. Minutes from the education committee meetings show typical scepticism for these new ideas, particularly in working-class communities: 'I suspect that Miss Lewis is trying to transplant into a coal village something she had admired in Switzerland without taking into account the change in altitude. Actually it is as much as we can do to get the Ilkeston children to speak good English by fourteen.' (Newell, G.N., 1981, *Steiner Education in England*, dissertation presented to the University of Nottingham, p. 52). Nevertheless, the school was established, and a kindergarten was added later.

2.4 An example of the 'traditional modernist' approach was the kindergarten at Karl Marx Hof, Vienna, by Karl Ehn, 1927. Seen in these terms, there is a clear connection between early educational philosophies and their expression in the best examples of early kindergarten architecture. Ehn's nursery school is a Montessori pre-school building in the form of a small pavilion that communicates its practicality and buildability rather than the spiritual expressionism of Rudolf Steiner's Waldorf schools.

2.5 Perspective view of the Caryl Peabody Nursery School. Unbuilt project by Walter Gropius (1937).

2.4

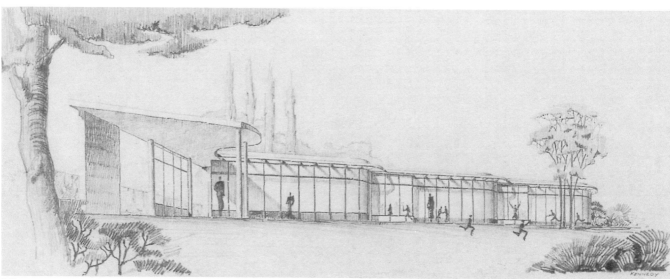

2.5

2.6 Axonometric of the rooftop playground at Le Corbusier's Marseilles Unité Nursery School, 1947–52. This included a paddling pool, integrated climbing ramps and water-play features that created an exciting futuristic children's landscape.

Key:
1 artificial mountains
2 children's play area
3 climbing ramps
4 paddling pool
5 crèche
6 ramp connecting health centre with terrace and day nursery

2.6

of the early theorists (Chapter 1).[4] Certainly, the rejection of an integrated approach to educational and architectural philosophies for pre-school was wholly at odds with the Steiner approach. In the Steiner schools, teachers and parents were not only to understand the complex philosophies supporting kindergarten education and architecture, but they were also to be in spiritual harmony with those philosophical ideas – a fusion between enlightened educational views and 19th-century mysticism. Unfortunately, Steiner's basic philosophy was always a little too esoteric for his enlightened methods to be widely adopted. It is clear today, however, that younger architects find many aspects of his architectural reasoning capable of producing particularly appropriate architecture for children.

The machine aesthetic

Following World War I, interest and concern for the well-being of young children continued with university child study centres in the USA encouraging the development of largely privately funded facilities. In Europe and to a lesser extent in Britain, interest in psychology's impact on child development and concerns for the improvement of the environment in general were expressed in a whole series of social projects. These were generally funded by private or public bodies or through charitable religious groups. Continental kindergarten movements developed apace: massive municipal housing schemes in Vienna, humanized by the incorporation of shops, clinics and particularly nursery schools, created a distinctly European form of social housing project.

The earliest known nursery school buildings had initially not been about education, but about social and medical care. The McMillan sisters' Deptford Nursery School, which was established in 1913 for poor and undernourished children, was little more than a scattered collection of Nissen huts and temporary canvas shelters supported by scaffolding poles. However, it influenced the thinking of the President of the Board of Education, who formulated a new bill to encourage the establishment of nursery schools. The Chelsea Open Air Nursery (1929) was accommodated in a house which had formerly been an artist's studio. There were no purpose-made kindergatens with any significant architectural qualities until the mid 1920s. Up until that time, nursery school buildings were largely accommodated in readymade houses, makeshift sheds and shelters.

Andrew Saint asserts that this remained the case in Britain during the 1920s and 1930s, except for a few notable exceptions.[5] However, Froebel nursery schools continued to be founded in Britain, North America, Europe and Japan, and the search for more appropriate modern forms of architecture developed. Montessori schools were very much in evidence during the 1930s; at the same time, nursery schools were being attached to existing Waldorf schools. A number of modernist architects were employed to produce buildings which would reflect the growing importance of children in society and the radical humanism at the heart of the kindergarten ideal.

The influence of European architectural movements brought about two significant developments before World War II. The overriding philosophy dictating the style of these key prototypes was the notion of the 'machine aesthetic' which incorporated kindergartens into its new social forms. Fundamental to this spirit was the use of new materials and innovatory technology. The second development was the pragmatic need for units of accommodation (houses, schools, factories) produced efficiently, economically and in great numbers using prefabrication techniques.

At Dessau in the 1920s, Bauhaus teachers prompted by the Dutch De Stijl movement were responsible for the propagation of both innovations. The Bauhaus school buildings

2.8

2.8 Kensal Rise flats and nursery school by Maxwell Fry, Robert Atkinson, C.H. James and Grey Wornum.

2.9 Exterior view, from the playground, of a nursery school designed by Hans Leuzinger on the outskirts of Zürich in 1934. The formal plan is given a more dynamic quality by its subtle twist to fit the site.

2.10 Plan.
Key:
1-2   classrooms (25 children in each)
3-4   sleeping area (five children in each)
5   play hall
6   cloakroom and entrance

2.11 Interior view of classroom.

and houses for teachers were exemplars of the machine aesthetic. Two houses by Walter Gropius at the Wiessenhof Housing Exhibition in Stuttgart (1927) employed unit construction as a prototype for mass-produced housing. In the following years, a number of modernist child care buildings followed these technological principles, taking the home as their social model and often using the new technology.

In 1937, Maxwell Fry and Elizabeth Denby designed Kensal House in northwest London. Primarily a social housing scheme, it included an elegant semicircular nursery school in the shadow of the housing block. This followed European social patterns of maintaining closer contact between the home environment and the child's first school. The whole scheme shows the modernist influence of Walter Gropius, understandable since both archi-

tects were partners in practice with him for some years. Elsewhere Le Corbusier proposed a heroic rooftop play space as part of his Unité housing block in Marseilles (conceived in the 1930s; built 1947–52), asserting the importance of child care in the new socially enlightened communities.

The influence of European ideas extended to the USA with the adoption of an appropriately termed 'international style' in a number of housing-related day care centres. Gropius, who had worked for the Froebel Society in Germany in 1926, emigrated to America and in 1937 designed an unbuilt nursery school for the Caryl Peabody Trust. It was significant not just because of its architectural style, but also because of its social programme; the building contained a library and a health visitors' room. It established important ground rules for enlight-

2.7 Plan of Kensal Rise flats and nursery school, showing an interesting variety of different-sized play spaces.

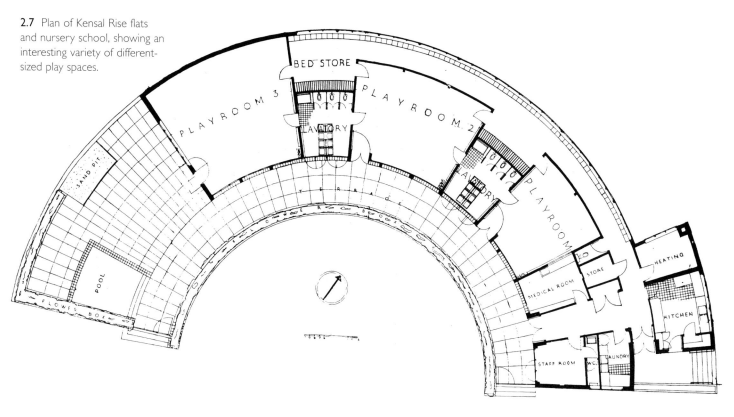

2.7

2.9

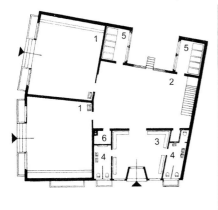

2.10

2.11

2.12 Ground-floor plan of André Lurcat's school at Villejuif. The kindergarten part is contained around its own courtyard, which is separated from the the main school by the head's office. It is considered to be one of the first examples of 'free' planning on open-air lines.

Key:
1 kindergarten
2 girls' playground
3 boys' playground
4 flower garden
5 vegetable garden
6 main entrance to kindergarten
7 porter
8 dining
9 head teacher's offices
10 medical
11 dormitory
12 plant room
13 classrooms
14 WC
15 junior school with classrooms over
16 sport/activity space

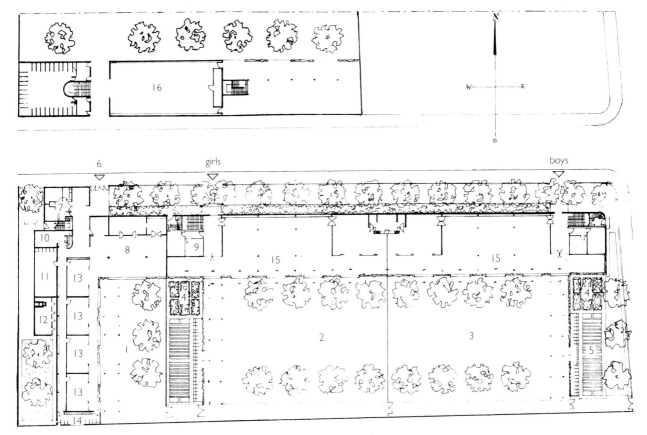

2.12

2.13

2.13 Timbe-frame kindergarten at Hartford, near Northwich, Cheshire, designed by Leslie Martin and Sadie Speight, 1938.

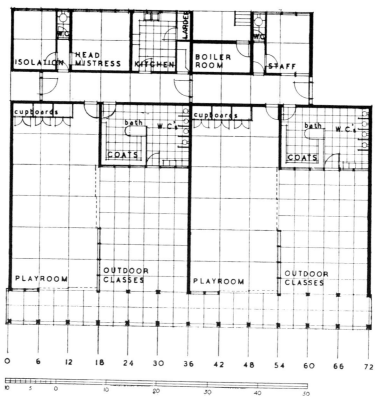

2.14 Plan of the expanding nursery school, by Erno Goldfinger and Mary Crowley, 1937. Goldfinger's expanding nursery school included three possible stages to accommodate 40, 80 and 120 children. Cloakrooms, lavatories and staff accommodation were integrated and positioned side by side. Constructional units were to be 6ft-wide wood-framed wall-sections, faced with tongue-and-groove weatherboarding, bolted together. (An internal perspective appears on the back cover.)

2.14

ened designers and educationalists in the USA up to World War II and reflected key pedagogic preoccupations.

Similarly, the influence of the Swiss ABC group permeated the USA when William Lecaze, who had trained in Zürich under Karl Moser, designed a campus nursery for Oakland School. The ABC Group were architects of a constructivist persuasion. They included Roth, Haefeli, Artaria, Schmidt and Moser who were influential in identifying the Swiss Modern Movement vocabulary. This was rather more modest than that appearing in the USSR and Germany at the time; nevertheless, it exhibited clear 'machine aesthetic' tendencies. In 1934, after the demise of the ABC periodical, Hans Leuzinger produced an exemplar of the style at a nursery school near Zürich. It incorporated ergonomically designed furniture, with the timber structure of the building seemingly harmonizing with the wooden toys.

Other nursery schools in Switzerland demonstrated the influence this group had on practising architects of the day.

Nursery school projects in the Paris suburbs during this period, particularly by Beaudouin and Lods at Suresnes, helped to establish a French tradition of good local state-funded kindergartens. In France in the 1930s a number of infant schools with attached *écoles maternelles* were built. One at Villejuif by André Lurcat was a notable example of this new architectural form in France. It had a spacious and open, but strictly orthogonal, L-shaped layout with classrooms placed over refectories and covered play spaces. The one-storey kindergarten contained four classrooms and a dormitory which occupied the short arm of the L. These structures opened on to a secure garden. The school at Suresnes was an open-air pavilion type, with its facilities describing a five-sided polygon with classroom pavilions dispersed on the two open sides, and the kindergarten as the centre of the continuous three-sided block. There was a covered court at its centre.

In Britain, perhaps in optimistic anticipation of a more coherent strategy towards the state funding of child care facilities, the Nursery School Association in London commissioned a prototype by Erno Goldfinger and Mary Crowley, intended to be mass produced by the joinery company Bolton and Paul (1934–38). Called 'the expanding nursery school', it was based on a gridded unit system and was organized in a modest but elegant form. Goldfinger's internal perspective shows an open-plan activity space with full-length doors opening on to the external play spaces. The children he includes in his drawing appear somewhat lost in the space, suggesting that Goldfinger may have had little idea of how nursery school children might actually spend their time in his anonymous setting.

Nevertheless, its intentions reflected the enlightened thinking of the time in relation to pre-school facilities. It combined the open-air health values of the 19th century with a weightless, machine-made image of the future; and, most importantly, it held a vision of nursery schools for all. Unfortunately, the exigencies of wartime meant that it was never put into production, although the germs of the idea did re-emerge in the post-war years.

Pre-fabrication and the post-war years

The notion of solving the urgent need for units of accommodation (houses or schools) efficiently and economically by mass production was a preoccupation of members of the developing Modern Movement prior to Goldfinger's commission.[6] In 1924 Walter Gropius was asked to design Friedrich Froebel House in Bad Liebenstein. The programme required a kindergarten, a day care centre, a recreation home for children, a youth centre, and a training school for mothers. The main building was surrounded by playgrounds, stables and vegetable gardens, and adjoined by eight identical play pavilions. The intention was that ten or twelve underprivileged children and a nurse could form a family group. The pavilions were to be of standardized light slabs for easy construction, a system that was later to be used by Gropius for housing at Törten, Dessau. The Froebel project was not built; however, the plan and intended construction method illustrate a belief in standardized, house-sized nursery units, and reinforce the 'home from home' concept for nursery school design. The complex programme could also be said to have been a prototype for the large European child care centres of today.

Two years earlier, in 1935, Donald Gibson and C.W. Lemmon had already designed an experimental nursery school. This was built at Lache, Chester, and had a timber-framed structure, asbestos cement sheet cladding and steel windows. In 1938, Leslie Martin and Sadie Speight designed an elegant nursery school at Hartford near Northwich, Cheshire. It had an expressed timber structure, clad with asbestos cement sheeting externally and internally. Both of these examples reflected the new spirit of rational, innovatory pre-school thinking. (With hindsight, the use of asbestos, in a children's building, seems scandalous.)

World War II caused an acceleration in the need for nursery school places, which was achieved by all kinds of temporary accommodation – from sheds and church halls to Nissen huts. In Britain, nursery school provision became a statutory requirement in the 1944 Education Act. Surprisingly, expectations were never fulfilled in the post-war years, because although prefabrication was developed and used to create a large number of schools (particularly the CLASP system[7]), few of these were nursery schools or designed with pre-school children in mind.

After the war, the economic and political will failed to produce a positive and coherent strategy for the provision of a state-funded nursery school system. Indeed, Bowlby's philosophy that young children should be with their mothers rather than in a nursery school helped to institutionalize an anti-kindergarten view which still prevails in some male-dominated sections of society.[8] One can generally sense a similar attitude in the USA during this period, whereas in Japan and most of mainland Europe private initiatives continued to develop alongside coherent state systems. These were seen as healthy and essential prerequisites of modern industrial and post-industrial societies.

Summary

At the outbreak of World War II the need for kindergartens to support the children of women working in armaments factories had been manifested in low-quality nursery buildings in Britain and elsewhere. Overall, the disruption of the war extinguished

2.15 Birchwood Nursery School, Hertfordshire, a temporary building constructed in 1943 for the needs of mothers working in the De Haviland aircraft factory. Although intended soon to be replaced, it is still in use more than 50 years later. The bomb-proof shelter is used as a materials store.

2.15

the higher architectural intentions that had been initiated during the 1930s. Elements of the Froebel philosophy appealed to the Nazis in Germany, however, and as a result kindergarten institutions proliferated, but the pre-war modernist architecture of imagination and innovation was felt to be ideologically unsound and many eminent educators and architects left Germany.

Despite the incoherent nature of early nursery school developments, it is clear that architects usually followed a distinct ideological philosophy – either looking backward to the 19th-century arts and crafts/organic tradition, or forward to the new architecture of the 'machine aesthetic'. This stylistic and philosophical diversity produced a number of clearly definable architectural categories, which were particularly applicable to kindergarten architecture.

At the end of the 1950s, therefore, we find kindergartens that reflect four broadly defined characteristics. First, there were those that exhibited experimental Modern Movement preoccupations, as explored by Max Fry; secondly, those that reflected Expressionist, Steineresque notions; thirdly, examples of a less adventurous sort that have the spirit of the late 19th-century arts and crafts movement; and finally those buildings that represent a traditional modernist approach – they are modern, but neither overtly expressionistic nor overtly experimental technically or philosophically.

It would appear that in the thirty years following World War II the connection between contemporary educational theory and pedagogical architecture was barely recognized. As we have explained, this was not always the case: one can justify the importance early childhood education had in the development of innovations such as the concept of the 'natural child', the Froebel 'gifts and occupations', and child art [section 4]. It will be seen how early experiences of kindergarten had a profound influence on important 20th-century artists, designers and architects including Paul Klee, Wassily Kandinsky, Frank Lloyd Wright, Theo van Doesburg and Rudolf Steiner. The act of drawing was a pivotal element in the new theory of child development; its use in the kindergarten may well have had a fundamental effect on various aspects of art and architecture in the 20th century.

Alternative religious beliefs – like Naturphilosophie, transcendentalism, theosophy, anthroposophy and Freudian thought – which mainly developed in the early part of the century were all inextricably linked to the concurrent awakening of interest in

childhood and childlike states. These ideas have played an important part in the development of innovatory architectural thinking, especially in the area of kindergarten architecture. Perhaps the most significant expression of this was the separation of theosophically influenced German expressionism and the rationalism of De Stijl, which occurred at the Bauhaus. In this chapter, one of our arguments will turn on how these new philosophies helped to shape contemporary approaches to kindergarten theory, and more broadly to architecture in general.

The nature of this patchwork history must make it apparent that there is no broadly agreed framework to define the historical development of the kindergarten as a recognized building type. This is mainly because pre-school attendance has (quite rightly in our view) always been optional. Consequently, these facilities have developed in a piecemeal fashion, architects playing a dominant role in their widespread procurement only over the past ten to fifteen years. Nevertheless, the historical development of the kindergarten movement is so inextricably related to an architectural understanding as to make it a fundamental part of any publication dealing with nursery school buildings.

2.2 Childhood before child care: London

We have already made reference to the social and demographic changes that took place over a relatively short period of time as a result of the Industrial Revolution. The impact of these transformations ultimately made the need for child care so transparently obvious that practical individuals such as Robert Owen and Margaret McMillan emerged. They responded in a more down-to-earth way than the philosophical thinkers of the Enlightenment who had first raised the issue of child welfare. How was the young child cared for and nurtured before this time? What structures, if any, existed that enabled the child to be protected and socialized prior to the invention of organized systems?

Extensive anthropological and social studies on this subject have been carried out, particularly since Philippe Ariès's influential and contentious study of 1960, *L'Enfant et la Vie Familiale sous l'Ancien Régime* [*Centuries of Childhood*].[9] In trying to paint a brief and generalized picture of the child in pre-modern society, we have referred extensively to Linda Pollock's excellent study of parent–child relations from 1500 to 1900, *Forgotten Children*,[10] and *Growing Up in Medieval London* by Barbara Hanawalt.[11]

Although London would not have been a typical European city of the medieval period, it is worth recounting the social conditions of its children during the period up to the end of the 15th century. Poll tax records of the period show that the population in 1377 was 35 000 and one can guess that the adult population was nearer 60 000.[12] By 1550 the population was estimated to be 150 000.[13] London was therefore a small town by today's standards. However, if we took a walk through London before the great fire of 1666 we would have been struck by the tightness of the city streets and the concentration of people living one on top of another:

Houses were packed together in streets no more than ten or twelve feet wide, with sudden gaps of vast open space. Indeed, as we approached new buildings near the walls of Paris or at no-man's land between the City of London and Westminster, we would perceive not a gradual diminution in the concentration of houses, but a sudden abrupt break between teeming streets and isolated houses . . .[14]

And although the strong patrilineages which we know characterized social structures in cities like Florence and Ghent were for various reasons less strong in medieval London, nevertheless even the orphaned child was part of large network of carers not necessarily related by blood:

Servants and apprentices and perhaps even a journeyman lived in the household. Neighbours were always visiting, so the [orphaned] child would not feel deprived of male direction or company. The stepfather might even already know the child and might well not be a stranger. And just as for children of divorced families today, the commonness of the experience [being brought up by a single parent] might have made it easier to accept.[15]

Care for young children was very much supported by these extended communal groups which characterized the City of London, even when the two-parent family structure was not in place. Male children would be given better care, because they had a higher social value. Although childhood mortality was high (30–50% in the pre-modern world), all the care and nurturing of babies and small children was in the main taken on

conscientiously by parents, godparents, family, servants, apprentices and neighbours. Barbara Hanawalt makes the point that 'child care in London may not have been organized, but the streets and houses were crowded with adults going about their business or pleasure'.[16] By the time children started to walk and could use the street as a sort of playground, passers-by would be as much part of the welfare structure as close family and friends.

From a health point of view, filth in this was much more dangerous for the young child than it was in the rural environment. To balance this, country life was physically harder, and parents would spend long hours toiling in the fields. Consequently, young children were often left all day with inadequate baby-sitters such as older sisters and brothers, whereas in the city, when a poor or socially disconnected mother had to go out on errands or to work, she would often carry her child with her. This practice, however, was by no means safe – one coroner's report gives an example of the risks: 'Margaret, the wife of John Hilton, worked as a brewer for a London baker. She brought her five-year-old child to work with her and claimed that the apprentice had beaten it so severely that it died two days later.'[17]

Many historians and scholars adopt the negative view that the arrival of a new child was a misfortune to be overcome, particularly in the puritanical societies of late 16th- and 17th-century northern Europe. Ivan Illich, talking about parent–child relations in 17th-century England and America, suggests the notion of 'breaking the will of the child' as being of primary importance: 'There is no denying that parents in 17th-century England were interested in their children, but that interest took the form of controlling youngsters – just as adults restrained themselves – rather than allowing autonomous developments'.[18]

Clearly, discipline as opposed to free play was the pedagogical pattern even during the early years for many children at this time. Some historians suggest that harsh physical punishment was common in the medieval and Victorian world; for example, de Mause puts the view that 'the further back in history one goes, the lower the level of child care, and the more likely children are to be killed, abandoned, beaten, terrorized and sexually abused'.[19] However, not all evidence confirms this view. For example, Ryerson in her 1961 study of child advice literature, concludes that a more gentle method of child rearing was proposed in advice manuals between 1550 and 1750.[20]

Certainly, some court records support the idea that children were physically abused as a social norm. The following quotation from 14th-century records depicts a society that appeared to condone the assault of young children: 'A five-year-old boy, for instance, was in a neighbour's house at vespers when he took a piece of wool and put it in his cap. The lady of the house, "chastising him, struck the said John with her right hand under his left ear". He cried out and Isabella, his mother, raised the hue and carried him home where he died.' Interestingly, when this case came to court it was dismissed as being an accidental death. The violent behaviour of the neighbour was presumably considered to be a necessary act of discipline.[21] 250 years later we can compare this to a similar court account which relates how 'a mother was charged with "barbarously beating and ill-treating her own child" – a daughter aged four. When the mother was taken out of the office after her trial, it was with the greatest difficulty she could be protected from the fury of the women on the outside.'[22]

J.H.P. Plumb argues that up to the end of the 17th century, the 'common lot [of the child] was fierce parental discipline'. He suggests that from that time onwards a new attitude to children was developing, which resulted in books, games and clothes designed especially for them. This, he believes, is the point where 'childhood' was invented.[23] Much debate has centred around the idea of when and why the notion of childhood came about. Philippe Ariès asserts in *Centuries of Childhood* that only in modern times have sentimental definitions of childhood and adolescence been recognized. If by sentiment we mean 'liberal thought', this may well be the case. However, it is possible to suppose that medieval social systems were in many ways more capable of nurturing and supporting the natural needs of young children than those of the modern world. Parents and carers would probably not have been as conventionally sentimental in their treatment, particularly of young children, as we are today, but the everyday physical closeness of parents (or carers) ensured that children were well looked after.

When society began to transform from a relatively ordered hierarchical semi-feudal system into the industrial and semi-industrial societies of the 18th and 19th centuries, it inevitably became more chaotic, with more fraying at the edges. Indeed, Ariès, when discussing the transformation of societies from the open feudal systems to the more closed nuclear families of the 20th century, supports this view: 'the extended "sociable" family of the middle ages allowed children a great deal of freedom but in the transition to the closed nuclear family a child became more constrained and disciplined'.[24]

Hoyles states that 'the invention of childhood as a separate state corresponds with the transition from feudalism to capitalism'.[25] Economic growth brought about the possibility for individuals and groups with ethical Christian views to begin to respond to evident needs in the newly industrialized cities. Influenced by the writings of key 18th-century libertarians such as Locke and Rousseau, the selfconfident, educated classes recognized the need to replace the extended socializing structures of the medieval period with something new, specifically to meet the needs of young children living in cities.

The Industrial Revolution, starting in about 1750, caused change on legal and administrative levels, but more importantly immense demographic transformations. Although the population of London doubled to 750 000 in the 18th century, in the 19th century it rose from 860 000 to 5 million.[26] Although the industrialization of the cities brought wealth to certain sections of society, making a degree of humanitarian legislation affordable, it also brought great misery as the *quid pro quo*, with children as young as six employed in factories, mills and mines during much of the 18th century. The poor parent was left with the often tragic choice between this and starvation for the family. Whereas social conditions were more apparent to the squire in the pre-industrialized village, and also in the teeming streets of medieval London, the new, massively enlarged cities concealed the condition of the poor from the middle classes who might have wished to do something about it.

Until determined investigators such as Chadwick and Engels, and the publication of the parliamentary blue books in the 1830s, the appalling plight of the poor, and particularly poor children, in British cities was not widely known. It was possible, Linda Pollock states, 'to see more human misery and suffering in one visit to one factory than in a tour round the countryside'.[27] Child care legislation came quickly after this period in Britain and throughout Europe and America.

When William Blackstone published his *Commentaries on the Laws of England* in 1765, it had set the agenda for the introduction in the 19th century of the Poor Laws and the Education Act of 1876. These placed a legal duty on parents to provide education for their children. However, different countries developed

2.16

their formalized responses to such legislation in different ways. According to Hugh Cunningham, 'the emergence of the idea of a "childhood" appropriate for all children was focused around three issues: the child at work, the street child, and the child who was abused in the home. The interplay between these three issues led to the articulation of the belief that the child's fundamental right was a right to "childhood"'.[28]

For millions who left the familiarity of their farms and villages in the 18th and 19th centuries, adapting to city life was about learning to live cheek by jowl with strangers, unable to even see, let alone experience, green fields and farm animals. Concern for the welfare of young children was clearly a reaction to this urban 'implosion' which brought the plight of children (along with those of the poor, the infirm and the insane) to the minds of the new liberal thinkers. They did not invent the notion of childhood, but they necessarily formalized it after the fragmentation of the social structures that had provided a framework for the support of children for generations.

The advent of smaller family groups tended to separate children from parents and family carers, increasing the risk of child abuse. It also cut children off from the important socializing influences of a wider society of personal contacts, and public life in general. One of the key roles of the new kindergartens was (and remains) to reconnect the young child to a coherent socializing system. In philosophical terms, another key role of the new institutions was to reestablish a bond between childhood and the natural world, felt to have been sacrificed in the new industrial conurbations. Childhood was not invented at this stage, but the social conditions within which childhood was lived changed irrevocably.

2.3 Educational thought from Rousseau to Froebel

Rousseau and Laugier

Laugier believes in an absolute, 'essential' beauty, independent of custom and convention. He believes this beauty is to be found in Nature alone; it is from Nature that all rules are derived, but all architectural rules so far proposed seem to Laugier to be 'rules of chance (*règles au hasard*)'. Architectural principles are imitations of the processes   of Nature. Just as Rousseau envisages a bliss-

condition, so Laugier posits a primitive hut as the origin of all possible forms of architecture.[29]

In the 18th century, towards the end of the French Enlightenment, Jean-Jacques Rousseau (1712–78) and Marc-Antoine Laugier (1713–69) developed similar notions. They were directed towards the idea of the restoration of man's natural being and habitat. Rousseau in the 1750s portrayed the primitive savage as a natural man; a noble and magnificent creature on a higher, more natural plane of being than contemporary man. Laugier depicted his habitat, the primitive hut which, unlike earlier illustrative precedents, was not fashioned in the image of a prehistoric cave-like edifice, but as a lightweight construction of trees and branches.

The belief in nature and the restoration of natural man were common ideals. Rousseau rejected the city in favour of a decentralized rural utopia. Although Laugier shared his belief in the picturesque value of landscaped gardens and parks, he was more pragmatic. Laugier was inclined to show how cities like Paris could be given a breath of natural life by the construction of wider roads with avenues of trees and parks. Although the visionary architect Étienne Boullée did not go along with Rousseau's 'rural utopia', his younger contemporary C.H. Ledoux saw in it great relevance. He also reacted positively to Rousseau's proto-political thesis *Discours sur l'origine de l'inégalité parmi les hommes* published in 1755 and *Du Contrat Social* of 1762 which repeated many of these ideas.

Rousseau had no idea that his *Discourse* would become such an important treatise for revolution; it was a fundamental text for the Russian revolutionaries and is still discussed today. He did, however, believe that his novel *Emile, ou de l'éducation* (1762) would have a far-reaching effect, and this was indeed the case. No other book had a greater influence on early educational ideas. Its publication and the thoughts it provoked disturbed the placid stability of 18th-century European education. The fusion of its ideas, combined with radical scientific thought, led to the creation of new perceptions on the nature of children, of teaching methods, and the aim and purpose of the educational process.[30]

The appeal of *Emile* was strengthened by the 'cult of the noble savage', which thrived in the 1770s. The legacy of Rousseau's architectural and educational vision was a kind of decentralized rural utopia, where the notion of creativity – making by doing – would flourish, and children would explore the content of language within the context of their immediate environment. The school was to be at the centre of rural village life. However, it would be in its readymade or vernacular form; this would develop in young children an inherent understanding of the 'natural' way of life from the earliest years.

> What were the leading ideas of Rousseau's *Emile*? Its originality lay in the fact that it was the first comprehensive attempt to describe a system of education according to nature. The key idea of the book was the possibility of preserving the original perfect nature of the child by means of the careful control of his education and environment, based upon an analysis of the different physical stages through which he passed from birth to maturity.[31]

The educational views expressed in *Emile* show a transformation in Rousseau's attitude towards society. He now seeks an equality, both moral and political, for man who is coming to fruition in society. He has discarded his 'noble savage' and the notion of innate knowledge for a belief in the social process and its effects on development. Rousseau was highly original in his thought and, as a political philosopher, could be described as the founder of modern democracy. His ideas on education were so radical that the theory and practice of nursery education has been influenced by them ever since. They were to be the philosophical basis for the key educational pioneers, such as Pestalozzi, Owen, Froebel and even Piaget in the 20th century.

David Michael Levine argues that the pedagogical ideas of Rousseau and his disciples have been largely ignored in the development of educational theory much beyond the nursery school.[32]

This may well be the case, as the value of 'rote learning' for school children is being advanced even today in some educational circles. However, the importance of Rousseau in the first stirrings of the kindergarten idea should not be underestimated. He originated the need to educate and thus socialize the young child in a holistic way, synthesizing the child's bodily needs with the development of the mind. He attempted (unsuccessfully) to put the theory into practice. Unfortunately, it took more than 100 years after the publication of his book and treatises on education for his enlightened views to be recognized, and for the unique needs of the pre-school child to be addressed in any coherent form.

Johann Heinrich Pestalozzi

Pestalozzi (1746–1827) was certainly inspired by Rousseau and Naturphilosophie. He spent years writing and teaching, during which time he had two overriding aims: the idea of social amelioration, and the desire to understand and discover the key to the educative process. Like Rousseau he was convinced that education should be in complete harmony with the nature of the child, and developed a child-centred approach that accepted the 'free spirit' but still maintained the importance of the teacher's direction in the child's learning processes. He disagreed with Rousseau's idea of the education of the child in isolation, and included stimuli such as drawing, writing and talking in the context of group learning. 'The means of making clear all knowledge gained by sense impressions comes from number, form and language.'[33]

Pestalozzi had belonged to the Helvetic Society, which was inspired by the literature of the French Enlightenment and naturally absorbed Rousseau's philosophies. He initially learned farming and, somewhat rashly, started the experimental cultivation of madder, the plant used in the production of red dye. This was a disastrous failure financially, and collapsed in the first year. In 1774 he founded an industrial enterprise at Neuhof:

The large house was there, his estate provided the basic essentials in food; workers (children!) were available in plenty. His ardent wish to help hurried him on. The idea was to teach poor, neglected, sometimes even physically unfit children to earn their living by their own work as cotton spinners or weavers. While working, they would learn arithmetic and catechism by repeating together what they had been told. In the evenings, by way of recreation, the boys would do gardening, the girls cooking and sewing. Pestalozzi placed great hopes in realising his plans.[34]

Neuhof worked for poor and orphaned children almost like an extended family. However, even in the early months of its development it was insolvent. Pestalozzi raised small amounts of money from wellwishers, but this attempt to create a self-supporting school also failed. It was 20 years before he had the chance to implement his dream of devoting his life to the education of the poor. Depressed with his failure during this interval, he turned to writing. One of his books, *Leonard and Gertrude*, was superficially a novel about village life, but it was socially didactic, its underlying message being reformist. It had a considerable influence as an educational treatise and, as a result, Pestalozzi was offered his first recognized teaching post, at the infant school at Burgdorf. He was given accommodation in the 13th-century castle, where J.R. Fischer (1772–1800) was also living, as government inspector of the Burgdorf schools. He had similar humanitarian ideals, believing in the furtherance of general education. He arranged for wealthy Burgdorf families to take evacuees from Appenzell, which had been ravaged by the Napoleonic war. Fischer was forced to leave Burgdorf without establishing his proposed teaching college, but he placed the education of the children from Appenzell in Pestalozzi's hands.

In 1800, Pestalozzi opened his first educational institute for children whose parents were willing to pay modest school fees. A teachers' training course was also proposed, and separately a school for poor children. Owing to inadequate financial support, Pestalozzi began to take on fee-paying children, and this – the private school for middle-class children – was the only part that flourished, although the school for poor children was eventually established some years later. This had always been Pestalozzi's most cherished project.

After the French announced a new constitution for Switzerland, the institute was transferred to Yverdon. The castle of Yverdon, a former stronghold of the Dukes of Savoy, was owned by the municipality when Pestalozzi arrived in 1805. It was repaired, slightly adapted to his needs, and given to him rent-free for life. The new institution was furnished simply; it had many spacious halls which could be used as classrooms and for assembly, and also dormitories for boarders. The layout included a large courtyard, a meadow, and broad avenues which were to serve as playgrounds.

At Yverdon Castle, Pestalozzi's new teaching curriculum was based on three crucial elements: language, number and form. His plea was for children to find out through their own senses before being informed about the origin and use of an object. He despised and condemned repetitive learning and factual cramming. The three activities of speaking, counting and measuring became the foundation of his theory of education. The theories could be summarized in three questions: what kinds of objects does the child see, what is their appearance or form, and how might they be represented? Primarily these exercises should be enjoyable and thus natural:

> The advantages of the Pestalozzian system of education . . . is the pleasure all Pestalozzian pupils take in mental labour and study. Thus from an early age learning and thinking can be made an enjoyment instead of a drudgery and any occupation useful to oneself or to others, hitherto regarded as beneath one's dignity, can be transformed into amusement by early habit.[35]

The basic principle for all subject areas was *Anschauung*, perception. Locke's principle of comprehension influenced Pestalozzi's intellectual understanding of education – the development of reasoning by the exercise of reasoning. Pestalozzi gave the name *Anschauung* to the basic processes of the mind. It applied to various stages of the evolution of ideas. Sometimes it was about reception of sense impression, and sometimes about the process of idea formation, combining sense impression and perception.

For a time Yverdon became the educational focus for the whole of Europe. Its occupants included pupils, teachers, servants and Pestalozzi's family. Numbers grew rapidly to over 250

2.17

pupils, who came from all over Europe, Russia and America. However, it did not cater specifically for very young children, and there is no evidence that any special systems were developed for children under the age of five. Younger children were undoubtedly accepted, though, and it was Pestalozzi's profound achievement that he devised a system of education that was enjoyable and capable of adaptation to the needs of children as young as three years old.

Pestalozzi's ideas were spread internationally by his many disciples. For example, in 1837 James Pierrepoint Greaves (1777–1842) went to Yverdon and stayed for four years. He devised various means of introducing the system to Britain. In 1837 he founded a Pestalozzian school at Alcott House in Ham, Surrey – a utopian world similar to Robert Owen's. However, neither Greaves's nor Owen's scheme was a lasting success: one was based on reason and one on love, rather than a coherent combination of the two.

W.H. Ackerman (1789–1848), who had experience as an assistant teacher at Yverdon, arrived in London in 1814, and later taught in Lancastrian and national schools based on the monitorial system.[36] The best-known follower of Pestalozzi in Britain was Dr Charles Mayo (1792–1846), who went to Yverdon in 1819 and stayed for three years. He started a school in Epsom for wealthy boys, and employed mainly Swiss teachers. There were other Pestalozzian schools in England at this time; however, the majority of them retained the Church of England system, with young children mixed in with large classes of older children.

The influence of Pestalozzi reached the USA much earlier than England. A wealthy philanthropist, William Maclure (1763–1840), pursuaded one of Pestalozzi's assistants to emigrate to the New World in order to establish a school. In 1806 Joseph Neeff became the first Pestalozzian teacher in America, and in 1809 he founded the first school based on these principles in Philadelphia. The relationship between Neeff and his pupils was relaxed: 'I shall be nothing else but their friend and guide, their schoolfellow, playfellow and a mess mate', he said rather naïvely, but then he was not working with particularly young children.[37]

In the 1820s Maclure stayed with Robert Owen in New Lanark for a few days, and was impressed by the projects which were being undertaken. Soon afterwards Owen helped to establish an experimental school in New Harmony, Indiana.

Maclure made a large investment in this venture, which was supported by the enthusiasm of his assistant teachers from Yverdon. He transferred his Philadelphia school to New Harmony, where he took control of the educational side. His wife, also trained in the Pestalozzian method, took over the teaching of girls, and infants from the age of two. Although described by Kate Silber as a 'play centre', the adoption of Pestalozzian methods in this pre-school institution enables us to define it loosely as one of the first American child centres.[38]

Although New Harmony collapsed after only two years, its influence was considerable. The ideas in education expressed by Rousseau, Pestalozzi and later Froebel were incorporated into John Dewey's pedagogical system, and become second nature to all those interested in kindergarten education in America.

Robert Owen

The Scottish mill owner Robert Owen (1771–1858) visited Yverdon in 1818. Like Pestalozzi, he believed that the aim of education was the development of children's intellectual, ethical and pragmatic sensibilities and that as a result the living standards of the whole community would rise. His methods were similar to Pestalozzi's: he began education at an early age, adapted it to the child's level of understanding, and encouraged active interest and cooperation. Owen's educational idea was simply to encourage the innate gifts and powers of the child.

No one was better known as a pioneer of education for young children in Britain than Robert Owen. In 1816 he had opened the first infant school in the country at his New Lanark cotton mills. He was impressed by the possibilities of industrialized production, and dismissed notions of the revival of a pastoral society. He foresaw that new sources of wealth might be used for the benefit of people, but also recognized the problems the new system might bring to the lives of young children.

His educational theory was influenced by the ideas of John Locke (1632–1704) and Pestalozzi. He viewed education as an instrument for social change, and the route to a new form of socialist society which would supersede the existing competitive class structure.

This experiment at New Lanark was the first commencement of practical measures with a view to change the

2.17 Interior perspective of the New Institution for the Formation of Character, New Lanark.

2.18 North-east elevation with plans.

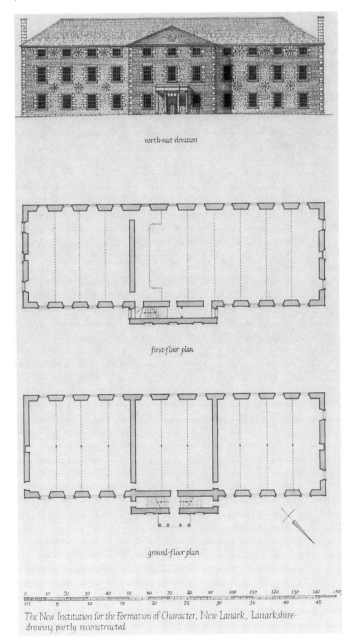

north-east elevation

first-floor plan

ground-floor plan

The New Institution for the Formation of Character, New Lanark, Lanarkshire drawing partly reconstructed.

fundamental principle on which society has heretofore been based from the beginning, and no experiment could be more successful in proving the truth of the principle that the character is formed for and not made by the individual.[39]

Owen devised three schools at New Lanark. Children between the ages of two and six years attended the infants' school, in which he had the most interest. Books were excluded, and activities such as singing, dancing, marching and basic geography took their place. The children spent three hours a day of free play in an open playground, unless the weather was bad. Initially, the school combined nursery and infant activities; later, separate rooms were used for the two- to four-year-olds, and the four- to six-year-olds. At the age of six or seven, children moved on to the school room. At ten, they left to work in the mill and attended evening classes with the adults. Owen's son Robert Dale Owen recalled the method of teaching and the apparatus and pictures employed:

> They were trained to habits of order and cleanliness; they were taught to abstain from quarrels, to be kind to each other. They were amused with childish games, and with stories suited to their capacity. Two large airy rooms were set apart, one for those under four years, and one for those from four to six. This last room was furnished with paintings, chiefly of animals, and a few maps. It was also supplied with natural objects from the gardens, fields and woods. These suggested themes for conversation, and brief familiar lectures; but there was nothing formal, no tasks to be learned, no readings from books.[40]

The school was part of Owen's model factory settlement which included apartments, a canteen, a recreational facility and the evening institute. Architecturally, the school building was similar in style to the rest of the factory settlement, conceived in a kind of late Georgian industrial form which the architectural critic the late Sir James Richards might have judged as an early example of the Functionalist tradition.[41]

The 'New Institution' or School . . . consists of two storeys. The upper storey which is furnished with a double range of windows all round is divided into two apartments; one, which is the principle schoolroom fitted up with desks and forms, on the Lancasterian Plan . . . The other apartment, on the second floor is of the same width and height as that just mentioned, but only 49 feet long. The walls are hung round with representations of the most striking zoological and mineralogical specimens; including quadrupeds, birds, fishes, reptiles, insects, shells, minerals, and &c. At one end there is a gallery, adapted for the purpose of an orchestra and at the other are hung very large representations of the two hemispheres . . .

The lower storey is divided into three apartments, of nearly equal dimensions, 12 feet high, and supported by hollow iron pillars, serving, at the same time as conductors, in winter, for heated air, which issues through the floor of the upper storey, and by which means the whole building may, with ease be kept at any required temperature. It is in these three apartments that the younger classes are taught reading, natural history and geography.[42]

Having successfully introduced the school and modified the mill's management, Owen's output improved remarkably. This provided funds to expand the facilities, and he immediately began another long-considered project, the construction of a large new building to be known as 'The Institute for the Formation of Character'. This was to accommodate schools, public halls, community rooms and, most importantly, what he called a playground or nursery school. The Institute and its nursery school were the basis of the educational work at New Lanark, and came to be admired by visitors from all over the world. 'The nursery school, which in fine weather occupied the playground of the Institute building and in wet weather, or when the children were tired of being outside, three lofty rooms on the ground-floor was Owen's chief pride and concern.'[43]

The whole school cared for children from the age of eighteen months to ten or perhaps twelve years. Infants aged from two to five spent only half their time in the school – during the afternoons they were allowed to play freely in the large paved external area under the supervision of a nurse. The approach to care was quite advanced pedagogically, using the principle of play. Children were not forced to participate in the activities, and sleep sessions occurred whenever the individual child wished.

Where the Owen system differed from the Pestalozzian approach was in the absence of arts and crafts activities: the emphasis was on the physical rather than the intellectual and emotional development of the child.

The sound originality of Owen's curriculum has been praised, but his methods were felt to be deficient in the more imaginative aspects. Owen was not himself interested in literature; although he was emphatic about the importance of speech and reading, this would largely be without any poetic content. There were simple lessons in drawing for the top classes, but no painting or craft activities were mentioned in connection with the nursery school curriculum.

Both Pestalozzi and Owen made significant contributions to nursery school education. Yverdon became something of a laboratory of early nursery school practice, visited by a number of English admirers who returned to open their own nursery schools. Owen could be described as being at the more practical Anglo-Saxon end of kindergarten practice. His importance in the context of this study is that his was the first UK institution where the environment was a primary consideration, and it can be assessed on the basis of the engravings and buildings which still survive. Although architecturally primitive, it was a building purpose-made for the needs of young children and perhaps the first real example of architecture for childhood.

Recollecting his schooling towards the end of the 18th century, Samuel Wilderspin said that it was mainly about corporal punishment where the teachers became objects of terror.[44] In Britain, the formal education of the under-fives was almost without support until after the Napoleonic wars. An increasing number of young city children whose mothers were working all day were clearly being inadequately looked after at so-called dame schools. Childminders in these large-scale day care centres were often old men or women who were untrained. The institutions were usually accommodated in badly ventilated rooms with few books or toys, and little play was possible.

In 1818 an early infants' school was opened in London by Lord Brougham and James Mill on behalf of a group of Whigs and Radicals. Impressed by Owen's ideas at New Lanark, they appointed James Buchanan, who had spent two years there as a master. Henry Brougham had visited Pestalozzi at Yverdon and returned to present the new theories to Parliament. The group founded a second school for infants a little later, with Samuel

Wilderspin as master. infants' schools were chosen because of the inadequacy of educational provision for the young, and the serious social problems of children who were resorting to crime and prostitution. Their establishment in turn brought the needs of even younger, pre-school, children to the fore.

Social rehabilitation was one significant aspect of early infants' schools in England; another was experimental pedagogic systems. Brougham believed that the group's first school was unique to Britain and, indeed, anywhere. He argued that those founded by Owen and Philip von Fellenberg (1771–1844, a neighbour and colleague of Pestalozzi, who founded a school on his estate at Hofwill) were not day schools in the normal sense, but were serving industrial or agricultural communities. Wilderspin's school at Spitalfields, opened in 1820, was from Brougham's point of view merely another exercise in developing early childhood institutions; it was not particularly radical.

Friedrich Froebel and his disciples

Without doubt, the most influential educational theorist during the second half of the 19th century was Friedrich Froebel (1782–1852). Froebel was born in Thuringia; his boyhood interest was in nature and initially he undertook an apprenticeship in forestry. From 1800, he studied biology and mathematics at the University of Jena where he first heard of Schiller's part in the formation of Naturphilosophie. Imbued with an interest in the sciences, he went to Frankfurt to commence a course in architecture. Although he did not complete it, the skills he acquired were to be put to later use in the design of his own houses and school buildings. He discovered his educational vocation when invited to teach drawing at a school in Frankfurt; this was a truly inspiring experience, as the school had adopted the progressive educational methods of Johann Pestalozzi.

From 1807 to 1810 he worked under Pestalozzi at Yverdon. Froebel recognized the importance of creative development through play as opposed to discipline. He began to see how important it was to cultivate the uniqueness and individuality of each child. He believed that children had an almost mystical understanding of the innate truths of life, and that this spirit could be reawakened by playing games which had symbolic meaning. For him, the kindergarten should represent an ideal society, hence its name. This did not refer to the importance of the garden, but rather to the total environment for the child: the

garden and buildings together should be representative symbols of the natural world. This was important, since according to his theories young children understood through a symbolic language which utilized metaphor and analogy. In this respect he disagreed with Pestalozzi's methods, and developed his own educational system that looked towards a communication of the unity of nature.

During the course of this development, Froebel visited a number of infants' schools founded by the followers of Johan Friedrich Oberlin, a pioneering educationalist who established an infants' school in Alsace in the 1770s where children were taught, among other things, singing, drawing, morals, speech training and manual tasks. To him these institutions appeared to be no more than day nurseries for the convenience of working mothers, without any educational philosophy. Convinced of the importance of new ways to teach young children, in 1837 he founded a new school which he called a school for the psychological training of small children through a system of play and occupations. This was located at Blankenburg in the mountains of Thuringia:

> This new institution was to provide an environment where children felt secure enough to match their inner life with the demands of the outside world, where opportunities existed for children to experiment through their play in areas not yet known, but vaguely surmised. Such a protected and predictable environment was more like a nursery where the gardener tended his plants, provided water and air and moved plants into the sunshine so that they could grow and flourish. It was going to be a garden for children, a Kindergarten.[45]

Although Wilderspin had earlier asserted the importance of allowing a child free play in an indoor playground, 'he favoured the rigid gallery form of classroom, which was a feature of 19th-century schools, and the system of learning by rote'.[46] It was Froebel who took Pestalozzi's ideas on the meaningful representation of concepts, with his invention of the structured play system he called 'gifts and occupations'. This was an expansion of the ideas of Pestalozzi, that there are forces within children that move them towards those activities that stimulate development. Therefore the physical and restless activity of children should be sustained and directed by the teacher towards these developmental goals. Thus the traditional role of the active teacher and the passive class would be reversed. Children would be given a wide range of materials 'and encouraged to carry out various sorts of creative and expressive handwork; self-activity became the means of education'.[47] This was to be the basis of a new education of particular relevance to the youngest children. We will return to examine Froebel's educational techniques in more detail and their lasting influence through certain key artists and architects.

Due to the religious and socialist movements that developed in opposition to the employment of child labour in the factories during the 19th century, Britain became something of a test-bed for the development of new ideas in the education of young children. After the failure of the revolution in Germany of 1848, many German liberals emigrated to Britain and America, bringing with them Froebelian educational ideas.

In England they settled in London, Manchester and other provincial centres. In 1851 the first kindergarten was set up in Hampstead, London, primarily for the children of these German immigrants.

Bertha Ronge and her sister Margaretha, from the wealthy Meyer family, had been pupils of Froebel in Hamburg; Bertha and her husband Johann had founded kindergartens in Hamburg before they came to London. Prior to his marriage, Johann Ronge had been a Roman Catholic priest in Bresslau until his renunciation of the Church. The child-centred principles of Froebel were fused with the humanistic approach of the Ronges, resulting in a progressive kindergarten for children from three to seven years of age, with classes for older children. In addition the Ronges considered including a training school for teachers. It moved to Tavistock Place, Bloomsbury, in 1855, and is described in their own manual, *A Practical Guide to the English Kindergarten*, as

having a layout greatly improved on existing schools which acted as a precedent in later practice in relation to space, light and air. The kindergarten consisted of two 'good, spacious, healthy and well arranged rooms'. One was furnished with forms and tables for six children and was used for seated exercises. Arrangement and order were stressed and each child had a number marked on his/her own box, slate, drawing-book, and plaiting-mat. The other room was

without furniture except for a piano and had access to a garden and it was here that the children performed their musical and gymnastic exercises, sometimes selecting their own games. Games were a very important part of the syllabus. One of these games was called The Pigeon's House and included singing and dancing.[48]

The Ronges visited Manchester in 1857, where they helped to form the Manchester Committee for the Extension of the Kindergarten System. Several kindergartens were founded there by German teachers. In 1873, the Manchester Froebel Society was established and a year later a similar organization was founded in London; the National Froebel Union is still in existence. Although the Ronges' schools lasted for only ten years, they were responsible for starting the Froebel movement in England.

After Froebel's death, Baroness Berthe von Marenholtz-Bülow became the leading propagandist of the 'New Education'. One of Froebel's personal friends and disciples, she lectured on kindergarten methods in London in 1854, and was a constant supporter and consultant to the Froebel Society until her death in 1893. *The Times* and the *Athenaeum* both published articles on the kindergarten in 1854. Well-informed descriptions were produced by Charles Dickens for his periodical *Household Words*. Dickens, who met the Baroness and visited the Ronges' kindergarten in Tavistock Place, wrote about the dire situation of children, particularly the underprivileged.

One of the visitors to the education exhibition held in St Martin's Hall, London, in 1854 was the American educator Henry Barnard. The exhibition was opened by the Prince Consort and a demonstration of Froebel's 'gifts and occupations' was given by Heinrich Hoffmann, another of Froebel's former pupils. Hoffmann, who was head of the training institution in Hamburg, remained in England to assist in the training of teachers. In 1893 the Home and Colonial Society became the National Froebel Union.

The English kindergartens differed in one respect from Froebel's German system as they expanded in the 19th century. More emphasis was placed on play organized by teachers, and less on children's free play. 'The teachers' justification was that games devised by them would more effectively serve the kindergarten's goals of intellectual training, ethical teaching, physical exercise, dramatic action, musical and rhythmical training, and the use of simple, concise, and accurate language, than the unorganized, perhaps aimless, pupils' play.'[49] Froebel's German singing games were replaced by English nursery rhymes.

English kindergartens were so successful that elsewhere in the British Empire educational bodies became interested. Kindergarten movements were active in Australia, Canada, India and New Zealand. Elsewhere kindergartens developed in Austria, Japan, Russia, Turkey, France, Switzerland, Norway and Sweden.

2.4 Pedagogical drawing, Froebel and learning to see

The key problem for all educationalists is the best way to *represent* ideas to young (pre-verbal) children. The importance of drawing in the development process perhaps holds a key to the affinity that developed between radical architectural ideas and the kindergarten. Rousseau's belief in drawing as a pedagogical benefit is found in *Emile*, where the development of the child's visual and creative faculties is emphasized rather than passive listening, learning and reciting.[50] The adoption of new ways of representing ideas as an educational reform led to three important tendencies, which had a significant influence on art and design in the 20th century.

The first could be described as the use of domestic and everyday objects as subjects for study in the education of the young child; this may have influenced the work of Le Corbusier, Ozenfant and others in their involvement with Purism. The second is the phenomenon of children as artists, and the perceived value of their freedom from inhibiting rules such as perspective and anatomical correctness. Around 1880 many educationalists felt that the benefit of allowing children the freedom to produce their own interpretations of the world held great developmental value. Allied to 'child art', the third of these tendencies came out of Froebel's conception of children learning through play, and his development of the famous 'gifts and occupations'. It is said that many influential artists and designers were trained in the Froebel method at kindergarten.

In Rousseau's treatment of drawing in education, he emphasizes the importance of the child recognizing basic symbols by sight – in other words, 'learning to see' – when previously it had been customary only to listen, learn and recite.

One cannot learn to estimate the size of bodies without at the same time learning to know or even to copy their shape; at bottom this copying depends entirely on the laws of perspective and one cannot estimate distance without some feeling for these laws. In *Emile*, Rousseau insists that drawing 'is not so much for art's sake as to give him exactness of eye and flexibility of hand.'[51]

Pestalozzi's key theory that counting, measuring and speaking could be coordinated by drawing was, in practical terms, about identifying individual forms, analyzing their shape and using language to describe them. The publication of Pestalozzi's influential manual *ABC der Anschauung*, written with the assistance of Christoph Buss in 1803, established drawing as an important part of educational reform. This vital new constituent in the education of children largely replaced the notion that drawing was merely a leisurely aristocratic pursuit. Thus initiated, pedagogical drawing was distinguished from academy teaching in that it began at an early age, and its exercises could be taught to groups within the new kindergartens.

Pestalozzi, Froebel and others in German-speaking Europe saw drawing as a form of writing, parallel to alphabetic writing. Pestalozzi believed that the square was the foundation of all forms and that the drawing method should be based upon the division of squares and circles into their constituent parts. Rousseau's and Pestalozzi's ideas on drawing differed, however, in that Rousseau believed that 'nature should be his [Emile's] only teacher and things his only model. A house should be drawn from a house, a tree from a tree, and a man from a man.'[52]

Rousseau was portraying the education of a child of good birth by a tutor of intelligence and taste devoting all his energies to the task of teaching a single individual. Pestalozzi took the new philosophy of child drawing further by the creation of a system of representation that could be used by a teacher of fairly modest academic skill to teach large groups of children. According to Clive Ashwin, Pestalozzi thought it vital to 'break down the complexity of nature into its constituent forms for the pupil, to identify and elementorize the underlying geometry of the visual world in a way which would make it comprehensible and assimilable for the child'.[53]

The exercises in *ABC der Anschauung* may seem somewhat dry and predictable to us today. To children at the beginning of

2.19 Illustration from Johannes Ramsauer's *Zeichnungslehre* (1821), showing different characteristics of drawing in a simple form.

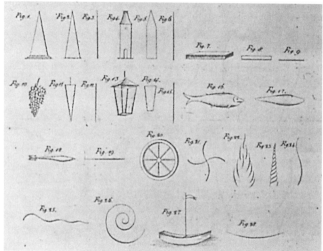

2.19

the 19th century who had been used to the inhibiting discipline of Victorian society, they must have seemed quite exciting. One particular example simply showed how a square form could be broken down into smaller and smaller forms of the same proportion but of different sizes. By limiting the complexity of the exercise to a few abstract moves, it was felt that important but hitherto unaddressed areas of learning related to a child's numerate and conceptual skills would develop quickly and relatively free from distracting images. Certainly, the remarkable quality of the exercises in *ABC der Anschauung* is the absence of a prescribed viewpoint. Their elemental geometric simplicity enables their meaning to be conveyed without confusion or distortion to large numbers of children.

Two of Pestalozzi's colleagues, former Yverdon pupils Josef Schmidt and Johannes Ramsauer, produced books on drawing. Ramsauer's *Zeichnungslehre* [Drawing Tutor] of 1821 used main forms (*Hauptformen*) to represent the abstracted essence of physical objects.[54] Each of the three main forms – objects at rest, objects in movement, and objects combining movement and rest – is given an abstract symbol describing its essential characteristic. Again, this was a way of communicating concepts about natural phenomena, but in a less abstract way than Pestalozzi.

Unlike Rousseau or indeed many contemporary academics, Pestalozzi's method of teaching drawing was to elementorize the subject geometrically. Schmidt and Ramsauer included net (grid) drawing and dot drawing in their teaching theories. The subject areas tended to focus on simple domestic and everyday objects. These examples may have influenced Le Corbusier, Ozenfant and others in their involvement in Purism, through an awakening of interest in the aesthetic quality of simple domestic objects which hitherto had been deemed to be of no cultural value whatsoever.

The difference of background between Ozenfant and Le Corbusier (born Charles Jeanneret) is startlingly manifested in paintings in their first Purist exhibition in 1919. Jeanneret's have the studious simplicity of schoolroom exercises, rendering regular geometrical solids, which is all that they are. The main drift of their argument depends on the unity, later doubted by both artists, of art and science:

> Nothing justifies us in supposing that there should be any incompatibility between science and art. The one and the other have the common aim of reducing the universe to equations. We shall prove that pure art and pure science are not watertight domains. They have a common mind . . . art and science depend on number.[55]

Child art

According to Anne Balif, 'asking a child to draw his house is asking him to reveal the deepest dream shelter he has found for his happiness. If he is happy, he will succeed in drawing a snug, protected house which is well built on deeply-rooted foundations.' It will have the right shape, and nearly always there will be some indication of its inner strength. In certain drawings, quite obviously, 'it is warm indoors, and there is a fire burning, such a big fire, in fact, that it can be seen coming out of the chimney. When the house is happy, soft smoke rises in gay rings above the roof.'[56]

What many psychologists, such as Françoise Minkowska, call the house-test alludes to the second of the influential tendencies; this relates to the importance of a child's drawing in general, not just in the kindergarten. Bachelard explains that a child will reveal tension or unhappiness by depicting a narrow, cold or closed house. The reason that the act of drawing reveals such truths and enables the child to express complex emotions in advance of speech development is that he or she can dream over the paper and pencil, and communicate spontaneous and therefore authentic 'psychic states'. This then was the important phenomenon of the child as expressive artist.

The roots of this interest can be found in Georg Hirth's *Ideas About the Teaching of Drawing* of 1887, which encapsulated contemporary thinking and interest in this area. It could be described as the elevation of the scribblings of the untrained intuitive artist to the level of high artistic merit; previously, child drawings would have been dismissed merely as crude attempts at realism. The catalyst for this movement was the reevaluation of primitive art by Paul Klee, Joan Miró and members of the Vienna Secession. The phenomenon of child art was an influential part of this reformist influence on art education.

The movement first gained recognition at an exhibition, 'The Child as Artist', at the Hamburg Museum in 1898. Drawings and paintings by children from local schools and by Indian children, together with a collection of Eskimo art, were exhibited probably for the first time. The idea of the child as artist and the liberalization of the teaching of drawing developed hand in hand. The exhibition coincided with a number of publications recording the art and culture of primitive peoples. The primitive, non-industrialized view allied to the child's view was beginning to be considered genuine; to have an authenticity that was missing from conventional 'adult' art of the time. Child art had a spontaneity and freshness because it was unencumbered by logic or social preconceptions.

Influential artists and architects could now look back to their time in kindergartens as having a renewed significance. As Carl Schorske has remarked, the phenomenon of child art 'recapitulates atavistically the childhood of peoples and the childhood of art'.[57] In other words, representations of this kind had primordial qualities, which could be created only by the so-called uncivilized individual or the young child. This concept is explained concisely by David Michael Levin in contemporary philosophical language as the 'pre-ego-logical existence' – when the child is fixed in a single view of reality, 'which contains within it something that is in a sense pre-psychic and pre-physical, that is still psychic and physical in one'. This idea perhaps touches on the spiritual uniqueness of the young child which was understood and explored by these early pioneers.[58]

Ten years after the 1898 Secession Exhibition, in 1908, the Kunstschau exhibition took place, celebrating the triumph of the neo-classical/art deco phase of the Viennese aesthetic move-

ment over the more organic, naturalistic theories of art nouveau. This coincided with a transfer of interest from large-scale urban concerns towards smaller-scale domestic architecture. A display of various arts and crafts demonstrated the principle of the unification of the fine and the applied arts, marking a move from organic interests to more formalistic concerns:

> Aesthetically, formalism and the new garden cult were reinforced by the shift from art nouveau to art deco, from organic and fluid forms to crystalline and geometric ones. Artists who in the 1890s under the name of 'Secession' had engaged in a dynamic search for new instinctual truth, now turned away from their unsettling findings to the more profitable task of beautifying daily life and the domestic environment of the élite.[59]

This ideological shift could be seen in the work of the designers Josef Hoffmann, Joseph Olbrich and Emile Hoppe, and their beautification of the residences of wealthy men. Allied to this move away from wider urbanistic concerns to the domestic was the cultural ideal, which praised the ordinary environment of man (*homo aestheticus*) above the more esoteric global interests that had been at the heart of the 1898 Secession Exhibition. However, part of the Kunstschau 1908 exhibition also had a room devoted to the 'Child as Artist'. Although its inclusion was intended to complement the domestic themes of Olbrich and others, elevating the child's drawing in a nostalgic way, nevertheless it also maintained interest in the uninhibited expressive quality of child art. It was the first room in the show and received a great deal of attention.

Closely involved with this exhibition was the young Oskar Kokoschka (1886–1980) who, it is said, was at the very birth of expressionistic culture. He rejected the work of the great masters in favour of primitive and child art. The 'Child as Artist' room at Kunstschau 1908 enabled him to demonstrate how childhood creativity was central to the principles of expressionistic art, a movement which was to explode into life and to continue to develop over the next ten years, becoming particularly relevant to Rudolf Steiner.

One of the key organizers of this exhibition was Professor Franz Cisek, Head of the Department of Education in the Arts and Crafts School, Vienna, where Kokoschka was studying to be

2.20 Haus der Kinder, Vienna, designed by Schuster. Like the kindergarten at Karl Marx Hof, it was a traditional modernist building in brick, with large windows. Here, children play within the exposed framework of the building.

an art teacher. Professor Cisek had been an associate of the Secession from its inception. According to Schorske, he took the contemporary notion of an aesthetic liberation and drew analogies with the child-like view. He became Austria's leading progressive educator in the plastic arts, dismissing the traditional educational emphasis on children imitating adult drawing and aesthetics. Cisek believed in free creative activity: 'everything elemental, subconscious and unconsumed is fostered and protected . . . Only the uninhibited, the instinctual becomes luminous here as essentially human.'[60]

Arts and crafts products designed for children were developed by the teachers of Oscar Kokoschka. The styling of book illustrations, tapestries and the like was in the form of folk art. A poster for Kunstschau 1908 by Kokoschka illustrates his skilful assimilation of child and folk art.

There is no doubting the influence of child art on a number of important 20th-century art movements; Robert Goldwater asserts that the phenomenon can be seen first in the paintings of Paul Klee associated with the expressionist group the Blaue Reiter (1911–12).[61] Certainly, Klee's diaries bear this out: 'Children also have artistic ability and there is virtue in them having it! The more helpless they are, the more instructive are the examples they furnish us, and they must be preserved from corruption at an early age.'[62]

Klee told Lothar Schreyer during his time at the Bauhaus that he did not object to his pictures being compared to 'children's scribbles and smears. That's fine! The pictures my little Felix paints are better than mine, which all too often have trickled through the brain; unfortunately I can't prevent that completely as I tend to work them over.'[63] Undoubtedly, Klee was the first and most coherent advocate of child art, firmly asserting its importance in the development of Primitivism, and much else. In Goldwater's view, artists such as Raoul Dufy, Marc Chagall, Otto Feininger, Johannes Itten, André Masson, and especially Miró and Jean Dubuffet, were all affected by the 'child as artist' movement. One could add to this list Picasso, the proto-Surrealist de Chirico and Max Ernst – indeed, Surrealists in general, who were interested in any form of spontaneous, psychic representation.

Child art and its developing use in different forms in the early kindergartens also had considerable significance for educational theory within the kindergarten movement. Allowing children to express themselves was, and still is, part and parcel of the whole concept of child-centred learning, which exemplified an important transformation in the way children were to be brought up in the new 'children's gardens' as free and natural individuals. In 'No more Play', Rosalind Krauss asserts that a natural sense of freedom and uninhibited pleasure is the driving impulse behind the young child's desire to draw, as opposed to the desire to depict reality. After this initial impulse, 'random marking changes gradually to intentional patterning, which in turn gives rise to a figurative reading'.[64]

Krauss's thesis – that drawing is an absolutely primal desire for self-expression within all of us as children – articulates the views of Rousseau, Pestalozzi and so many others over the last 200 years, hence the importance drawing has had on pre-school educational theory. What Krauss describes as 'a will to art' which, she feels, is within all of us, is first seen as a process in the markings of young children who discover condensation on the inside of the window, or random scrawls made with a pen on a sheet of white paper.

How far this is 'natural' and 'within us' is open to speculation, since every parent is all too aware of the 'will to copy' in their own children. However, there is no doubting the potential for the drawings of children with characteristics like 'the profiles of faces endowed with two eyes and two ears, or the rendering of houses and bodies as transparent in order to display their contents, or the free combination of plan and elevation'[65] to stir the senses and to bring about new and startling conceptual discoveries, both in the young child and in the adult gently guiding that child. The spontaneous dialogue that often results is no doubt an important encouraging factor in the development of the child during the ages of three to six.[66]

The 'gifts and occupations'

The third tendency, of particular significance to architect Frank Lloyd Wright, was Froebel's invention of his play system called 'the gifts and occupations'. Robert Owen concentrated on practical activities in the nursery part of his school, such as dancing and physical games. He was not in the least interested in literature, drawing and art, or other aesthetic pursuits as aids to the personal development of his young children. Owen's view was largely anti-intellectual, whereas the developments of Friedrich Froebel came from a profoundly intellectual impulse. Froebel's

2.20

2.21

2.21 Shapes and building blocks from Froebel's 'gifts and occupations'.

2.22 Pestalozzi with his children. On the wall are tables to aid the teaching of counting and drawing, from *ABC der Auschauung* by Pestalozzi and Buss, 1803.

2.22

career up to his involvement in teaching had included the study of the natural sciences, which gave him a clear conception of the importance of geometric forms and their underlying relationship to natural phenomena such as plant forms and crystals.[67]

Between 1812 and 1817 Froebel worked with Professor Christian Samuel Weiss (1780–1856) as his scientific assistant. This period, prior to his involvement in education, is of considerable historical importance. Indeed, John G. Burke states that this work probably led to the transformation of Froebel's beliefs.[68] It is clear that many of Froebel's teaching methods and his general philosophy of education emanated from his experi-

ence in crystallographic science. In the first German edition of his *Education of Man* (1826), he makes the observation that 'whether organic or inorganic, crystalline or non-crystalline, developmental processes seemed to be the same; in essence they tend to develop outward from within, striving to maintain balance between inner and outer forces'.[69] In addition, Froebel's training as an architect probably supported the importance of precise and unchanging relationships between things as the foundation of his educational philosophy.

Thus Froebel's background encouraged him to believe that the random nature of child-like play should be directed into an organ-

2.23 Froebel's building block pattern for a farmyard, which Manson compared with Figure 2.24.

2.24 The garden entrance, Imperial Hotel, Tokyo, by Frank Lloyd Wright, 1916–22.

nized system of learning, initially through the child's contact with simple crystalline objects in the form of three-dimensional toys. These, in primary colours and made of natural materials, were known in the early days of kindergarten education as 'gifts'. Starting to play with the first gift, six coloured worsted balls or a sphere on the end of a piece of string, the child was understanding concepts of colour and individuality. A sphere was felt to be the first plaything for the child after Froebel witnessed children playing with a ball in a meadow in Burgdorf around 1835.[70] After the sphere, the second gift was a small cube, a ball and a cylinder strung together. Here, the primary elements would become known to the child. The third gift comprised eight one-inch cubes, together forming a two-inch cube. Similar to the Pestalozzi exercise (Figure 2.21), this exercise communicated the concept of numbers and divisibility. The system of gifts would become more and more complex, developing into forty-piece constructions.

The most well known of the Froebel gifts was number five: the 'building boxes'. These were comprised of building blocks of three differing mathematically derived forms, together with triangular and square wooden shapes. The child could make forms which became less and less abstract as he or she became more confident. Thus a bridge or a house might be the imagined outcome of a half-hour spent playing on the floor.

> In this way the child perceived without prompting the mastery he had gained over these materials, giving him the self-confidence to progress another step on the Froebel ladder . . . the child familiar with the Froebel gifts would have the very unusual advantage of developing a sympathy for basic forms, simple materials, and true colour.[71]

Froebel's 'occupations' developed more complex skills such as clay modelling, cardboard work, paper folding and cutting, painting and thread games. Although today these activities seem to us dry and somewhat preconceived, at the time they were considered to be a revolutionary approach to children's education. The system enabled many opportunities for children to produce symmetrical patterns of their own artistic invention. Froebel encouraged children to make shapes from sticks and rings which could be laid out to form letters – in theory the first stage of writing. As in the world of natural science, all of the activities were intended to be built upon mathematical principles. Man's

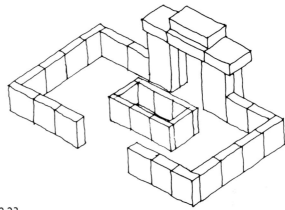

2.23

2.24

proximity to the natural world was constantly stressed by the importance of the garden in the learning environment:

> The child is unaware of course of the mathematical significance of his playthings; but his eye unconsciously becomes accustomed to correct mathematical forms. Thus, his sense of form, proportion, and harmony are being developed. Froebel fostered a sense of art in the kindergarten children and also aimed to keep his pupils in harmony with nature through cultivation of their gardens and observation of the nature and habits of small animals.[72]

Buckminster Fuller and Frank Lloyd Wright, Le Corbusier and Kandinsky were all educated in the Froebel method: the Bauhaus programme clearly reflects this. Johannes Itten (1888–1967) trained as a Froebel primary schoolteacher in Berne before becoming a painter. He established a private art school in Vienna in 1916, where he developed and adapted child art techniques to the training of adult art students. The notion of elementary ways of releasing the intuitive (or childlike) as opposed to the intellectual, through techniques such as automatism, blind drawing and rhythmic drawing motions, encouraged a mystical approach to modern art. Itten became Vienna's first abstract painter before becoming a tutor at the Weimar Bauhaus in 1919, where he probably instigated the radical development of elementary geometrical forms in art.

Buckminster Fuller said of his first days at kindergarten:

> The teacher brought us some toothpicks and semi-dried peas . . . I found that a triangle held its shape when nothing else did. The other children made rectangular structures that seemed to stand up because the peas held them in shape . . . the teacher called all the other teachers in the primary school as well as the kindergarten to look at this triangular structure . . . I began to feel then that all nature's structuring and patterning must be based on triangles.[73]

2.5 Maria Montessori, Frank Lloyd Wright, Rudolf Steiner

Maria Montessori

Maria Montessori died in 1952, a century after Friedrich Froebel's death. During that time there had been great changes to the social context of early years education. One might contrast Froebel's first kindergarten, located in a beautiful wooded valley in Thuringia, with Montessori's House of Childhood (Casa dei Bambini) in the most squalid district of urban Rome. Their differing viewpoints and preoccupations are reflected in this disparity. Froebel, in an ideal rural environment, focused on the natural gifts in the development of the child. Montessori centred her attention on the immediate environment, emphasizing its importance in her more pragmatic methods.

Initially, she had attended a technical high school with the intention of training as an engineer. However, in 1896, she

became the first woman to graduate in medicine in Italy at the University of Rome. She then worked on the staff of the psychiatric clinic at the university, specializing in the treatment of retarded children. She studied the methods of Jean Itard and Edouard Seguin in Paris. Her success with backward children led to an interest in general education, and she returned to Rome University to take up a seven-year course in experimental psychology and anthropological pedagogy. During this time she assisted at the teachers' training college for women in Rome. She was appointed Professor of Anthropology in 1904.

Within three years, Montessori launched an educational project of immense social significance, thanks largely to the philanthropy of Eduardo Talamo, and from 1906 the Case dei Bambini were developed. The object was to care for children close to their homes in the tenements, which were being upgraded by the Roman Association of Good Building. All small children between the ages of three and seven living in a tenement were brought together in a large nursery room or space. A teacher was appointed, and given her own apartment in the building. The costs of the school were met by the Association as part of the reconstruction budget.

In 1906, Maria Montessori was officially appointed as organizer of the infants' schools in these newly upgraded tenements throughout Rome. Her success with retarded children was phenomenal; she was able to teach some of her 'backward' children so effectively that eventually they could read and write to examination standard. Believing that her methods would be even more effective if used in the training of normal children, she applied them to the education of the very young who were believed to be at the same stage of mental development as the older, retarded, children. The Montessori method can be best analysed by examining the basic tenets of her training of 'defective' children.

> The first principle is to train the pupil to be independent of others with regard to the ordinary practices of life; it appears also to necessitate an approach to the child's mind at a lower level than can be adopted with normal children, and appeal to the senses rather than the intellect.[74]

The sense of touch was an intrinsic factor in this approach to preschool education. If not developed during this period of the child's life, sensitivity required at a later stage could be lost. Pestalozzi wished to psychologize education, but during his time the theory was not recognized in relation to the schoolchild. In education the psychological method means that the process is tuned to the stage of the child's mental development rather than wholly to the needs of the curriculum. In practical terms, a particular child may be at a stage where he or she is able to fit correct weights into their sockets and identify little packets through sound or smell, but may not be ready to formulate simple words from sandpaper letters. These stages would be recognized and respected in relation to each individual child. The freedom of a child is perfected in the psychological method and adheres strictly to the laws of the child's natural self. Montessori recognized an interrelationship between mental and physical powers in mankind, and categorized three types of activity: the exercises of practical life; the exercises of sensory training; and the didactic exercises.[75]

The first stage of training in the House of Childhood is freedom, freedom to be able to perform ordinary tasks by oneself. So pupils learn personal cleanliness and the actions necessary in undressing and dressing, by the use of apparatus designed for this purpose. All furniture in the House of Childhood is at the height and scale of the child. There are no fixed desks, and the tables and chairs are specially designed for lightness and movability, thus providing motor dexterity training. Montessori devised a completely new set of gymnastic exercises to develop coordination – for example, a circular wooden staircase with very shallow steps enabled the child to become practised at going up and down stairs safely. Over the years, other more imaginative sense-training apparatus were added, which combined physical coordination with natural thought development. The gifts of Froebel and the didactic apparatus of Montessori are different in form but similar in their psychological methodology.

The Montessori movement has become so widespread in the 20th century that it has gained an important place in the history of education. For 40 years Montessori travelled throughout Europe, India and the USA giving lectures and papers, and establishing teacher training courses. In 1922 she was appointed Government Inspector of Schools in Italy, leaving in 1934 after Fascist rule was established. She lived in Spain and Ceylon, finally settling in the Netherlands where she died in 1952.

The Austrian Lili Roubiczek, a pupil at her London training course of 1921, decided to aid the relief of poverty for underprivileged children in Vienna. With two other former pupils, one an architect, she collected subscriptions for the construction of a Montessori school. She received financial support from England, and opened the Haus der Kinder in Favoriten on the outskirts of Vienna.

Her original group of helpers consisted of five young women, 16–18 years of age, who formed a working commune called Arbeits Gemeinschaft. Life was difficult; food, clothing and fuel were scarce and expensive, as was furniture and equipment. The Haus der Kinder opened in the summer of 1922 with a rollcall of 25 children aged between two and four. 'The children, inadequately dressed and underfed, some surly and rebellious, some just listless and unresponsive, came at six in the morning, half-frozen in the winter, and stayed until six in the evening when their mothers picked them up . . . The unprepossessing group of children settled down, began their work/play, learned, became enthusiastic yet orderly and thrived.'[76] It was a model of its kind, and ran from the early 1920s to the late 1930s.

The new building was attractively furnished by the young teachers. In addition to Montessori materials, there were child-sized plates and bowls from Dresden and small tables and chairs built by a local carpenter. Later, a special set of drinking mugs designed at the Bauhaus was sent as a gift from the Montessori school in Jena. The Haus der Kinder building was linear and symmetrical, with three isolated classrooms. The building consisted of one storey, except for a central classroom and staffroom on an upper floor. The classrooms were acoustically isolated, with adjoining cloakrooms and lavatories forming sound baffles. Medical inspection was on the left of the main entrance, with the kitchen on the right. Externally, there were two terraces, but these were contained within the structural framework of the building to give a sense of shelter and containment. A large garden of quasi-symmetrical layout extended to the south of the school, with the main classrooms looking on.

Pestalozzi and his school of freedom, Froebel's kindergarten for early child care, Seguin's and Itard's methods for educating the retarded – all were synthesized in Maria Montessori's educational practice. Concealed in Froebel's list of somewhat repetitious and mystical works were indications of concepts that Montessori was to pragmatize in her own more down-to-earth style.

In the final decade of the 19th century, the kindergarten idea had become increasingly institutionalized; the whole movement was rigid in its interpretation of Froebel's methods. Radical

2.25 Exterior view of the Avery Coonley play house.

2.25

change was inevitable, as new answers to new problems were identified. Montessori took over from Froebel, utilizing many of his ideas along with those she discovered in her practice of medicine and teaching retarded children. Maria Montessori's methods in nursery and infants' schools were contained in *The Montessori Method*, published in England in 1915. Today, many hundreds of Montessori schools exist throughout the world. Their philosophy has a universal appeal as a humanistic, rational approach to the education of young children, which is very much focused on the environment.

Frank Lloyd Wright and the kindergarten connection

Without doubt, the most widely researched and quoted architect said to have been influenced by his childhood experiences was Frank Lloyd Wright. On many occasions Wright described the significance of the Froebel 'gifts' and how his thinking developed from these experiences to create an original, modern, organic architecture. It can be argued that his vision was crucial in initiating the beginnings of a 20th-century view of modern architectural form and space, which stemmed partly from Froebel.

At the Centennial in Philadelphia, after a sightseeing day, mother made a discovery. She was eager about it now. Could hardly wait to go to Boston as soon as she got home – to Milton Bradley's. The Kindergarten! She had seen the 'Gifts' in the Exposition Building. The strips of colored paper, glazed and 'matt', remarkably soft brilliant colors. Now came the geometric by-play of those calming checkered color combinations! The structural figures to be made with peas and small sticks: slender constructions, the joinings accented by the little green-pea globes. The smooth shapely maple blocks with which to build, the sense of which never afterward leaves the fingers: form becoming feeling. The box had a mast set upon it, on which to hang the maple cubes and spheres and triangles, revolving them to discover subordinate forms.

And the exciting cardboard shapes with pure scarlet face – such scarlet! Smooth triangular shapes, white-back and edges, cut into rhomboids with which to make designs on the flat table top. What shapes they made naturally if only one would let them!

A small interior world of color and form now came within the grasp of small fingers. Color and pattern, in the flat, in the round. Shapes that lay hidden behind the appearances all about.

Here was something for invention to seize and use to create. These 'Gifts' came into the gray house in drab old Weymouth and made something live there that had never lived there before. Mother would go to Boston, take lessons of a teacher of the Froebel method and come home to teach the children. When her housework was done mother and the two children would sit at a low mahogany table with a polished top, working with these 'Gifts'.[77]

He goes on to cite the square, the triangle, the circle and the straight line as the constituent forms of a new architecture.[78] It has been suggested that these ideas were initially developing in the design for his Midway Gardens leisure building, Chicago, in 1913. This thinking came at a crucial time: art nouveau was expiring, and architects and artists in Europe were experimenting with new abstract forms. Over the past 40 years, a number of separate studies have been carried out examining the relationship of these kindergarten ideas to the development of Frank Lloyd Wright's architecture. We will describe briefly the significance of these studies.

Grant C. Manson was probably the first writer to demonstrate the relationship between kindergarten building block constructions and some of Wright's built projects. For example, he illustrated the farmyard pattern made from Froebel blocks taken from the Froebel manual, relating it to the form of Wright's Imperial Hotel in Tokyo (1916–22). The main thrust of his thesis was devoted to Wright's manipulation of the Froebel toys and their relationship to the external form of his completed buildings. Manson believed that his first designs displayed a way of thinking which must have been instilled in childhood through a particular kindergarten experience with Froebel building blocks.[79]

Fifteen years later, Richard MacCormac also suggested that the Froebel discipline had made a deep impression on Wright and instilled in him an understanding of how aesthetic beauty was inextricably linked to the principles of compositional form.[80] Perhaps based on his own experiences, MacCormac argued that kindergarten lessons had given Wright a confidence in his own

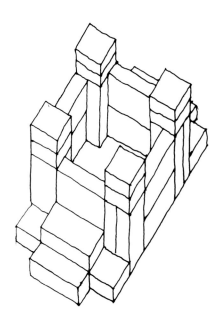

2.26

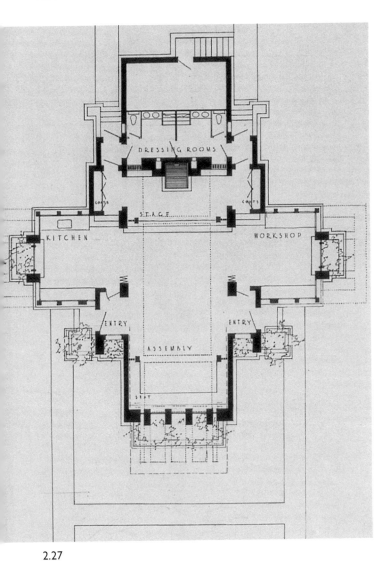

2.27

2.26 'The characteristic intersection of square and cruciform in plan into three dimensions', discussed by Richard C. MacCormac.

2.27 Plan of the Avery Coonley play house by Frank Lloyd Wright, Riverside, Illinois, 1912. Apart from its Froebel-inspired forms, its programme included a kitchen with child-height worktops, and a stage with a dressing-room. The fireplace, behind the stage, acted as a permanant backdrop and symbolic heart of the building.

innate understanding of form and space. More importantly, Mac-Cormac asserted that the patterns described in the Froebel 'gifts' and their potential for three-dimensional form making related to a number of Wright's house projects from the period 1892–1908: 'the inner modules of the grid are represented by components of various heights, flower boxes, balustrades and bay windows arranged so that they overlap but do not obscure one another. With this assembly of parts characteristic of the mature Prairie period, Wright translated the patterns of the kindergarten into a three-dimensional system of architecture.'[81] MacCormac successfully analysed strategies inherent to the Froebel patterns for the complete comprehension, internally and externally, of the Prairie Houses.

Edgar Kaufmann Junior, writing in 1981, criticizes both of the above theories. He asserts the importance of social issues in Wright's work. Nevertheless, he declares the significance of Froebel whose 'gifts' awakened the youthful Wright to his own innate artistic sensibilities and the essential poetry of visual arts: 'form became feeling'.[82]

Kaufmann believed that Wright's debt to Froebel was immense and all-encompassing. He felt that Froebel's kindergarten ideas, seized upon by Wright, had inadvertently affected the entire course of early modern architecture.

Professor J.S. Rubin's 1987 study places greater emphasis than previous research on Froebel's interest in crystallography. Her analysis reveals the contribution of crystallographer C.S. Weiss (1780–1856) to the course of science.[83] She suggests that Froebel's didactic materials in the 'gifts' and his general philosophy of education are based on the science of crystallography. Quoting from the first German edition of *The Education of Man* (1826), where Froebel makes the observation 'whether organic or inorganic, crystalline or non-crystaline, developmental processes seem to be the same: in essence they tend to develop outward from within, striving to maintain balance between inner and outer forces', as being 'essentially the same developmental formula Wright proclaimed for organic architecture'.[84] She makes further observations about Wright's projects and the principle of rotation in his plans; Froebel's windmill shapes and their connection to naphthalene crystal chains, she claims, are related to Wright's Crystal Heights Hotel leisure complex of 1940. Professor Rubin goes on to state that Wright's kindergarten training taught him to see and appreciate the forms of

Kindergarten Architecture

2.28 A child's buggy designed by Gerrit Rietveld in 1918. The furniture for children designed by Rietveld (1888–1964) included high chairs, cots and playpens, with the openness and elemental simplicity that he was then employing in his early furniture for adults. Here again he used colour, and these pieces had a relaxed, play-like quality. They were lucid, and often resembled the educational and constructional toys fash-

ionable among middle-class parents throughout Europe following the ideas of Froebel and Montessori.

2.29 The Schroeder House in Utrecht, Holland, by Gerrit Rietveld, which was used for two years, from 1936, as a Montessori nursery school. It might be described as having the characteristics of a 20th-century Froebelian 'occupation'.

2.29

2.28

nature, for example shells and plant stems. This general observation is perhaps of more value than the somewhat obsessive rationalization she makes in relation to the crystal.

Kaufmann is undoubtedly in tune with the duality of Froebel training: the holistic appreciation of the natural life forces, which gave Wright the ability to conceive buildings; and open social programmes. This, linked to a simplistic yet aesthetically pleasing ability to use forms as abstractions within his architecture, helps to underline how important the Froebelian cultivation of imagination and spatiality was to Wright.

The research which has been carried out on Wright develops an understanding of the influence of the kindergarten system, both philosophically and practically. Over the years this research has advanced, linking the work of the architects and artists of De Stijl and then of the Bauhaus. The scope of this publication does not allow us to develop this any further, but one can hardly imagine concepts like the Rietveld Schroeder House or the pin-wheel configuration of the Bauhaus building at Dessau without the influence of Froebel and Wright. 'If one were making a plea for the "kindergarten" idea in education, one could adduce no better living example of its value as a factor in the development of the creative faculties than by referring to architect Frank Lloyd Wright.'[85]

Rudolf Steiner and organic expressionism

An important theorist and sculptor of the early 20th-century expressionist period, Hermann Finsterlin (born 1887), defined the essential nature of his own house as follows: 'In the interior of the new house you will not only feel that you are an inhabitant of a fairy tale crystalline gland but also a privileged inhabitant of an organism, wandering from organ to organ, giving and receiving symbiant of a "gigantic fossilized parent body".'[86]

This radical interpretation of a new organic architecture – that it was to be a natural living organism in its own right – goes some way towards distinguishing it from Frank Lloyd Wright's view of organic building. Steiner's interiors would become spacious caverns, liberated from the constraints of the right angle. This, he believed, was the appropriate context within which young children should live and grow in a naturalistic way.

Steiner, like Froebel before him, believed that pre-school children needed to play rather than engage in formal educational tasks, in order that all their spiritual, intellectual and physical powers could emerge unimpeded. However, he added that this awakening should happen in harmony with the natural world. Steiner went further than Froebel in evolving an architectural theory which set out to be in tune with the psychological needs of early childhood. His influence instigated a powerful synthesis between architecture and pre-school education, which was given expression in pre-school buildings largely by his later disciples. It remains the clearest manifestation of a pedagogic and architectural convergence during the past 40 years.

Steiner was born in Kraljevec, Croatia, in 1861. At an early age, two crucial influences developed: he became fascinated by mechanical objects, and also greatly attracted to the mountainous countryside of the region. At school he was not a good student: he was a poor speaker and had difficulty mastering the written word. Despite this, he was an avid reader and had an ability to comprehend concepts and ideas quickly. A geometry textbook left by a teacher became a source of considerable interest to him.

The entire direction of Steiner's life seems to have been influenced by his profound view of geometric forms which were 'perceived only within oneself, entirely without impression upon the external senses'.[87] He was profoundly moved by this perception, seeing in it the reconciliation of the material and the spiritual. Thus he set out to construct spatiality which combined these two seemingly contradictory concerns, harmonizing with the innermost subconscious senses of the mind to create 'therapeutic environments'.

Despite the significantly slow start to his academic career while at first school, in 1879 he entered the Vienna Technische Hochschule at the age of 18, having matriculated with distinction. He carried his scientific interests forward into his Hochschule studies, specializing in natural history, mathematics and chemistry. He also attended philosophy lectures at the University of Vienna, where he developed what he believed to be his own innate sense of truth and reason. In 1884 he contributed to a symposium on Goethe, having become acquainted with Karl Julius Schroer, a professor of German language and literature and a recognized authority on the works of Goethe. Schroer's enthusiasm was boundless, and he encouraged Steiner to explore relevant academic areas such as Goethe's work on the natural sciences and colour theory.

Having completed his college studies, Steiner became the tutor of four boys, his attention being mainly directed towards the education of ten-year-old Otto, who was suffering from hydrocephalus and was believed to be uneducable. Steiner quickly identified the symbiotic relationship between bodily functions and spiritual wellbeing, and sought to liberate Otto through gentle encouragement and the gradual stimulation of his senses. The boy achieved *gymnasium* entrance standard in two years and eventually became a doctor of medicine.

In later years, this experience helped Steiner to formulate a new art of education. By the end of the century he had studied the work of Kant, Fichte, Herbart and Nietzche, Marx and Engels, and later Breuer and Freud. He also became aware of the theories of Hume and Darwin, and Einstein's work on relativity. Through this academic immersion he arrived at his basic philosophy, which was to become known as anthroposophy, 'the wisdom of man combined with his spiritual being'.[88]

In 1900 Steiner identified with many of the principles outlined in the newly emerging theory of theosophy.[89] In 1902 the Theosophical Society set up a German section and Steiner agreed to be its general secretary. However, he had certain reservations: he did not approve of the impartial support of alternative religions, nor of the general erosion of Christian belief. He also believed theosophists lived in the past and had little awareness of profound scientific advances. Steiner wanted to accept what

for him were the realities of the modern world as the context within which anthroposophists were to develop self-knowledge. After a short period in Weimar doing research related to Goethe, he returned to Vienna and joined a group of architects, writers and artists who met at the home of theosophist Marie Lang. Returning to his own cultural circle in Weimar involved him in a Nietzche archive. He began to see himself as an interpreter, combining the spiritual science of Goethe with the spiritual mythology of Nietzche.

In 1907 he arranged an international theosophical congress in Munich. Here, perhaps for the first time, music, recitation and drama were linked in a dynamic interaction appealing to the senses of the whole person. In 1912, the first Anthroposophical Society was founded; by 1913 Steiner, surrounded by a group of artists, architects, actors and musicians, set out to establish a centre for this artistic revival.

On a site at Dornach outside Basel, they erected a theatre for the enactment of mystery plays and later a number of houses and related buildings including a kindergarten (although this was not in the Steiner style). The first Goetheanum (identifying a connection with Goethe as one of the founding fathers of Naturphilosophie) was the ultimate *Gesmapkunstwerk,* with artists and architects from many different nations gathered together to work on the building. Artists and craftsmen worked together, oblivious to national boundaries, entering into the experience of a harmonious building process which defined the essential nature of his philosophy. Steiner showed how 'vitality of form could be achieved, how a concave surface leads into a convex one, creating a living curving surface. He described the different kinds of wood that were being used and their intrinsic qualities. He talked about how to create a painting by identifying with the different possibilities offered by the colours.'[90]

Later, Steiner's wider architectural influence was almost exclusively on kindergarten and school buildings. It was an expressionism which Kenneth Bayes described as having three characteristics: movement (particularly of line), sculptural form and metamorphosis of form.[91] These ideas were explicitly demonstrated at Dornach, which became an ideal Steiner community where a number of organic buildings were constructed; these included the Duldeck House, the Eurhythmeum and Brodbeck House and, centrally, the second Goetheanum, constructed after the first had burnt down.[92] Dennis Sharp suggests

2.30 Duldeck Haus, Dornach, Switzerland, by Steiner (with Hermann Moser and Ernst Aisenpreis), 1915–16.

2.30

that Steiner's Goetheanum had references to the Vienna Secession, and to Van de Velde who was head of what became the Bauhaus at Weimar. Steiner's own command of sculptural form and movement give his buildings a plastic, moulded appearance that resembles distorted crystalline shapes. Froebel's experiments with crystalline form predated Steiner's work in the same medium. Froebel's interest, however, had been overtaken by more cubistic concerns with the regular coloured geometry of the gifts; these found expression in De Stijl and the architecture of the Bauhaus.

'Metamorphosis of form' is the quality identified in Steiner sculpture and architecture, an idea that has become a recognized architectural term. According to Kenneth Bayes, it originated in Goethe's analysis of the plant as an 'earthly image of a spiritual archetype. Budding and sprouting, the archetype being of the plant embodies itself through successive metamorphoses of form until it reaches its full expression' – hence the term metamorphosis.[93] Steiner's idea was that one inorganic form would be added in sequence to another to create a system which resembled an image of growth – incomplete (and therefore dynamic), and natural. It was this sense of spiritual metamorphosis, an embodiment of the process through which the pre-school child passed, that has made the style so appropriate for some anthroposophical architects and educationalists since the 1950s.

The Waldorf schools

Dr Emil Molt, Managing Director of the Waldorf–Astoria cigarette factory in Stuttgart, was highly regarded by his workforce. In an attempt to improve conditions for his employees, Molt provided funds to establish a programme of education. He felt that education for children, rather than adults, would ultimately reduce the social division between rich and poor more effectively:

The original idea which led to the founding of the school was a social one, to provide for the children of workmen and employees the same teaching and education as that enjoyed by children of families with means. The insight was involved that the social chasm might begin to close if the problem of education were no longer dependent on money and that our cultural, economic and political

advancement would be possible only if all children, without distinction of the class to which their parents belonged, were permitted to share in the same educational system.[94]

Molt asked Steiner to establish and run the project, his first major opportunity to test his theories pragmatically. Die Freie Waldorfschule in Stuttgart opened in 1919, and was the first of many Steiner schools. Although not architecturally organic or distinctive, evidence suggests that this first building adopted Goethe's colour theories and a number of Steineresque details.

In the Steiner curriculum, no formal instruction is given to children at the nursery stage. 'The pre-school years, the kindergarten period, are the most important of all in the education of the child,' said Steiner in the first of a series of lectures.[95] The importance Steiner placed on the kindergarten is generally believed to have come about after a visit he made to Margaret McMillan's school at Deptford during a visit to England in 1923. McMillan wrote to a friend: 'Yes, Steiner is a wonderful glorious man . . . [He] came here to Deptford and everything seemed new and wonderful when he entered the room . . . No-one need tell him anything about themselves. He seems to see one . . . He never condemns or criticizes or has bitter thoughts like me.'[96]

The first Waldorf school in England was opened in Streatham, south London, in 1925, largely as a result of this inspirational visit by Steiner to London. Later, it was relocated to Forest Row in Sussex, and became known as the Michael Hall School. It is still thriving today, located in what could be described as a typical Steiner building. By 1939, 16 schools had been opened in Europe and the USA. By 1990 there were 521 Waldorf schools in 25 countries throughout the world, a number expanding by 100 schools per year.

Though still a comparatively minor educational strand, it nevertheless carries with it a consistent form of architectural expression. Indeed, the style is sometimes adopted by kindergarten architects who are not designing to Steineresque principles. To a certain extent, it has become the 'alternative style' for kindergarten architects, although Steiner would never admit to its being anything as transitory or ephemeral as a 'style'. Perhaps surprisingly, considering Robert Owens' earlier industrial workplace school at New Lanark, the original Waldorf school had no

2.31 Classroom block at
Peredur Home School, East
Grinstead, Sussex, main
entrance, 1965, by Kenneth
Bayes. Bayes suggests that his
building has no stylistic
dogma because its form is
intrinsically free.

2.31

kindergarten; today, however, pre-school and nursery education
are seen as fundamental to the Steiner educational philosophy.

Steiner's work was not taken seriously until the 1950s. Willy
Rotsler's article in the Swiss journal *Werk* was followed by
Dennis Sharp's *Modern Architecture and Expressionism* (1966).
The newly emerging style seemed to appeal particularly to the
Nordic nations, which were more in tune with its naturalistic
expressionism, as opposed to the intellectual abstraction of
modernism. In Sweden, this was mainly represented by the work
of Erik Asmussen, whose Rudolf Steiner school in Stockholm
engaged the teachers in the planning process and resulted in

a particular form of Nordic architecture, inspired by Steiner's
educational and architectonic ideals.

2.6 Summary

Much is written on the subject of education, but only a small proportion of it deals specifically with the architecture of pre-school.
The reason for this may be due to the historic failure to validate
an architecture tailored specifically to the needs of the pre-
school child. Particularly in Britain, nursery school facilities have
been (and still are) often dealt with merely as add-on classrooms

Kindergarten Architecture

2.32 Plans of the Michael Hall Waldorf kindergarten at Forest Row, near East Grinstead, Sussex, by Denis Devaris and Barbara Manteuffel, 1972. Contemporary organic Steineresque architects may believe that there is no direct stylistic precedent for their work, and that their architecture is a spiritual manifestation of what is within their souls; their architecture could therefore never be described as a style.

However, comparing this with the earlier Duldeck Haus, it is apparent that strong formal similarities prevail. For example, they are both symmetrical in one direction, contain five distinct spaces, are entered by way of a raised terrace and are volumetrically articulate.

Externally, the treatment of window openings and portals, and the moulded flowing forms of the roofs are also tied to the Dornach elemental vocabulary.

It can be argued that this was in turn influenced by such contemporaneous thinking as evidenced in other expressionists of the period. In the work of non-Steiner architects – such as Gaudí, van de Velde, Hermann Finsterlin and, most particularly, Erich Mendelsohn, who built the Einstein Tower in Potsdam, 1917–21 – there is clear evidence that Steiner's thinking was in line with some of the stylistic preoccupations of his time.

Key:
1–4 playrooms
5   hall
6   staffroom
7   kitchen

2.33 Plans of the Duldeck Haus.
Key:
1   terrace
2   dining hall
3   library
4   living room
5   entrance hall
6   kitchen
7   larder

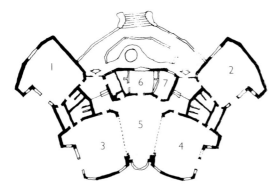

2.32

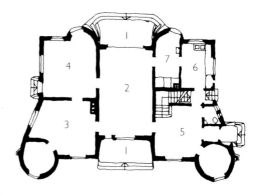

2.33

to existing primary school accommodation or conversions of existing buildings with no real concern for the needs of the child.

Traditionally, the European kindergarten was designed as a distinct institutional building, physically separate from the upper school, the church or community centre. However, the European nursery school model was more usually integrated into the urban environment, being both physically close to residential quarters and encouraging the involvement of parents and others from the wider community. We have briefly set out what we perceive to be the essential originators of the diverse strands of contemporary kindergarten practice. The list is neither complete nor exhaustive; however, it provides a useful summary of the most important pre-school theories and their relationship to space and the environment.

Child-centred activities in nursery school environments from the time of Pestalozzi and Froebel were always innovatory. The examples of nursery school architecture featured here are chosen to demonstrate an architecture of new ideas: radical educational ideas promoted in radical settings. This is the unique basis upon which the roots of kindergarten architecture can be viewed and assessed to form an understanding of the kindergarten idea – that of the broader humanization of children prior to the positivistic methods of the first school. It is, however, puzzling how little the key educationalists from the earliest times had to say about the role of architecture and architects, except in the realm of spiritualist educational theories exemplified by Steiner kindergartens.

That is not to say that we advocate the Steiner approach merely because it attempts to take a holistic view of pre-school education, including as it does architecture as a primary element in the educational method. Modern architecture, devoid of the overt Steiner ideology, can be as holistic and spiritual as organic expressionism. However, it is clear (Chapter 3) that an organic philosophy is becoming attractive to young contemporary architects (indeed, as a philosophy, attractive to young people in general), as disillusionment with 20th-century industrial capitalism sets in.

Although the Naturphilosophie of Froebel has been snubbed and derided as merely romantic, the alternative philosophies of Montessori, Piaget and many more of the pragmatists have proved to be limited in the wider humanization of mankind. The notion that man can continue to stand apart from nature, that the external world can be the object of man's exploitation, is being rejected, and has never been a part of the true kindergarten idea. Therefore it must, to a degree, be a rejection of 'the conceptual shallowness of pragmatic problem-solving' in the contemporary design of kindergartens. 'The way ahead is surely to fulfil Robert Owens' vision of the "new moral world", reconstructed now on the basis of the recognition of the totality of mankind as part of nature, and therefore to develop a new unitary theory of knowledge and morals in the interest of producing a genuinely humane world.'[97] In kindergarten architecture as a reflection of the the natural spirit of childhood, this impulse could be said to be happening right now.

2.34 The Froebel-trained Le Corbusier illustrates the simply defined forms of Purism in L'Esprit Nouveau, 1923, suggesting that they release primary emotions that are themselves modified by the individual's own culture and history.

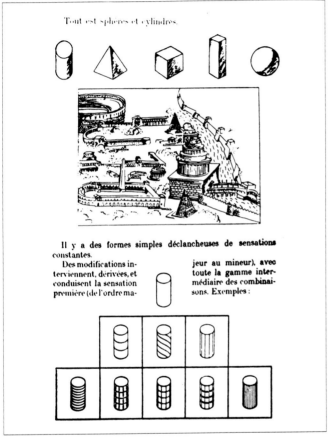

2.34

References and notes

1. 'The "work" of the Mother School was concerned with the training of the senses and the mastery of elementary facts and words – much the type of thing now taught in nursery school and kindergarten', Comenius, quoted by Cole, L. (1965), *A History of Education*, New York, Holt Rinehart Twinson, p. 338. This idea originated from Keetinge, J. A. (trans.) (1908), *J. A. Comenius: The Great Didactic*, London, A. and C. Black.

2. This is an interpretation of Meyer's statement: 'All things on this earth are a product of the formula (function times economy)', which appeared as part of a manifesto in the fourth issue of *Bauhaus* magazine, 1928. See Whitford, F. (1984),*The Bauhaus*, London, Thames & Hudson, p. 179.

3. Morris, Henry, *Nation and Athenaeum*, 25 August 1929. The quotation relates to a book review of *A Modern Philosophy of Education* by G. H. Thomson, which can be found in Rée, H. (1984), *The Henry Morris Collection*, Cambridge University Press.

4. We make this statement admittedly without a great deal of supporting evidence; however, architectural principles were certainly at the heart of Froebel's thinking. He was a trainee architect before becoming a teacher.

5. Saint, Andrew (1987), *Towards a Social Architecture – The Role of School Building in Post-War England*, New Haven and London, Yale University Press, p. 49.

6. Examples of the new architecture do not relate to the sort of prefabricated dwellings built after World War I by a number of British local authorities. Nor did the modern nursery school evolve from hutted camps or emergency hospitals, as has been suggested. That is not to say that some aspects of pre-school architecture were not eventually influenced by these cheap and cheerful exigencies.

7. CLASP (The Consortium of Local Authorities Special Programme) was originally developed by a group of local authorities in England who combined in 1957 under the leadership of Sir Donald Gibson at Nottingham. The system, which became well known, was for buildings to be economically put up on undermined land prone to subsidence, using a light steel frame construction.

8. My own experience of this came at an interview for an RIBA Research Award, when the all-male panel was unconvinced that a nursery school study was necessary. The attitude of some members of the panel was stated to be personal ('I was nurtured by my mother until the age of five, therefore what is the need for pre-school facilities?'). This appears to be an attitude inherent to many middle-aged, middle-class Englishmen.

9. See Blenkin, G.W.A. and Kelly, A. (1988), *Early Childhood Education*, London, PCP Education Series, p. 36.

10. Pollock, L.A. (1983), *Forgotten Children: Parent – Child Relations from 1500–1900*, Cambridge University Press.

11. Hanawalt, B.A. (1993), *Growing Up in Medieval London*, Oxford University Press.

12. Russel, J.C. (1948), *British Medieval Population*, Albuquerque, NM, pp. 285–7.

13. Beier, A.L. and Finlay, R. (1986), *London 1500–1700: The Making of the Metropolis*, Longman, London.

14. Sennett, R. (1974), *The Fall of Public Man*, Cambridge University Press, p. 53.

15. Hanawalt, *op. cit.*, p. 94.

16. Hanawalt, *op. cit.*, p. 64.

17. Public Records Office Cl/14/18.

18. Illich, Ivan (1973), *Deschooling Society*, Harmondsworth, Penguin, p. 4; quoted in Pollock, *op. cit.*, p. 7.

19. De Mause, Lloyd (1976), 'The Evolution of Childhood', in *The History of Childhood*, London, Souvenir Press, pp. 1–74; quoted in Pollock, *op. cit.*, pp. 18–19.

20. Ryerson, Alice (1961), 'Medical Advice on Child Rearing 1550–1900', *Harvard Educational Review*, vol. 31, pp. 302–23; quoted in Pollock, *op. cit.*, p. 45.

21. Sharpe, R.R. (ed.) (1913), *Calendar of Coroners' Rolls of the City of London 1300–1378*, London, p. 83; quoted in Hanawalt, *op. cit.*, p. 66.

22. Pollock, *op. cit.*, p. 93.

23. Plumb, J.H.P. (1975), 'The New World of Children in Eighteenth-Century England', *Past and Present*, no. 67, pp. 64–93; quoted in Pollock, *op. cit.*, p. 15.

24. Ariès, Philippe (1960), *Centuries of Childhood*, 1973 English edition, London, Jonathan Cape, pp. 13–14; quoted in Pollock, *op. cit.*, p. 27.

25. Hoyles, Martin (1979), 'Childhood in Historical Perspective', in Hoyles, Martin (ed.), *Changing Childhood*, London, Writers and Readers Publishing Cooperative, pp. 16–29; quoted in Pollock, *op. cit.*, p. 31.

26. It is worth quoting from *The Fall of Public Man*, p. 50, to illustrate the incredible transformation in the population of London: 'Here is how London grew. In 1595, it contained about 150 000 souls; in 1632, 315 000; in 1700, about 700 000; at the middle of the 18th century, 750 000. The growth of London in the industrial period of the last two centuries makes these changes seem pale; in the 19th century London grew from 860 000 to 5 million.'

27. Pollock, *op. cit.*, p. 62, citing the following sources: Altick, Richard (1973), *Victorian People and Ideas*, London, J.M. Dent; Briggs, Asa (1972), 'The History of Changing Approaches to Social Welfare', in Martin, Ernest (ed.), *Comparative Development in Social Welfare*, London, George Allen and Unwin, pp. 9–24; Bruce, Maurice (1968), *The Coming of the Welfare State*, London, Batsford; Perkin, Harold (1969), *The Origins of Modern English Society 1780–1880*, London, Routledge & Kegan Paul, pp. 60–2.

28. Cunningham, H., *et al.* (1994), 'Rights of the Child from the Mid-Eighteenth to the Early Twentieth Century', *Journal of the Institute of Education*, The University of Hull, 50.

29. Cruft, Hanno-Walter (1994), *A History of Architectural Theory*, Zwemmer Princeton Architectural Press. See also *Laugier Essai* (Paris, 1765), 2nd enlarged edition facsimile reprint 1966, New York Gregg Press.

30. Stewart, W.A.C. and McCann, W.P. (reprint 1970), *The Educational Innovators, 1750–1880*, London, Macmillan St Martin's Press, p. 28.

31. Stewart and McCann, *ibido* p. 28.

32. Levin, M.L.(1985), *The Body's Recollection of Being*, London, Routledge & Kegan Paul, p. 226.

33. Ashwin, C. (1980), 'Drawing and Education in German-Speaking Europe 1800–1900', dissertation submitted to the Institute of Education, London University, p. 46. Reference to Pestalozzi, J.H. and Buss, Christof, *ABC der Anschauung*, originally published 1803.

34. Silber, K. (3rd edn, 1973), *Pestalozzi, the Man and his Work*, London, Routledge & Kegan Paul, p. 22.

35. *Ibid.*, p. 313, essay by American philanthropist and social reformer W. Maclure, entitled 'The Advantages of the Pestalozzian System of Education', New Harmony, 1831.

36. Older children were used to look after groups of slightly younger ones. The classes were large and based on rote learning. Ackerman attempted to introduce the Pestalozzian method, without success.

37. Monroe, W. S. (1894), *Joseph Neef and Pestallozianism in America*, Boston MA, Monroe, .

38. Silber, K. (1973), *op. cit.*, p. 311.

39. Owen, R. (1857), *The Life of Robert Owen in Two Volumes*, London, Effingham Wilson.

40. Stewart, W.A.C. and McCann, W.P. (reprint 1970), *The Educational Innovators, 1750–1880*, Macmillan St Martin's Press, p. 67.

41. Richards, J.M. (1958), *The Functionalist Tradition*, J.M. Richards Architectural Press; reprint 1968.

42. Owen, Robert Dale (1824), *An Outline of the System of Education at New Lanark*; quoted in Silver, Harold (1969), *Robert Owen on Education*, Cambridge University Press, pp. 149–50.

43. Cole, M. (1953), *Robert Owen of New Lanark*, London, The Blatchworth Press, p. 86.

44. Wilderspin, Samuel (1840), *A System for the Education of the Young*, London, James S. Hodson, pp. 56–80.

45. Liebschner, J. (1991), *Foundations of Progressive Education*, Cambridge, The Lutterworth Press, p. 15.

46. Read, J. *et al.* (1992), 'A Short History of Children's Building Blocks', *Exploring Learning: Young Children and Blockplay*, ed. Pat Gura, with the Froebel Blockplay Research Group directed by Tina Bruce, p. 9.

47. *Ibid.*

48. Ronge, J. and B. (1855), *A Practical Guide to the English Kindergarten*, London; quoted in Stewart, W.A.C. and McCann, W.P. (1970), *The Educational Innovators*, Macmillan St Martin's Press, p. 305.

49. Downs, R.B. (1903), *Friedrich Froebel*, 1978 edition, University of Illinois, Twayne Publishers, G.K. Hall and Co., Boston, p. 92.

50. Rousseau, Jean-Jacques (1762), *Emile*, trans. and ed. Foxley, Barbara, (1974), London, Everyman's Library.

51. Foxley, B., *ibid.*, p. 108.

52. Foxley, B., *ibid.*, p. 108.

53. Ashwin, C. (1981), *Drawing and Education in German-Speaking Europe 1800–1900*, Ann Arbor, MI, UMI Research Press, pp. 16–17.

54. Ramsauer (1821), *Zeichnungslehre* , Part 2; quoted in Ashwin, *op. cit.*, p. 46.

55. Le Corbusier and Ozenfant, Amedée (1918), 'Après le Cubisme' (Purist manifesto), quoted in Banham, R. (1960), *The Theory of Architecture in the Machine Age*, London, Architectural Press, p. 207.

56. Balif, Anne (1949), *De Van Gogh et Seurat aux dessins d'enfants*, illustrated catalogue of exhibition held at the Musée Pedagogique, Paris.

57. Schorske, C. (1981), *Fin-de-Siècle Vienna*, New York, Random House, p. 328.

58. Levin, D. M. (1985), *The Body's Recollection of Being*, London, Routledge & Kegan Paul, p. 219; quoting from Neumann (1976), 'The Child: Structure and Dynamics of the Nascent Personality', p. 12.

59. Schorske, *op. cit.*, p. 325.

60. Franz Cisek, quoted in Schorske, *op. cit.*, p. 20.

61. Goldwater, R. (1986), *Primitivism in Modern Art*, London, Thames & Hudson, p. 195.

62. Klee, F. (1964), *The Diaries of Paul Klee 1898–1918*, Berkeley, University of California Press, p. 226.

63. Klee, F. (1962), *Paul Klee*, New York, Braziller, p .1872.

64. Krauss, R.E. (1985), *The Originality of the Avant-Garde and Other Modernist Myths*, Cambridge, MA, and London, MIT Press, p. 53.

65. Krauss, *op. cit.*, p. 53.

66. Bachelard, *op. cit.*, p. 72, where the 'intellectual realism' of psychologist G.H. Luquet is discussed in relation to the views of Georges Bataille on primitive representation.

67. Gura, P. (ed.) (1992), *Exploring Learning–Young Children and Blockplay*, with the Froebel Blockplay Research Group directed by Tina Bruce.

68. Burke, J.G. (1966), *Origins of the Science of Crystals*, Berkeley, California, University of California Press; quoted in Rubin, J.S. *et al.* (1989), 'The Froebel Wright Kindergarten Connection: A New Perspective', *JSAH*, vol. XLVIII, March 1989, p. 24, n. 4.

69. Froebel, Freidrich (1826), *The Education of Man* (trans. W.N. Hailmann), D.

New York and London, Appleton and Co., 1887, p. 68. See also Rubin, *op. cit.*, p. 25.

70. Froebel, *The Education of Man*, *op. cit.*, p. 287. The distinction between the gifts and occupations is, according to Hailmann, not clearly defined by Froebel, but is very important: 'The *gifts* are intended to give the child from time to time new new universal aspects of the external world, suited to a child's development. The *occupations*, on the other hand, furnish material for practice in certain phases of skill. Anything will do for an occupation, provided it is sufficiently plastic and within the child's powers of control; but the gift in form and material is determined by cosmic phase to be brought to the child's apprehension, and by the condition of the child's development at the period for which the gift is intended . . . The gift gives the child a new cosmos, the occupation fixes the impressions made by the gift.'

71. Manson, G. (1953), 'Wright in the Nursery – the Influence of Froebel Education on Frank Lloyd Wright', *Architectural Review*, vol. CXIII, June 1953, p. 350.

72. Downs, R.B. *Friedrich Froebel*, *op.cit.*, pp. 50–1.

73. Snyder, R. (ed.) (1980), *Buckminster Fuller Autobiographical Monologue/Scenario*, New York, St Martin's Press, p. 9.

74. Rusk, R.R. (1918), *Doctrines of the Great Educators*, Macmillan, London, reprint 1948, p. 196.

75. *Ibid.*, p. 198.

76. Maria Mills, one of the original helpers, quoted in Kramer, R. (1978), *Maria Montessori – A Biography*, London, Hamish Hamilton, pp. 286–7.

77. Wright, F.L. (1943), *Frank Lloyd Wright – An Autobiography*, New York, Duel, Sloan and Pearce, pp. 13–14.

78. Denevi, D. (1968), 'The Education of a Genius: Analysing Major Influences on the Life of America's Greatest Architect', *Young Children*, March 1968, p, 239. Wright did not attend a kindergarten as such. His mother introduced him to kindergarten activities at the age of nine when she bought a complete set of Froebelian toys and kindergarten 'chests'; she felt he would derive more value from them at this age than at four.

79. Manson, G. (1953), 'Wright in the Nursery – the Influence of Froebel Education on the Work of Frank Lloyd Wright', *Architectural Review*, vol. CXIII, June 1953, pp. 349–51.

80. MacCormac, R. (1968), 'The Anatomy of Wright's Aesthetic', *Architectural Review*, vol. CXLIII, February 1968, pp. 143–6.

81. *Ibid.*, p. 146.

82. Kaufmann, E. (1981), 'Form Became Feeling: a New View of Froebel and Wright', *JSAH*, vol. XL, May 1981, pp. 130–7.

83. Rubin, J.S. (1987), 'The Froebel–Wright Kindergarten Connection: a New Perspective', *JSAH*, vol. XLVIII, March 1987.

84. *Ibid.*, p. 25.

85. Denevi, *op. cit.*, p. 239.

86. Sharp, D. (1966), *Modern Architecture and Expressionism*, Longman, p. 98.

87. Childs, G. (1991), *Steiner Education in Theory and Practice*', Edinburgh, Floris Books, p. 9.

88. Sharp, *op. cit.*, p. 146. The name derived from the Greek *anthropos*, man, and *sophos*, wise. Man was then placed at the centre of all perception.

89. Stewart, W.A.C. (1972), *Progressives and Radicals in English Education 1750–1970*, London, Macmillan, p. 190: 'Theosophy is based on belief in immutable, all-pervading principles which pre-exist creation and from which the universe, spirit and matter, growth and decay, all flow.'

90. Klinborg, A. (1992), 'Rudolph Steiner and His Ideas on Building', *Byggekunst*, p. 328.

91. Kenneth Bayes, unpublished lecture, quoted in Sharp, *op. cit.*, p. 149.

92. Sharp, *op. cit.*, p. 156. The Goetheanum was a centre for the Anthroposophical Movement and is described by Dennis Sharp as a 'vast temple of spiritual science'.

93. Sharp, *op. cit.*, p. 149.

94. Wachsmuth, G. (1955), *The Life and Work of Rudolf Steiner*, New York, Whittier, p. 363.

95. Steiner, R. (1923), *Understanding Young Children: Excerpts from Lectures by Rudolf Steiner Compiled for the Use of Kindergarten Teachers*, German edition 1975, Stuttgart, International Association of Waldorf Kindergartens; trans. into English 1994, Waldorf Kindergarten Association of North America, p. 8.

96. Stewart, W.A.C., *op. cit.*

97. Bowen, J. (1981), *A History of Western Education*, vol. 3: *The Modern West*, London, Methuen, pp. 557–8.

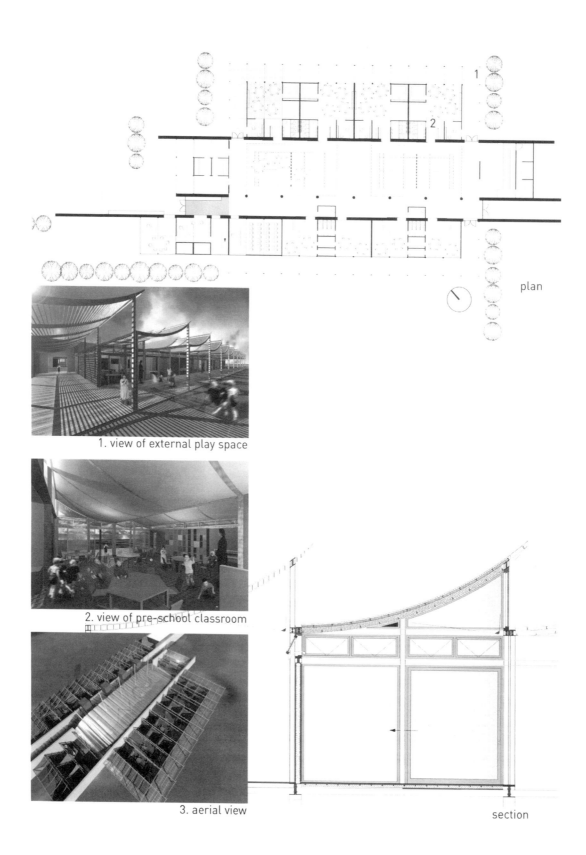

plan

1. view of external play space

2. view of pre-school classroom

3. aerial view

section

3.1

Meaning in contemporary kindergarten architecture

3.1 Didactic versus neutral

Since the beginning of the 1980s the growth in kindergarten architecture has been marked, partly because of previously explored social needs. However, it is also important to recognize the often pioneering activities of groups and individuals in a number of different cities throughout the world, who have been able to employ good architects in the design of pre-school facilities. There is a growing recognition that architecture for pre-school is neither exclusively for care (and therefore relating typologically to the hospital), nor is it wholly educational (relating to the school). Over the past ten years, it can be said that a new synthetic building typology has emerged.

Contemporary 'state of the art' kindergarten buildings, while typologically similar, exhibit perplexingly diverse theoretical approaches. Often the architectural expression goes far beyond functional meanings, adopting highly playful metaphor or extreme organic forms to create an architecture which 'fascinates'. Many of our featured case studies exhibit radical architectural poses ranging from the naturalistic 'ideal children's environments', beloved by Rousseau, to more overtly modernistic forms.

3.2

The latter may be seen to be reacting against more sentimental views of childhood. The notion that children are not innately innocent but can carry within them 'diabolical carnality' was explored by Henry James in *The Turn of the Screw* (1894) and in much other literature about children. It suggests that a less romantic and tougher architectural expression would be more appropriate for contemporary children's culture. These radical meanings are being discreetly reflected in some contemporary kindergartens.

We have already identified a number of architectural categories relating to important historic kindergartens, conceived predominantly during the 1920s and 1930s. Today, despite the pluralistic condition of contemporary architectural theory, it is still possible to identify at least four clear 'types'. The first of these encompasses organic projects such as Christopher Day's Nant-y-Cwm Steiner Nursery in Wales, and the Jardin de Niños la Esperanza (Children's Garden of Hope) in Tijuana by James Hubbell. We also include the extreme metaphorical expressionism of the Luginsland 'boat' Kindergarten in Stuttgart or the Bungawitta Children's Centre in Tasmania, since this is an architecture derived from an overtly expressive design sensibility.

3.3

3.1 The community nursery designed in modular units by the Education Design Group and Ed Mullett.

3.2 View of the courtyard, Poplar play nursery, east London, by Proctor Matthews.

3.3 Interior view of main activity space.

The second category, which might be described as 'late modernism', is a definition that covers a multitude of extremes: from technically experimental proposals such as the unbuilt Frankfurt projects by Arup Associates and Future Systems (not featured as case studies), to the somewhat mechanistic day care centres by Greenhill Jenner in south London and Rudolphe Luscher in Lausanne, Switzerland. The style of the architecture is clearly directed at the child's innate sense of inquiry into systems, mechanisms and machines. By the age of three or four, explorations of this nature are undoubtedly beginning. They hold immense fascination and have considerable developmental value, particularly for boys.

To describe an architectural theory as 'moderate' or 'neutral' may be viewed by some architects and critics as a contradiction in terms. They might argue that contemporary architecture, particularly architecture with a social programme, must by definition be extreme, reflecting a vision of constantly evolving social structures. Equally, some educationalists believe that it is harmful to assume that an environment for young children can be neutral in any way, because infants and toddlers are particularly 'sensitive to all qualitative aspects of its setting: its movements, sounds, volumes, textures, visual and kinesthetic vibrations, formal colours and rhythms.'[1] However, in defining this third category we hope to show that a 'moderate', or what we call a 'contextual', approach is as much a part of meaningful contemporary kindergarten architecture as more extreme forms of architectural expression. In certain circumstances it may even constitute a more appropriate approach, particularly when an opportunity for the later adaptation of the building is made possible, or when economic strategies are required that are allied to a clear pedagogical view.

This category is broad and contains a great range of diversity within the framework of what is usually a conservative or moderate style. Its adoption has educational implications to which we will return. However, despite its inherent conservatism, it represents a valid approach which we include as part of this architectural study. It covers those projects made as adaptations of existing buildings and kindergartens that are extensions to existing buildings. The architecture is usually moderate, responding to an existing context or simply redesigning the interior of an existing building. Nevertheless, it can illustrate an important manifestation of excellence in contemporary kindergarten architecture.

The fourth and newest category is what we have described as a 'modular' approach. Here the technical innovation lies in the principle that on site labour is up to three times as expensive as its factory based equivalent for a number of reasons. The nursery is constructed in complete units which are then transported to site and bolted together to give economies of scale and time. Despite the contentious nature of the process (is this really kindergarten architecture or merely product design, some might say) and problematic environmental control problems, this is nevertheless an important and expanding type.

In this chapter, through critical analysis and the comparison of a number of our featured case studies, we discuss the ways in which successful kindergarten design can be imbued with all sorts of meanings, which ultimately encourage and enable the young child to explore, develop and learn in a pleasurable yet secure way. Are there established principles to guide the architect in the creation of an authentic kindergarten architecture that reflect these cultural concerns? How can the diverse philosophies, particularly those of the organic tradition set against overt modernism, be explained and justified?

3.2 Metaphor

From the very beginning, curiosity and learning refute whatever is simple and isolated, but rather yearn to discover the measure and relations of complex situations . . . to create analogies, metaphors, anthropomorphic and realistic logical meanings.[2]

Architects have widely differing opinions on how best to incorporate these principles. Christoph Mäckler, who designed one of the Frankfurt 'Kita' day care centres, states that 'there is no such thing as architecture for children'.[3] Consequently, in his Sossenheim project, he does not include any 'child oriented details'. Mäckler adopts a design metaphor: the notion of the building as a small town. A series of classrooms ranged along either side of a central corridor is articulated as a terrace of houses, complete with gable ends facing the street. Within the building, circulation runs through the centre of the plan, passing, so to speak, 'through' the house party walls. The structure of the cross walls is identified externally by the gables. This organization is further clarified by the use of a white wall running along the central cir-

3.4 Axonometric drawing of
Christoph Mäckler's Sossenheim
'Kita', 1989.

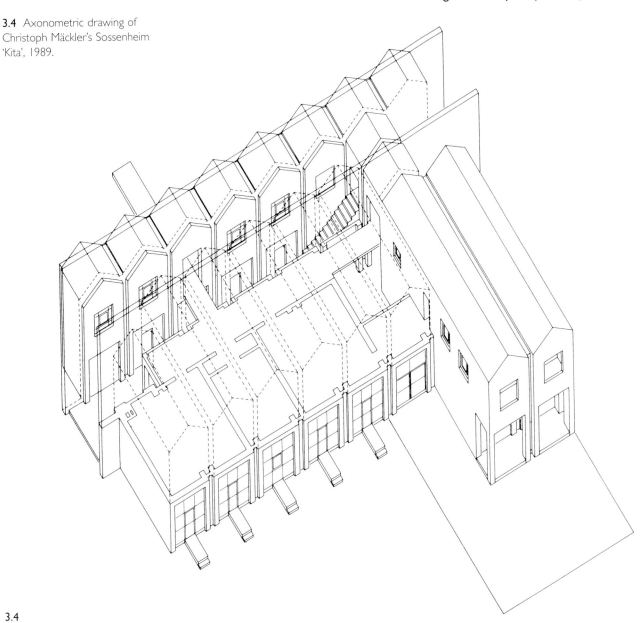

3.4

culation spine, in contrast to the dark red brick of the 'houses'
themselves. Urban typologies are referred to: the street, the
square, an entrance bridge and an alleyway. The building not
only makes reference to the single-person houses opposite, but
also provides spatial diversity within which children can explore
a range of differentiated interior rooms.

The Lützowstrasse Kindertagesstätte in Berlin by architect
Klaus Zillich develops a similar idea, albeit in a less literally
metaphorical way. Here, the intention is to create a sort of
child's world within part of an existing city block, complementing
other community activities. The nursery school is both part of
this community of child-related activities, and a separate self-
contained building. The kindergarten accommodation is
arranged in three 25-children 'apartments' which are organized
in a rigorous north–south section, allowing optimum levels of
daylight to penetrate deep in to the heart of the building.

In providing full-day care for 75 children up to the age of six,
the school divides children into mixed age groups in the three
'apartments'. Play, sleeping, eating and toilet areas are provided
within each self-contained unit. Each has its own sun terrace
where children can have lunch, using the east-facing winter garden with its external play space in the mornings. This solar
geometry helps to give structure to the long days and lends a
natural, almost symbolic significance, to the building and the site.
Primary colours – used so wilfully in many nursery schools – are
almost absent. Instead, a diverse range of natural materials is
used to create a diffuse if sombre atmosphere.

Zillich creates a sophisticated urban spatial hierarchy; the
whole block within which the nursery school building sits is a children's park. In turn, the school building has its own self-contained
gardens on a section of the east side of the city block. An east-facing morning garden and a west-facing afternoon garden, adjacent

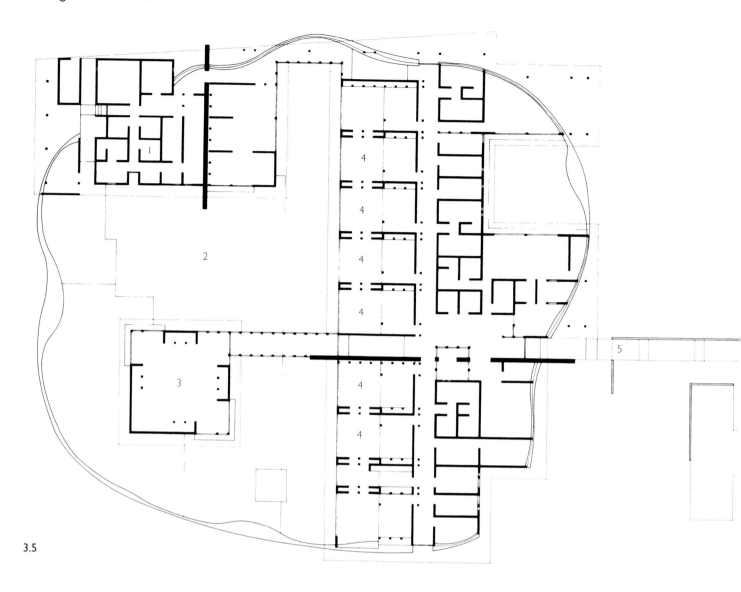

3.5

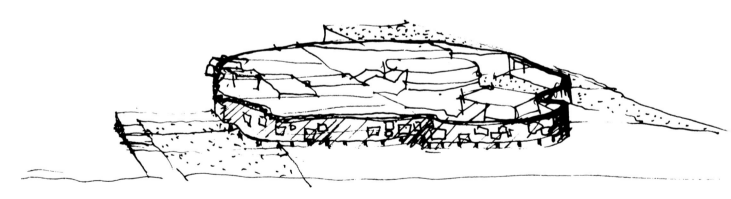

3.6

3.5 Plan of Christoph Langhof's project for a children's centre in Berlin, with the entrance at the base of the drawing. Unbuilt.
Key:
1 staff areas
2 garden
3 assembly hall/music space
4 kindergarten classrooms

3.6 Sketch perspective.

to the entrance where parents appear to collect their children, forms the context for the school building. Within the building itself, there is a large winter garden, a space where all the children, teachers and parents can gather for special events. The children's apartments are the secure base for individual daily activities. This is a hierarchy which goes from the intimate and almost private terraces of the 'apartments' to the safe but semi-public territory of the gardens. The construction of the block is incomplete, but will eventually provide a child's world in miniature.

The Poplar Play Nursery in east London includes a recently designed 'drop-in centre', where local parents can come with their children and use the facilities of the main nursery school. Architects Proctor Matthew's initial inspiration was to take a popular children's story – C.S. Lewis's *The Lion, the Witch and the Wardrobe* – and structure the architecture around a three-dimensional interpretation of it. Thus the rear wall in the play area is punctuated by seven spaces, intended to relate to the idea of the mysterious wardrobe. This forms a 'backdrop' for the play spaces of the building and the semi-covered external loggia. The children may act out their own version of 'The Tales of Narnia' within a secure child's world. Using this metaphorical method, the designers establish a rich sequence of architectural events within the overall framework of a secure courtyard.

The story is abstracted and diluted into a building form that can be interpreted as a contemporary version of the arts and crafts tradition – neither overtly modernist nor relying solely on traditional forms. Not only does this metaphor create a structure that is descriptive without being too literal or patronising, it also forms the kind of spaces that children would naturally inhabit, with lots of niches and useful storage. Quite clearly a narrative is supporting the architecture, which appeals to both imaginative and practical requirements.

A less literal narrative supports the approach taken in Christoph Langhof's proposal for a nursery school in Besselstrasse, S. Friedrichstadt, Berlin. Nevertheless it uses metaphor, and perhaps some of Rudolf Steiner's child theories of anthroposophy. The architect attempts to create what he calls an 'island for children'. A curved wall symbolically opposes the orthogonal grid of the city. At two points the orthogonal grid of the interior containing the school rooms breaks through the organic curved wall, suggesting that the fortress of the kindergarten is not or should not be wholly separated from the reali-

ties of the city: 'The island is removed from the mainland. The "mainland", in this case, is Berlin; the island is something separate, different for children. The city is for the adult (in all of us?); the island is for the child (in all of us?).'[4]

According to architect and critic Douglas Clelland, the project can also be read on the level of 'l'Esprit Nouveau': 'The notion of the island . . . for children, intact and separate from the city, will continue to be hotly debated. But it is encouraging to see such commitment from an architect. And, in this centenary of Le Corbusier's birth, it is good to see Langhof's understanding of the vitality of this particular strand of tradition.'[5] Although this scheme was not built, its multilayered child-orientated themes touch on the particular seduction that children's architecture holds for the contemporary architect.

A similar curved wall meets the street in architect Robert Morris-Nunn's Bungawitta Children's Centre in Launceston, Tasmania.[6] This time the curved wall has a bluff, fortress-like quality which, rather than opposing the orthogonal grid of the city, is perhaps more at one with it. The context is, in this case, a suburban one. However, the grid of the inner kindergarten world again breaks through the outer wall. Whereas this would have remained an abstract collision of architectonic forms in the Langhof project, here the protrusion is an entrance portico which gives a strong suggestion of what is to be revealed within: it is the image of a house that could have been taken from the drawing of a young child, complete with pitched roof, chimney, door and two square windows above. The door and windows are eccentrically proportioned to underline further the child-like image. The question being posed is: which is the real world and which is fantasy? The answer is not as obvious as adult perceptions may appreciate.

Once inside the wall, the full extent of the fantasy is revealed in the form of a child-scaled street, naturally lit by a linear rooflight. The street takes on the form of a series of dolls' houses, scaled to the height of a five-year-old, with every building that can be found in a typical suburban high street: there is a post office, a bank, shops, a garage and a Georgian town house. Roads and street crossings are delineated, etched into the vinyl floor covering. There are also street lamps and traffic signs. This is not so much a metaphor, more a theatrical experience of a 'stage street'. Go behind the curtain, and the 'back stage' unfolds: four activity areas relating to age groups (babies; one- to two-year-olds; two- to three-year-olds, and three- to five-year-olds) are conventional spaces – some enclosed, some more open-plan. The rear of the building allows access on to a pleasant north-facing garden.

Whether or not the architect is imposing too inflexible an image of play, to which children *must* relate, is open to question. As with many of these radical kindergarten projects, the children take more readily to the theatricality of this experience than the teachers, who may not appreciate the joke. Equally contentious on an architectural level is the extent to which the false façade is expendable. Take away the gimmicks, and do you still have a vital, expressionistic piece of modern architecture? Would allowing the children (with the aid of parents and teachers) to create their own street have been a more positive way to engage them with their environment?

One suspects these questions will be answered only with the benefit of hindsight, when teachers and care workers are able to assess the longevity of this particular architectural folly.[7] However, when young children first encounter the space, the pleasure is visible on their faces. The effect is both to amuse and to calm the natural anxieties of parent and child at what may be their first separation. One suspects that the tranquillising of the parents in this way (so that they do not communicate their anxieties to the children), and the breaking down of social barriers are the real benefits of this therapeutic interior space.

One of the most extreme metaphors structures the entire form of a new building: this is the 'sinking boat' Luginsland Kindergarten in Stuttgart by architects Behnisch and Partner. The idea was suggested by an earlier project at Neugereut, where the architect's intention had been to take an old boat from the Neckar river and transport it to the land-locked hillside site. Christian Kandzia, the project architect, felt that this would create a distinctive but economical solution; at the time, his Lutheran clients were not persuaded by its appropriateness. Consequently, that project was developed along more conventional lines. However, the idea remained, and the boat metaphor was rejuvenated as the inspiration for the Luginsland project.

Its value in the context of this study is that it is radical in its adoption of an architectural theory that may be only loosely related to conventional pre-school pedagogic ideas. Perched on a steep hillside rising from the Neckar valley, the building is an eccentric addition to the surrounding suburban landscape of pitched-roof houses and gardens. The legibility of the boat form is extremely clear, leaving little room for individual interpretations. The prow of the boat, pointing in a south-easterly direction, contains the main activity areas, which consequently gain a wide angle of solar exposure. It appears to sink to its rear, slightly listing, with the toilets and plant room in the half-buried stern. The head teacher's room is placed at the stern, which is, observes Peter Blundell Jones, 'precisely the position of the captain's quarters in wooden sailing ships . . . Though less literal (and less symmetrical) in execution than it might have been, the marine imagery is nonetheless unavoidably there, strikingly exuberant. Here is a building that is the opposite of reticent, which declares the new importance of child care facilities, and not without controversy.'[8]

Initially, the proposal drew a great deal of criticism from local residents who attempted to obtain a legal injunction to prevent its construction. However, it was believed (incorrectly) that as this was to be the last Stuttgart kindergarten to be built, an architectural statement – a Stuttgart landmark – would be appropriate. Even now it remains a contentious edifice on the horizon, but a highly memorable one.

However, it is not impractical. Contrary to what one might expect in a ship, the only sloping floors are the roof deck on which, for obvious reasons, the children are not permitted to climb. There are two teaching areas, one on each floor, containing entrance hall, main activity area and a quiet space. The conjunction of odd angles and indefinite forms creates child-sized niches that match the play patterns of young children who need to appropriate and dominate their space. Similarly to the Bungawitta kindergarten, it is quite noticeable how the children take to the building in an uninhibited way, in contrast to adults whose sense of unease is often demonstrable.

In a sense, this disharmony occurs where the fantasy meets the reality (or where the eccentric meets the prosaic); for example, in the selection of standard school furniture, which does not appear to fit comfortably into this strange quirky world of skewed angles and elusive scales, or in the relationship between the human (growing) body and the angular forms of the architecture that tend to challenge and perplex the young child. Does one wish to live a fantasy? After all, Disneyland is a 'once in a lifetime experience': to visit it every week may transform the experience into something banal. This is perhaps where the boat

3.7

3.7 Ortolanweg 'Kita', Berlin, by Woolf and Partner. The detailing is deliberately made legible for the benefit and understanding of young children, in the tradition of Günther Behnisch.

concept – so totally imposed by the designers – comes slightly unstuck. If the architects had taken the programme to its logical conclusion, they may have considered the design of similarly quirky furniture to complement the rest of the interior. But where does one end? It is almost as if the architecture is trying a little too hard to be childish.

Some critics suggest that its proximity to the baroque of southern Germany places this architecture in a cultural context. The late baroque/rococo style of 18th-century Catholic Germany was a rejection of the staid and the ordinary for more exuberant, optimistic forms. But this argument is not wholly convincing: baroque was always a complex, overlayered form within a highly structured framework. On reflection, a more appropriate historic analogy would be to the strange, jaunty work of Antoni Gaudí in Barcelona or Victor Horta in Paris. It is an architecture of the surreal – grave, fascinating and complex. It does, however, leave questions and concerns for 'rational' adult minds, as it may not take children's space seriously enough for some tastes.

Paradoxically, one can also interpret this as a building that recognizes and celebrates the new rights of children. It may even be a personal milestone in the architectural thinking of Behnisch himself. He drew the initial sketch, so this is not the whim of some unknown assistant. The roots of Behnisch's architecture lie in the immediate post-war climate of international modernism, which tended to inhibit more expressive architectural taste. For Behnisch, this architectural confection may be the ultimate liberation from the self-imposed artistic conservatism of much modern German architecture.

An earlier kindergarten designed by the same architects provides an interesting contrast to the 'boat'. The Neugereut Kindergarten, Stuttgart, was completed in 1975 and is more relaxed in its response to the needs of children. Comprising two activity areas for 50 full-time pre-school children with a central assembly space, it is a generous and warm 'home from home' for children. The triangular plan is completed by a beautiful (and now mature) garden which seems integral to the building itself. Vines and flowering blossoms drape over a trellis that gently dissolves the solidity of the building into its natural setting.

By comparison to the 'boat', the detailing here is less experimental and more refined. Equally, environmental factors such as light and ventilation tend to be more easily controlled in the less eccentric form. It is safe to assume that young children do not pay too much attention to architectural detailing. However, the deliberate way in which the structure is revealed may be seen to aid them in their development of spatial perceptions. The architecture of Günther Behnisch always has a constructional sophistication which is more than just academic. The way in which structure, fabric and services relate to each other in a modest but highly articulated manner produces a lightness of touch that suits its educational purpose well. The use of natural materials, mainly timber steel bracing and steel jointing brackets, gives the whole building a light feel. This structural clarity reveals the inner workings of the architecture, without imposing too strong an image. It is, therefore, more open to different imaginative interpretations.

In some ways this is a building which characterizes Behnisch's architecture much more than Luginsland. Its articulate simplicity is a reference point for many designers, such as Thomas Woolf whose Ortolanweg Kindertagesstätte in Berlin is an unapologetic tribute to early Behnisch. This is a recognition of the therapeutic effects of an architecturally neutral approach, which takes the aesthetic sensibilities of young children seriously.

3.3 The organic

According to architectural historian Nikolaus Münster, the architecture of Christoph Mäckler's Sossenheim project also takes children seriously, viewing them as 'small adults'. Some critics, interpreting his use of metaphor as a somewhat patronising stance, would not agree. They see metaphorical architecture as an attempt to create a synthetic Disneyesque world which, to a certain extent, avoids reality. A project developed on these metaphorical lines but adopting a more extreme expressionistic strategy is the Heddernheim-Nord 'Kita' in Frankfurt by Viennese painter Friedensreich Hundertwasser. Münster describes this as 'a kind of fairytale castle whose onion domes and cosy corners make it seem very playful'. For Hundertwasser, children's architecture should reconcile the imagination of the child with expressive images, almost like a baroque stage set, using very literal metaphors and narratives as an alternative way of structuring the architecture.

A secondary, but perhaps more crucial, reference for Hundertwasser would be his declared attempt to reconcile the relationship between man and nature. Rather than articulating abstract cubistic qualities in an overtly modernist way, or

3.8 Frederick Kiesler, 'The Endless House', 1959.

3.9 Christopher Day, Nant-y-Cwm Steiner Nursery, 1990.

structuring the architecture around a set of architectonic symbols in the way Mäckler does, here the architecture is subsumed into the land – the roof is a growing sediment of the landscape with meadow grass and trees, almost as if the building has been gently slid under the earth. 'It's high time we did the opposite for once and went underground. To have the earth above our heads in no way means dwelling in dark caves or damp cellars . . . for it is our duty to restore the nature we destroy when we build a house to the roof of that house. The nature that we have on the roof is that part of nature that we destroyed in placing a house there.'[9]

This reference is reminiscent of Rousseau's educational ideal in wishing to provide an environment which defers to nature and thus preserves 'the original perfect nature of the child' (Chapter 2). This is achieved not only through a deliberately close pedagogic relationship between the school curriculum and nature, a theme which is generally universal in pre-school education, but also through the physical form of the architecture. A harmonious relationship with man's rural environment is reflected through the mimicking of natural forms in the architecture itself. It is a comment that perhaps inadvertently echoes the phenomenological view, commonly expressed in certain forms of contemporary kindergarten architecture. Bachelard, who speaks of using the house as 'a tool for analysis of the human soul', talks in this context about it possessing 'the verticality of the tower rising from the most earthly, watery depths, to the abode of a soul that believes in heaven.'[10] This is appealing to an altogether more complex set of design intentions than the purely functional. This organic approach usually goes hand in hand with a highly developed pedagogic philosophy, which is intuitively understood and appreciated by teachers and parents alike.

One of the most obvious examples of this can be found in the design of a number of contemporary Steiner nursery schools. For example, Christopher Day's kindergarten for Nant-y-Cwm Steiner School attempts to infuse the Steiner philosophy into everything architectural. From the outset Day felt that the environment would have a positive influence on the way in which the children behaved.

The quality of their surroundings also affects their play. Fast moving, loud and over-stimulating or dreamy, gentle, magical environments induce different responses. Not only do

children play differently in a street, beneath a motorway flyover or in a woodland glade, but also in rooms of different qualities. They also play differently with inflexibly formed and simply experienced solids, and fluid materials such as water, sand, or clay. Elusively formed and coloured, textured and so on, things like tree roots, soft dolls and cloth, support their vivid powers of imagination, whereas harder, harsher, unambiguous ones, such as brightly coloured 'play' cubes depress, although they rarely completely suppress it.[11]

The rural site was the primary reference for Day: a conifer plantation on a south-east sloping hillside, between a quiet minor road and a river. This provides an atmospheric context within which to blend the new building into the topography. The natural incidents of the landscape create a child's world which is at one with Rudolf Steiner's spirit of anthroposophy. The building comprises two classrooms which are essentially circular, designed to enhance sociable games and offer a feeling of protection. However, according to Day, the circle is too perfect a form, a mathematical geometry not in harmony with nature and 'a somewhat lifeless shape'.

So the classroom forms are incomplete circles, which actually have corners. By distorting and twisting the geometry, using some straight lines within the construction of the curves, the circular form remains but the feeling is more variegated. Not only does this give the classrooms a more natural organic shape, like huge ancient tree trunks from a Grimm fairytale, but the corners themselves become little alcoves for small group activities. Reading takes place in a soft corner, and other related activities in a home corner and a kitchen corner.

The external form of the building continues to develop this dialectic, imitating nature rather than contrasting with it. The external walls taper out towards their bases, seemingly moulding the building into the earth. The use of earth-coloured render and the incorporation of a roof totally covered with grass reinforce this sense. The softly curving walls are welcoming, encouraging movement around the building, particularly as sharp corners are avoided. Thus the territory immediately surrounding the building enclosure becomes one that encourages exploration. The building seems to be fulfilling the paradoxical requirements essential to the contemporary kindergarten: on the one hand, its homely

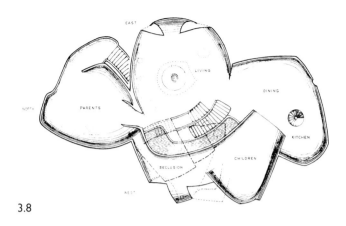

3.8

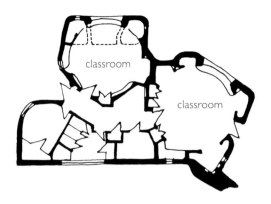

3.9

warmth encourages feelings of permanence and security; on the other, its presence casts a pleasurable glow over the entire area, to encourage the young child to go out and explore.

Christopher Day would, one suspects, be quite dismissive of much contemporary architecture. His references are almost entirely natural or organic; using forms which imitate nature. In explaining the careful positioning of the building on its site, he touches on the way he hopes that through its harmony with the whole environment it will transform the inner state of being of the children.

He describes how the children will have almost certainly travelled by car to arrive there, having had a 'kaleidoscopic' experience. They are in tune with only one of their senses, that of sight. The effect of this synthetic experience may be to make them raucous and fractious: 'They have therefore about a hundred metres of woodland walk, crossing several thresholds to leave that world behind them. First a leaf archway, then a sun-dappled cliff edge above the shining, singing river, then shady woodland, then pivoting past the firewood shed, through a gate to a sunlit play-yard and sandheap. Then an invitingly gestured, but slightly asymmetrical, so not too forceful, entrance. Then a blue purple-green corridor, quiet, low, twisting, darker. Then again a sunlit stopping place for de-hooting.'[12]

The language Day uses to describe his building matches the intensity of the architecture. Modern design is rarely this florid; at first sight the building has a rather disturbing presence. Rightly or wrongly, the modernist tendency is to create buildings that are minimalistic, a calming foil to the pace of contemporary urban life. The Nant-y-Cwm Nursery is almost anti-architecture, avoiding pure geometry and straight planes, consciously imitating the irregular forms found in nature. One has to admire its eccentricity, and young children absolutely love it! The composition of the plan is reminiscent of a project by environmental architect Frederick Kiesler called 'The Endless House' (1924–65). On many symbolic levels it is, observed Hans Arp, like an egg: 'in these spheroid egg-shaped structures, a human being can now take shelter and live as in his mother's womb'.[13]

The integrated child care centre on Gerbrandsvej, Amager, Copenhagen, is, according to architects Jørgen Raun and Ulla Poulsen, a more relaxed reworking of some of these Steineresque notions, albeit on a much larger scale. The building is based on organic ideas, the plan perhaps loosely derived from

the tree in that it has centrality in the main entrance hall, with branches that house the activity areas. The external cladding is almost totally of roughly finished fir, finally given a vibrant painted finish of blues and greens. Poulsen states that the organic theme is reflected in the internal planning, where no two corners of the same room match. Just as Christopher Day's tapering walls express permanence and stability, similarly the accentuated projecting eaves at Amager create a tree-like protective canopy, encouraging the children to go out and explore within the secure shadow of the building.

Prior to this building, the architects had never designed for children. However, through the experienced assistance of the Copenhagen Municipal Building Department, clear guidelines and safety regulations were defined and adapted to the needs of this unusual design. A room schedule was provided that stipulated merely that the kindergarten should have five 42m² areas, each comprising an activity or nursery room, toilet room and kitchen. There is an entrance 'stem' with an office and staff room.

Apart from these practical matters relating to safety and environmental standards, the architects were given a free hand. The resulting design is, to a certain extent, a reaction to the unlikely context, which is a conjunction of semi-industrial leftover land adjacent to Copenhagen's airport, and a sub-suburban residential quarter close to the anarchic Christiania Community of self-built houses. Partly as a response to this environment, the architects felt they could be more radical than in their previous projects, creating a strong, slightly idiosyncratic architecture. This radicalism could be further justified by rejecting the notion that kindergarten should be a 'home from home'; instead, their approach celebrates difference by using a vivid yet calming architectural language totally removed from that of the surrounding residential apartment blocks.

The building is unorthogonal in plan and uses some of Goethe's theories on colour. The group rooms are calming peach and yellow, and the central atrium spaces are blue and green, colours that are 'thought to unite people in activity'. The fan-shaped layout is referred to as having five leaves, each of which supports 20 kindergarten children or ten nursery children. This unpretentious yet imaginative response dissolves the institutionalizing nature common to much social architecture of this scale. The building encourages children to play and develop their own sense of independence within a secure umbrella. The pavilion building was opened in 1993 and a second, essentially identical, pavilion on the same site was completed in June 1994 to provide full-day care for 220 children. The project won a national civic architectural award in the year of its opening, and is clearly an economical way to provide a humane environment for many children.

Jardin de Niños la Esperanza (Children's Garden of Hope) in Tijuana is a kindergarten that benefits from a similar 'inside–outsideness'. Located on the Mexican border, approximately 200 miles south of Los Angeles, it has a positive social programme aimed at improving life in this grindingly poor community. Designed by San Diego-based environmental artist James Hubbell, it is not only a sensitive reworking of spiritual values in architecture, it is also a primary example of working with the local community to produce a building of exquisite beauty.

Comprising two large classrooms, an office and bathroom, all arranged around a central courtyard, the school provides full-time care for 140 children in two morning and afternoon sessions. The children are divided into separate groups of three- and four-year-olds, who attend for either morning or afternoon sessions. One would have thought that the simple programme would have resulted in a simple plan, but this belies the spatial complexity the architect has worked into his design. The basic building system is an in-situ concrete shell cast on to steel-mesh reinforcement that twists and curves down to the ground to create a complex, three-dimensional plastic form. The roof form extends beyond the rooms themselves out into the playground/courtyard to provide arcade-like shelters, protection against the hot sun. When it rains, the roof channels the water into the central courtyard, which provides a visual and social focus with its turtle-shaped tiled fountain.

The anthropomorphic references are further reinforced, according to Hubbell, by the form of the roof and the feet-like columns that spread down to the ground to make the building appear like some sort of friendly prehistoric animal, a turtle writ large. This is all part of the strategy to create a building that is architecturally subtle, yet at the same time provides a positive distraction for the children; an anthropomorphic fantasy which touches upon the mythic roots of the community, protecting and sheltering them from a harsh natural environment.

The parents have also been considered as an important factor in the construction process. The local women, many of whom have been abused in one way or another, are gently drawn into the process of building and making. Their involvement in the setting of mosaics and even bricklaying has not only benefited the hand-crafted finish of the building, but has acted as a kind of therapy, restoring their selfconfidence to become involved in the communal process. 'We have discovered [through our involvement] that education transcends class barriers. Beauty also transcends such barriers. It communicates a different sensibility to what they are accustomed to; like music, it changes the nature of space.'[14]

The careful control of daylight entering the classrooms through specially shaped windows and skylights, and the use of tile mosaics that swirl over walls and floors, make this a building of considerable decorative pleasure. Hubbell has used his sculptural sense to create the 'turtle fountain', a wall niche ringed by a mosaic of abalone shells and occupied by a tiny statue of Bart Simpson (which the children have dubbed St Bartholomew), to provide animated points within the architectural plan. The decoration creates a spiritual focus, calming the natural exuberance of the children very much in the way that Day uses the trees and natural topography of the site in his Nant-y-Cwm kindergarten, lifting dispirited or downtrodden parents, and assimilating the natural enthusiasm of the children into the whole project.

3.4 Late modernism

Compare these organic approaches to that taken by Bolles Wilson Architects at Greisheim-Sud 'Kita', also one of the Frankfurt projects; here, the architectural details are highly playful, but within a serious, modern 'white' architectural language. Peter Wilson explains his approach as being about the frame and its adjacency: 'Where the frame is the form of the building, which is neutral, without narrative content, a sort of abstract volume – the adjacency is a second order of event, a specific and localized event.' Thus the playful, child-related details are placed within the overall frame, independent of each other, creating specific localities within the building. Architecturally, the spirit of the building pays great homage to the Modern Movement which is coherent and largely functional, therefore a serious architecture. Yet it also has a series of amusing or ironic architectural details (the 'events'), which appeal to children and lighten the earnest pretensions of much modern architecture.

Interestingly, Wilson states that his later projects, designs for a library in Münster, use less and less of these adjacencies or events: 'I have enormous respect for the Modern Movement but I think there is a synthesis of the abstract volume and the incident which is more engaging . . . since the Frankfurt 'Kita', the incidents have become less important. The major turning point for me were the Japanese projects, or the encounter with Japan in general, where one came across a complete reversal of approach. In the west one tries to put meaning in – the Japanese try to take it out. This to me was most liberating, and I think our projects since have been trying to get back to more essential forms.'[15]

Despite his allegiance to Modern Movement philosophies, Peter Wilson believes that German architects and critics find his approach to architecture difficult: 'The whole school of thought that I come from is foreign to German rationalist thinking, whereas schoolchildren and normal people accept and understand the humour and inversions of the incidents. Some architectural critics find the frivolity unforgivable. With our kindergarten the children really related to the little things scattered around it . . .', whereas trained architects found it difficult to take, seeing the details almost as unnecessary decoration. Wilson believes that the German approach is going in the direction of 'a stone-faced historicism' of which he does not wholly approve. He defines the qualities of the Frankfurt kindergarten in a very down-to-earth way: 'I think the kindergarten we built was actually quite tough spatially. It certainly appeared so when it was photographed before the furniture and toys went in. The relationship between inside and outside is very important, children are free to run in and out from each group room. It's really about group management, ensuring the spaces are comfortable, the loos are located in the right place, and are spacious and architecturally reassuring.' Wilson defines a level of concern that is frequently cited as of great importance: that the kindergarten environment should 'have space' – each of the functionally explicit areas, such as washrooms and lavatories, are therefore considered in equally careful detail to the main activity areas.

Although the spirit of the Modern Movement is very apparent in the way the building appears superficially, this is far more than the neutral frame devoid of any narrative content suggested by the above quotation. In both plan and section, the important issue of scale informs the way in which the form grows from one end to the other. The tapering of the plan and the ele-vation creates a deliberate scale variation – from small, tight spaces around the entrance, equating to the rooms for the smallest children, to the large, open 'play hall' at the far end. Perhaps the strongest influence on the form of the building is the site, which has a busy motorway to its north. Therefore the building turns its back on this noisy road, opening up to the quiet, sunny, south side. 'It is also a clear solid form in response to the amorphous context.'

The building has strong anthropomorphic qualities, reminding children of a very large snail or some other almost pre-historic animal. This image is not mentioned by the architect in quite the same deliberate way in which anthropomorphic claims are made for Hubbell's building. The end result is the natural outcome of the financial and practical restrictions placed on the architect after the original design was conceived. The way in which the form was subsequently enriched without dilution is a tribute to the strength of that initial concept, which one suspects developed from Wilson's painterly or sculptural preoccupations. Indeed, these compromises have brought about many positive child-orientated details. For example, black stripes set into the linoleum floor finish (specified to be a single colour throughout by the client) not only relieve the uniformity, but also create the context for children's hopping games. The balance between solidity and frivolity creates a children's environment of great quality.

The basis of Charles and Elizabeth Lee's UCLA campus work-place nursery in California is also a serious modern architecture. However, in this case it is in the purer, unadorned style of Mies van der Rohe rather than the organic phase of Le Corbusier. The slightly mechanistic spirit of the building was adopted not only because of the short four-month building programme which validated a simple prefabricated building process, but also because it was felt to be an appropriate foil to the lush campus setting.

The partners worked for Norman Foster in Hong Kong prior to opening their own office in 1989. Their declared interest in Japanese simplicity is perhaps best exemplified by their main inspirations, the work of Charles and Ray Eames, and Rudolph Schindler's Kings Road House in west Los Angeles: 'They took as much care in the making of a project as in its concept.'[16]

Here is an admitted throwback to the pioneering period of radical modernism, where the economy of means becomes the architectural concept for the building, and can consequently be carried through with serene rigour to create the ultimately

3.10 Schindler House, Los Angeles, California, 1928. This was the inspiration for Charles and Elizabeth Lee's UCLA Child Care Center.

3.10

neutral container for the activities of the children. Elizabeth Lee cites the 'serenity' of abstraction as a precise 'material interpretation' of the age in which we live, and therefore an appropriate way to design for children.

However, this building adopts further meanings that also hark back to earlier West Coast social values. June Sale, former child care coordinator and the project's client representative, originally expressed this around the idea of the family, where there is space for more private individual activity and reflection (in the classrooms); however, at its heart there is an open courtyard where everyone comes together. Inadvertently, this ideal is echoed in Rudolph Schindler's explanation of his ideal family house. In 1926 he wrote that 'our rooms will descend close to the ground and the garden will become an integral part of the house. The distinction between indoors and outdoors will disappear. Our house will lose its front-and-back-door aspect. It will cease being a group of dens, some larger ones for social effect, and a few smaller ones (bedrooms) in which to herd the family. Each individual will want a private room to gain a background to his life. He will sleep in the open. A work and playroom, together with the garden, will satisfy the group needs.'[17]

The site for this 80-place child care centre is a former orchard on the UCLA campus. The site contains wild woods, a more conventionally landscaped area running along the side of Sunset Boulevard and, most importantly, a vegetable garden which is tended by the children under the guidance of the teachers. The kindergarten buildings, which sit in the centre of this beautiful site, consist of three pavilions containing an administrative block at the centre and two classroom wings. The classrooms comprise three areas: the activity area, a broad communal terrace on which it opens, and a sleep/quiet play area at the rear. To quote Schindler again: 'This theme fulfils the basic requirements for a camper's shelter: a protected back, an open front, a fireplace and a roof.'[18]

The pavilions, which overlap each other at their corners, are arranged in a U-shaped pattern that forms a secure and sheltered courtyard. Two broad covered loggias or porches run along each side of this courtyard, providing shaded outdoor play areas that protect the children against the hot Californian sun. The slightly tapering plan form of the courtyard is orientated towards the south-east, optimizing the least severe sun angles. The tapering of this space has the effect of engaging the wider landscape into the environment of the building. It does not seek to 'dominate' the landscape in the way that some pavilion-type buildings tend to do. The modest, relaxed nature of the architecture ensures that the relationship between building and nature fulfills the ideals of early educators such as Froebel, who sought this harmonious quality in his own pre-school environments.

The system-built steel modules (based on their transportability from the factory) form the frame for the alternately solid and translucent infill panels. These panels are either fully glazed in solid painted timber plywood, or of semi-translucent fibreglass 'Kalwall'. The lightweight fabric of the building is inevitably sensitive to solar heat gain; an air conditioning system was integrated into the floor slab, which was the only component cast *in situ*. The shaded loggias help to maintain a comfortable inner sanctum on the hottest days. The structural system was designed and specified by engineers Ove Arup and Partners. This elegant and sophisticated solution reveals the innermost workings of the building technology to the children. Perhaps more importantly, it acts as a positive and perhaps honest reflection of the modern world, yet is still at one with its natural setting. The notion of honesty in the somewhat synthetic world of Los Angeles creates an intentionally neutral backdrop, rather than a more synthetic 'home from home' in the Disneyland city.

Elizabeth Lee believes that the success of the project had much to do with their openness to new ideas, both educational and architectural. She recognized the experience and knowledge of June Sale, who accommodated the original concept of lightweight pavilions from the outset, and then helped to establish the practical needs of the children, staff and parents within this powerful architectural framework. Of equal importance in this process were the structural engineers, Ove Arup and Partners, who committed a great deal of time to this, their first project in Los Angeles. When we visited recently, some five years after the completion of the building, the children and teachers had adapted a great deal of this neutrality towards a more positive play environment, with paintings plastered across the partitions and windows. However, the quality and clarity of the architecture within the natural environment, communicate to the children their own value, helping to foster a more positive self-image. 'The character of the whole site says something to the children, that we think they are important and that we care about their future.'[19]

The building is a successful amalgamation of technology and poetics. The spirit of the architecture is of the greenhouse, an open transparent world within which children can see and be seen. Its lack of child-like details and down-to-earth organization is part of a tradition that originated in this region. It has a strong contextual flavour, which would perhaps work less well in other settings.

Rudolphe Luscher's Centre de Vie Enfantine, in Valency, Lausanne, Switzerland, expresses a more technical purpose through its external form, according to critic Peter Blundell Jones. On some levels it is reminiscent of a laboratory or a hi-tech factory 'and challenges the widespread notion that everything built for children must be warm and cuddly, or at least a reinterpretation of the gingerbread house. But children are just as much at home these days with space ships and robots and take to computers with astonishing alacrity.'[20]

In a similar way to those of the UCLA Child Care Center, the Luscher pavilions reveal much of the inner workings of the technology of the building, to heighten the children's perceptions of their space. For example, the lavatories for the younger children (up to the age of three) are open-plan and feature cisterns which have been adapted to make whistling noises when flushed. It is a modern pedagogic approach which, according to Rudolphe Luscher, 'is an effective teaching tool which helps the children to be sociable, and to understand the workings of the architecture itself.'

The original idea for the building was for three pavilions linked by bridges on a single level, which were to accommodate three functionally explicit areas: a nursery for babies from six months up to two years, two- to three-year-olds, and three- to six-year-olds. This, according to project architect David Linford, was seen to be too Cartesian and one-dimensional, and the design team developed a more complex, layered approach. The pavilion idea was a modernist response to the green park site, with the intention of accentuating the building as object, rather than contextualizing it in a naturalistic way, reminiscent of Le Corbusier's Villa Savoye in its contrasting – even shocking – effects on the landscape.[21]

However, there the similarity to Villa Savoye ends – the building has an architectural autonomy of its own which, to a certain extent, is unrelated to its social programme. What began as a clear composition of three largely autonomous pavilions in the landscape evolved into a more complex series of mixed forms accommodating the functional programme in a deliberately post-modernist manner. Thus the ground-floor plan dissolves the original clarity of the pavilion idea into an open-plan sequence of fluid spaces, one overlapping the other. The three pavilions become stair towers, which give rhythm to the plan at ground-floor level, emerging at first-floor level in three identical

studio rooms with views over the park. These rooms are for
four- to ten-year-old children to use after infant school finishes in
the early afternoon.

The sequence of functional areas at ground-floor level comprises entrance, open-plan kitchen, laundry (area one), assembly
room/dining area and day nursery (area two), open-plan circular
toilet space with activity area for two- to four-year-olds (area
three) and, finally, activity areas for two- to four-year-olds with an
external play courtyard. The building on this level exhibits two
paradoxical architectural tendencies: the fluidity of the modernist free plan, and a solid order overlaying the whole. This synthesis of free plan and clearly defined structural zones is almost
inadvertently expressive of the way in which contemporary
pedagogical structures work: there is a clear order, yet freedom
within that order for children to use other parts of the building,
or at least to remain aware of their context (this is similar to
Diane, Chapter 1). It also combines the traditional 'closed' classroom arrangements with more open-plan layouts; the latter
alone can be too open to provide enough security and privacy.

The original teaching staff – who came from more conventional school buildings comprising closed cellular spaces – were
unable to cope with the flexibility of this new building. According
to Head Teacher Mme Buchs, all but four of the original staff
were replaced with teachers who were more adaptable to new
ways of working with children. Initially, the adult instinct was to
reduce this openness by keeping the partitions closed. However,
this was stifling for the children, so the partitions were removed,
and the children then appeared to be more stimulated and in
less need of adult attention. This was tempered by the incorporation of cubby-holes and niches in which to hide, seemingly balancing young children's need for privacy and secrecy with their
natural sociability.[22]

The building is clad externally in shiny zinc titanium panelling,
which gives it a somewhat space-age feel. Fair-faced concrete is
used effectively as an internal finish in the stair bays, with dry wall
plaster and sliding timber partitions that recess into the wall bays
when not in use. Interestingly, the children used the building
much more effectively in the first three months of its life prior to
the introduction of toys, as if they were able to adapt it to be
used as a toy in its own right – they occupied niches and moved
panels and partitions as the architect had intended, experimenting and playacting freely in the different functional areas without

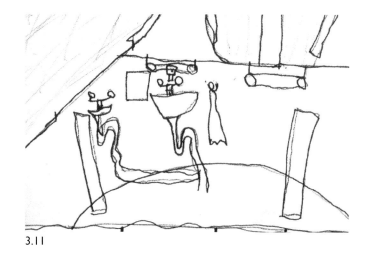

3.11

distraction. 'The children's house was designed as a complete
toy. The children noticed this immediately.'[23]

A project that generates its narrative almost entirely from
functional concerns relating to energy-saving technology is the
so-called 'low entropy' project. It was proposed for a site at
Sossenheim, Frankfurt, and was designed by architects Arup
Associates. It remains unbuilt, but is worthy of analysis as the
technology would probably have formed very appropriate
spaces for young children.

The plan of the building is a semi-circle of four large group
rooms, flanked by the smaller activity areas that form the outer
part of three functionally distinctive 'layers' of accommodation.
The middle of this sandwich comprises curved lavatories and
cloakrooms that protrude into the central assembly or dining
area. This is all organized along a solid spine wall, which acts as
the entrance (at either end) and a circulation corridor against
which lean the servicing accommodation, kitchen storage and
plant room. The section (Figure 4.36) illustrates the dialectic
which is developed with the rear, north-facing 'heavy' wall covered by insulating earth, and a sophisticated, south-facing 'light'
solar wall which also acts as an acoustic baffle to the main road.

Clearly, the composition has formal similarities to Christopher
Day's Nant-y-Cwm Steiner Nursery in its use of a grassy roof,
adopted ostensibly for its high thermal properties. Both projects
use curved forms to create niche spaces around which children
can lose themselves. In the case of the Sossenheim project, it

would appear that the building has been turned inward, as if in recognition of its urban context. The form is much more instantly comprehensible than the Steiner project, but similar in its use of curves and indents within the plan. Yet the end result is radically different. Here the forms are regular and in some ways more reassuring to the urban child. Its metaphor is technological, whereas the Day project is consciously removed from any reference to the real world.

The Ringrose Kindergarten in Malaysia by Akicipta Associates is a somewhat synthetic response to the needs of contemporary nursery schoolchildren. It adopts overtly elemental forms, which the project architect Teng Kok Seng describes as being reminiscent of Lego, an effect heightened by the use of primary colour. One is struck by the playfulness of this project, and its appeal to non-architects is instant.[24] However, of all the case studies featured, it is the most difficult to categorize architecturally. It is neither modernist nor organic, neither technically advanced nor architecturally neutral. It is dressed in almost Disneyesque clothes, and yet provides comfortable, well-planned spaces in a form that stands out in the rather dull landscape of the region.

The Scuolo dell' Infanzia Diane in Reggio Emilia is a moderate form of interior architecture that has considerable value in the context of this architectural study, even 20 years after it was conceived and built. It is similar to Charles and Elizabeth Lee's UCLA Child Care Center in that it does not impose any child-orientated details directly through the architecture. The building to a certain extent becomes a neutral container for the children's activities, an 'aquarium' for the fluid movements of developing minds and bodies. But Diane is pedagogically very successful.

Originally developed through a dialogue between the local authority architects and Loris Malaguzzi, then Director of Child Care Services in the city, it is a building of no obvious architectural merit externally. It is modest in its use of materials, orthogonally planned and clearly structured. This solid, no-nonsense order is further reinforced by a well-proportioned system of gridded window framing which is used throughout the building, both inside and outside. The school provides full-day education for three groups of 25 children between the ages of three and six.

On entering the building through the centrally positioned porch, one is greeted by a beautifully open and vibrant space that is described by the coordinator as a 'public piazza'. Brightly coloured banners are draped from the ceilings, and two small

courtyards are visible within which trees and plants grow. To the left is the open dining area, a space where all 75 children can sit at differentiated group tables. This exemplifies the social purpose of the building: lunchtime is a school-wide experience which allows the children to experiment socially by joining different lunchtime groups, making social connections of their own choice.

The dining room furniture, while old and somewhat home-made, appears to fit comfortably within its context, painted leaf green to harmonize with the lush planting draped down from the top of the courtyard windows. The whole atmosphere of the space is one of lightness and genuine transparency; beyond the courtyard, other, more enclosed, activity rooms are visible. But this transparency is selective, avoiding the goldfish bowl phenomenon. Hints of what is going on in the distance are only suggested: semi-glazed partitions ensure that a sufficient degree of privacy is maintained. This enables staff and children engaged in the activity areas beyond the 'public piazza' to feel private, without the sense of enclosure or claustrophobia felt in conventional schoolrooms. The philosophy that the child is engaged in his or her own activity, yet within the distracting world of a public institution, is seen as a positive quality and is subtly maintained and supported by the way in which the interior architecture works.

This clear, light atmosphere is enhanced by the generous glazing and, in particular, two small inner courtyards which allow light into the depths of the plan. The artificial lighting is not particularly effective, and this is one area that School Coordinator Tiziana Filippini wishes to improve. However, this expansive environment is 'littered' with architectural and educative moments or focal points. For example, running along one wall of the dining space is a marble bench seat which, in contrast to the chairs and tables, has a feeling of solidity and permanence inviting the visitor or the child to 'sit on me'. Moving through to the activity areas beyond the piazza space, there is a circular drum form cut down the middle, which holds the children's coats and shoes. On the other side is a strange, triangular form that has mirrors on its three inside surfaces — children lie within it and experience infinite reflections of themselves and their friends, an imaginative distortion of reality which they greatly enjoy.

These objects have all been carefully added to the interior over a period of 20 years since the building opened in 1971. Totally unpretentious 'interventions', they seem integral to the overall experience of the space. While the Bolles Wilson

3.12 Ground-floor plan of the Honjo Kindergarten by Team Zoo. The plan shows enclosed and open-plan spaces with level changes and wall niches to create a rich and diverse environment.

Key:
1 entrance
2 three- to five-year-olds' classrooms
3 working rooms with storage
4 dining hall
5 kitchen
6 playroom
7 staffroom
8 utility room
9 toilets
10 wash/cloak corridor
11 waiting/meeting room

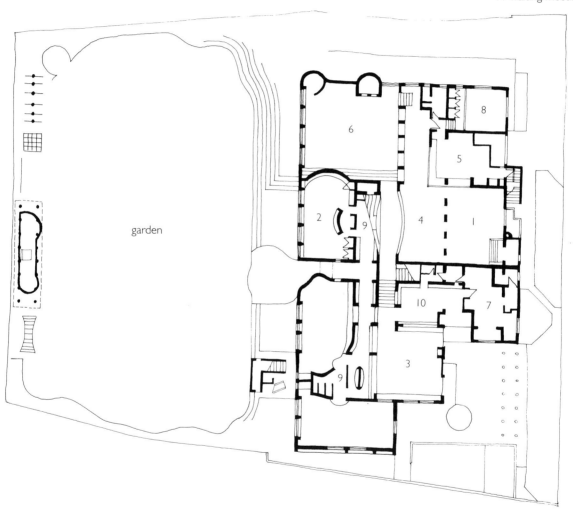

garden

3.12

Greisheim-Sud 'Kita' looked superb in the photographs taken immediately after its completion. As soon as the furniture (and children) were introduced it appeared cluttered and slightly over-elaborate. Of course, this is partly due to the difference in size of the two buildings. Diane has an area of 770m² with 75 children, giving a ration of 10.25m² per child, whereas the Frankfurt 'Kita' has a total area of 682m², giving an area of approximately 7m² per child.[25] The Diane nursery school is extremely practical, supporting a rich programme of activities, yet always appearing elegant and ordered. Equally, the garden is arranged as a series of highly imaginative activity areas, accessible from all parts of the building.

Since its opening, Diane has continued to evolve and improve its environment, adapting to changing pedagogic values. It provides more space per child than most of the other examples we viewed; however, the space is used totally and without waste. The public square at its heart has enabled the teachers to generate new social points of contact and enriches the overall spatial quality. It lacks some basic facilities, such as a proper office or staff room; however, there are plans to develop a new building in collaboration with the architects' department at Milan University. The basis of its form will be guided by the shortcomings and the inherent qualities of the present building.

We now consider the work of a Japanese group, who produced five kindergartens over the space of ten years between 1972 and 1982. Atelier Mobile, a practice working within the overall philosophical umbrella of the Team Zoo group, adopt an architectural stance that has similar qualities to a Frank Lloyd Wright house in its inherently child-centred spatiality. Whereas the Diane kindergarten is moderate, architecturally orthogonal, light and open, offering a sense of freedom within the secure knowledge of a class-based structure, the Honjo Kindergarten is all of these things and a little bit of Rudolf Steiner, too.

Located in the business area of this small town, the building caters for babies and infants up to the age of five. The accommodation comprises closed rooms as bases for mixed age range groups, with open-plan areas between. The predominant feeling is one of openness. However, the Closed rooms appear to be bonded together by the open spaces between them; which are never simply corridors. The public spaces are taken up by a dining area and a kitchen, which is glazed so that children can look in (and staff look out), an open-plan play space, and working rooms for art and potting plants – all of these seem to celebrate and encourage 'journeys' within and around the building. The open spaces have playful changes of level, with raised stage-like platforms – so-called 'rostras', which may be a reference to the theatre or to the surrounding undulating step-like topography of the region. This provides a variety of volumetric experiences, which succeed in their intention of encouraging the children to move around the building during the long days. Children love to experience different spatial perspectives, climbing up or jumping down, looking down on other children, constructing elaborate games. It is a testimony to their enhanced environmental perceptions that there are very few accidents.

The walls of the kindergarten are both orthogonal and curved, yet within the framework of the grid. The undulating roof is reminiscent of a large slumbering animal, or it might be an allusion to the wind. The form is multidimensional, inviting a range of interpretations. Team Zoo's architecture is described as humanist, but is neither sentimental nor architecturally unsophisticated. The kindergarten presents itself as a little town, in an uncannily precise echo of Margaret McMillan's 1920s' reference to what it should represent for the child: a small town of child-sized buildings (the classrooms) which are linked by the 'idea' of open spaces, replicating green fields between. In this example,

the 'fields' are of course still within the internal envelope of the building. The whole building is a place for children to play at being future citizens, representing a safe, stimulating microcosm of the city. 'Its ultimate aim seems to be "the human being and his blossoming" . . . Let us add then that this blossoming can only take place in open and sensitive surroundings.'[26]

3.5 The modular nursery

The task and responsibility of the new men will be to build in sufficient quantity and therefore at an industrial rate, schools first, but not just school buildings but schools for real children, and children who later will travel to the moon; universities different from those under construction at present; houses by the million with their ancillary extensions.[27]

During the 1950s, Jean Prouvé designed pre-fabricated building elements and structures in France in order to satisfy the need for a rapidly expanding school roll. Prouvé stated that by incorporating advanced methods of pre-fabricated construction, it would be possible to radically transform the school environment to create more appropriate places in which children learn. Spurred on by the need for large-scale production during the immediate post-war years, he established a factory at Maxéville and developed pre-fabricated systems which radically transformed the spatial quality of what had previously been viewed as low-quality buildings.

His thesis was that a school should display the architecture of the epoch rather than some sort of regressive historical form. The new designs were highly engineered constructions using state-of-the-art methods of fabrication. However, it was necessary to observe higher than average standards of design within his new systems, as the education board were uncomfortable with the idea of pre-fabrication. Despite much resistance, Prouvé won a competition with his experimental approach, which resulted in two building commissions. He also took part in the construction of schools in some communities headed by enlightened mayors. School buildings constructed at Villejuif in 1953 were made with robust cantilevered structural frames which were propped at the edges and infilled with planar steel frame windows to create extremely elegant and robust buildings.

3.13a,b The Forest Kindergarten (interior). Modules developed by Helle Grangaard for Kompan in Denmark. They are used as shelters for activity days in the country.

However, despite their advanced design they were condemned as temporary buildings within 15 years of their completion. The irony is that many huts with negligible architectural and very little environmental quality were subsequently built in France which then remained in use much longer than the Prouvé system. Many UK local education authorities will still refuse to commission pre-fabricated buildings because of the stigma attached to the temporary concept. Nevertheless, a number of manufacturers are working on the development of factory-built systems for use as schools, and more critically perhaps, as nurseries. The demand for nursery education and full-day care with an educational agenda has resulted in all the major political parties promising nursery places for all three- and four-year-olds within the UK. Whether the UK local education authorities like it or not, the whole issue of pre-fabrication is very much in the air.

The Lilliput nursery evolved out of a two-year development process and is arguably the first UK system to take the needs of pre-school children seriously, within the framework of a pre-fabricated system. The design was a joint effort involving the Portakabin technical team headed by development engineer Chris Hogarth, in collaboration with architects Richard Cottrell and Brian Vermeulen and the author. The conventional Portakabin is an advanced steel framed 'box' system, which is rigid enough to be transported from site with all its finishes in place, including almost everything from plaster work and light fittings to toilet roll holders in the bathrooms. Portakabin build pre-fabricated buildings – the design of which has evolved over a number of years; technical problems relating to thermal performance and longevity are no longer an issue. The system does impose limitations on the design, since the format is dependent on a module of pre-sized rectangular 'boxes' (to enable transportation). These fit together side by side once delivered to the site.

One of the key concerns during its development was the image and appearance of the 'box'; rather than attempting to disguise the Portakabin with a pitched roof or other devices to make it appear like a more conventional nursery building, the design team took the view that the Portakabin 'box' image should, if anything, be enhanced. Children, they felt, would appreciate the caravan-like qualities of the building. The format of the initial prototype comprises four zones: the wet/toilet area, the entrance/play area, the quiet room and a covered play deck accessible directly from the activity area. Storage walls are provided, one with the play/activity area and another externally on the covered play deck. Low windows are fitted which are designed to be safe yet child friendly. Much of its interior is ergonomically designed specifically with younger children in mind. The first prototype has a yellow external colour with a white slatted rain screen which gives it the striking appearance of fair-ground architecture. It is bright, gay and thoroughly inviting for children. Yet it actually provides an anticipated 40-year period of maintenance-free life.

The Portakabin prototype was designed as a school reception class for a specific client in Harlow, where four- to five-year-old children were in attendance only during school hours. As such it does not cater for full-day care for younger children. The intention is to extend and increase the range of its facilities to cater for full-day care, if a commission presents itself. However for the moment, the proposal is a limited, yet stylish alternative to a conventional, one-off nursery class. In contrast, the community nursery is intended to provide all the benefits of full-day care, part-time education for three- and four-year olds, and after-school facilities within the framework of a single building. The scheme is currently being developed by the Education Design Group (EDG).

Established in 1998, EDG is a collaboration of educationalists and architects working together to produce an integrated child care package. The initial idea for the building came about through individual members of the group, who recognized the potential of modular hotel bedrooms for adaptation to the needs of nursery education. The hotel bedrooms were constructed in a factory and transported with all their fittings to site, where external brick cladding walls provided a robust external finish. The concept of a nursery made up not of large open-plan spaces, as would usually be the case, but of 'cosy' little rooms, like hotel bedrooms, seemed particularly appropriate for the needs of young nursery children.

From this beginning, the concept of a complete package developed incorporating precise costing, advice on staffing levels, ideas about parental involvement, food, sleeping and play. Benefiting from economies of scale, the modular prototype provides a speedy, yet high-quality solution to the needs of pre-school care. A radical pre-school care and education strategy,

3.13a

3.13b

integrated with an economic high-quality building, to fully support the educational philosophy, could in theory be implemented within a period of 22 weeks from the receipt of an order; all the client requires is the site and the funding. The typical readymade package provides accommodation for ten babies (0–12 months), 25 one- to two-year-olds, 25 two- to three-year-olds, and 100 three- to five-year-olds, and space for after-school children. However, it can be adapted for smaller group sizes.

An open approach to parental access is encouraged, which takes the notion of community involvement seriously. The building takes a more continental view of the rights of children, locating a semi-open access kitchen as its communal focus, the symbolic heart of the project where children have access; indeed it is intended that the children would use the kitchen as a play/education space. Central to its philosophy is the notion that fresh food would be prepared in full view of the children. Perhaps most importantly, all parts of the building will (at certain times of the day) be open to all of the children. It is a socially advanced model where children support and learn from each other and (among other benefits) have the right to select the spaces they wish to inhabit.

As with the Portakabin project, the modular principle imposes limitations in terms of the architectural aesthetic. Whereas Portakabin presents a design that is clearly and proudly prefabricated, the architecture of the community nursery is a little more circumspect. A range of cladding options and alternative roof profiles are offered which allow for a certain amount of customization to each site context. The cladding could be either a shiny metallic rain screen panel or a heavy masonry parapet wall. The roof is a high-performance flat element, which is integral. However, in theory, a client can select a roof profile to his or her own taste, which could be pitched and tiled. Other add-on options include canopies, fences, walls, pergolas and play terraces to suit the needs of the site. It is, states project architect Mike Stiff, a building that will mould itself to the site.

Both of these schemes deal with the problem of appropriateness in different ways. Where Goldfinger's Expanding nursery (see Chapter 2) fails is in its ability to fulfil the needs of young children in providing the context for a variety of learning experiences, both inside and outside. By contrast, these two projects offer purpose-designed environments for pre-school children with space for movement, small intimate areas for rest and quiet, with warm, comfortable, child-scale bathrooms. The limitations of the Portakabin nursery are reflected in its lack of provision for full-day care, and its failure to provide a personal space for adults. However, through its quirky design, it is 'owned' by the children and organized to be as accessible to the children as possible, promoting their development as autonomous individuals.

One of the earliest examples of this new generation of modular nurseries was the Forest Kindergarten. Its ethos was to support the outdoor activities of Danish children spending activity days in the country. Its lightweight transportable structure means it can be sited in different rural locations to support this rich element of the curriculum. A similar initiative was established recently by the Bridgewater College Children's Centre after a visit to Denmark.

The environment for the forest school is an enclosed wood of approximately 1.6 acres located five miles from the children's centre. The organizers usually accompany groups of approximately 15 pre-school children to the site, where they spend three to four hours exploring the flora and fauna of this unusual setting. It acts as the perfect natural playground for the children. Rather than hard tarmac, the floor is made of soft wooded earth with a roof-like canopy of mature trees. Unfortunately they have no building on the site and children must use the mini-bus when in need of shelter. This would be the ideal location for a modular building.

3.6 Summary

The conjunction of the organic projects by Christopher Day and James Hubbell, set against the more overtly modernist designs of Bolles Wilson and particularly Rudolphe Luscher in Lausanne, point the way towards a growing confusion that has relevance to a much wider architectural debate. Architect and writer Kenneth Bayes described this dichotomy in the following way:

It may be stretching credibility too far to suggest that in time to come – perhaps early in the 21st century – the 'new organic' architecture may be seen to resolve the dichotomy of the two streams of the Modern Movement. Perhaps it should even be anticipated that before this can

3.14

happen the two extremes may become more exaggerated, the organic becoming ever more fantastic, the inorganic becoming even more inhumanly mechanistic.[28]

These comments are clearly pejorative, as Bayes was a Steiner disciple. Nevertheless, he is expressing a sense of exasperation at this confusing polarization of the debate currently raging in the world of kindergarten architecture. In the face of these philosophical extremes, so clearly expressed in the architectural style of these buildings, how does one choose between them? It could be argued that the mechanistic response of Luscher is as appropriate in reinforcing the modernistic myth of the electronically switched-on, computer-literate five-year-olds of contemporary European culture as any naturalistic references. Equally, the more primordial organic forms of the Tijuana project are appropriate in a less harmonious culture and landscape that is hardly able to exploit the benefits of new technology. In fact, it could be argued that the Tijuana children are actually being inadvertently exploited by this technology. There is clearly equal

meaning in the way both of these buildings relate to their own culture and particular contexts.

On another, altogether more pragmatic, level the approach taken in each example is regionally based. Hubbell's building responds to the hot, arid climate of Mexico with a building fabric that is solid and cave-like in its construction and therefore remains cool. The theme is further authenticated by the use of free-flowing water as the central motif. The location of Luscher's building is less environmentally problematic, yet still responds to the climate in its use of non-corrosive titanium-coated zinc panels, which resist the effects of atmospheric pollution and provide economical, highly insulated wall finishes.

Bearing in mind the current pluralistic condition of architectural theory, how does one justify the use of such blatantly arcane architectural forms as those utilized by Christopher Day in his Nant-y-Cwm kindergarten? The context is that of an advanced, industrialized nation; climatic criteria do not appear to have driven the building's architectural style, although there is a selfconscious environmental concern expressed in its use of

3.14 View from the kindergarten part of the Lund Ladugardsmårken (child care centre), Sweden, designed by Olaf Meiby, an example of low-key architecture for young children. With five different departments catering for children up to the age of nine, it is a large institution. However, the designer diffuses the scale by ensuring that every department has its own entrance and play space, and is articulated as a separate building within the overall framework of the larger institution. There are no corridors; all the departments focus on an internal multipurpose hall or 'square'. The 'Lillgarden' is shown here (one- to three-year-olds), divided into two providing full-day care for eight–ten children in each session.

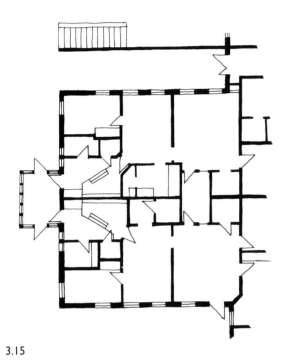

3.15

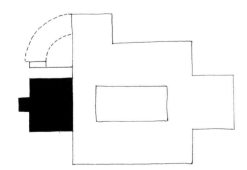

3.16

3.15 Plan of the kindergarten.

3.16 Kindergarten (shaded), part of a much larger main school building.

heavy 'green' architecture.[29] Taking an extreme view, it appears to be an architecture that refers backwards to the nostalgia of a pre-techno-imagined world of pixies and dancing fairies.

Equally, how does one make sense of the agglomeration of such clearly synthetic shapes and colours as those employed by Teng Kok Seng (Akicipta Associate Architects) in Malaysia, or even Toyo Ito in Frankfurt? Although popular opinion suggests that both buildings are instantly appealing to parents and teachers alike, there is something jarring, almost too new and ungrounded in culture, to situate this approach in any of the traditions of kindergarten discussed in Chapter 2. Both strands appear to be equally problematic for the contemporary critic searching for more general guiding principles.

One level considered valid in the search for broader meanings could be the notion of continuity. Rousseau's concern with the plight of the poor in the pre-industrialized cities of 18th-century France made him yearn to return to a more natural past. This somewhat nostalgic sense that man had lost something in his enforced engagement with the newly industrialized 19th-century city was a primary impulse in the development of the first kindergarten movements. They were responding initially to a tangible sense of social fracture, the genuine abuse of young children (particularly in factories) and other extremes of human exploitation connected to unbridled capitalism. Although these attitudes began to be transformed as 20th-century humanistic movements stopped child labour and emancipated women, the romantic sense remained that the city was an unhealthy or unnatural habitat for young children.

This current distrust of the urban environment is viewed with some unease by many contemporary architects and educationalists. The organic tendency may be instilling negative or false ideals into the developing personality of the child. What Andrea Branzi describes as a 'memory-village' is a myth that the child will carry with him possibly for life, if it is instilled by the environment of certain types of urban kindergarten. An interior reminiscent of a ploughman's cottage from the 17th century, only with electricity and piped music, must be a confusing contradiction for the young child.[30] Rather than being tuned into the fast-moving world of the modern city, Branzi argues, children may grow to see their own environment as being harsh or artificial. Although in this context he is referring to educational strategies rather than architectural ones, the overall theme has relevance:

Both in modern progressive nursery schools and in those run on more traditional lines I still see children being offered examples to make contact and reference with a universe which is an alternative to the real one, which consists of nature, leaves, trees, villages, cottages, country churches and flowers.[31]

These false realities may be forming entirely erroneous attitudes. In the deformed cosiness of some modern forms of kindergarten interior are we forcing children to believe in an arcane utopian world, which perhaps never really existed? And even if this world – in which reality was governed by an ordered distance between man and his history, space and time – did once exist, today it does not. In two generations, initially with the advent of the television age and now with more profound electronic advances, the urban milieu has become a sort of 'aquarium' where children find themselves floating in a fluid world of multitudinous experiences. The past, the future, time and space are blurred. The child is bombarded with messages and experiences that can no longer be understood in a linear way. To paraphrase John Dewey's view (in *Democracy and Education* of 1920), if the body in its totality is the channel for all human experience at pre-school age, then at the tail end of the 20th century, as the range and diversity of these experiences multiply, the need to make sense and give order to this world is ever more important.

Children are more adaptable and therefore better equipped for the world of machines, computers and electronic forms of virtual reality than our present adult view may be able to comprehend. There is a kind of certainty implicit in the integrated circuits of the computer which, like a game where the rules do not have to be continually questioned, can be used as a tool to aid and elaborate meanings, and encourage instant autonomy. The young child, given the space, can 'get on' in a way that he or she could never do previously.

However, one must be cautious about taking this too far. The over-synthesized environments of some kindergarten buildings has already been mentioned. Some may view Disneyland as the ultimate architecture for children. For us, from a developmental viewpoint, Disney's use of high-pressure selling techniques is exploitative rather than beneficial. While one does not wish to appear too reactionary about this (Disneyland is after all not intended to be an educational environment), the over-literal rep-

resentation of the image somehow negates the need for children to resort to playful imaginings. It is all there and laid out, even down to plastic birds that replicate and replace the real thing. In the end it can only let children down, and encourage them to seek even more predetermined images of greater and greater electronic and technical sophistication. When set against these excesses, the synthetic quality of Akicipta Associates' Ringrose Kindergarten in Malaysia, with its primary colours and idiosyncratic forms, appear restrained and tasteful; while the exploitative nature of the Disney 'experience' makes one appreciate the spiritual quest implicit in the work of Christopher Day and particularly of James Hubbell.

Luscher's building is, to a certain extent, an exemplification of this modern approach to children's culture. It is much less directly influenced by pedagogic theory, being more purely architectural and therefore experimental in its approach. Its pedagogic style is formed by the architecture, reflecting more general cultural preoccupations. One suspects that the passage of time will be its critique; however, its avant-garde style is part of a strong and continuing tradition of radical kindergarten architecture, looking idealistically and optimistically towards the future.

The Bolles Wilson Greisheim-Sud 'Kita' is equally well loved by parents and children. It would appear to be the most successful of all the Frankfurt projects; located in a tough area, it is still (three years after its opening) largely devoid of any grafitti. However, its architect, when discussing his creation of 'the events', inadvertently touches upon a fundamental conundrum. Should the architecture be a truly 'neutral frame', within which teachers, parents and children develop their own events or focal points, rather than expect the architect to 'design in' the distractions? This is certainly the way in which the Diane nursery school in Reggio Emilia was conceived, and it has evolved into the ideal pre-school environment. Diane's architect collaborated with the pedagogic experts to create a building 20 years ago that was architecturally moderate, not overtly organic, nor technological in its themes. Its total lack of architectural pretension has helped to make it the most successful pre-school environment we experienced during the course of this research. Why, then, should events be created by the architect, and imposed upon the children in an inflexible way, as is the case with the Bolles Wilson project or, in a more extreme way, in the Bungawitta project in Tasmania?

The answers are inevitably complex, and our conclusions would not lead one either to condone or condemn any of these diverse approaches. Diane succeeds primarily because the environment works on the functional level of optimum light, air and space, which is combined with a pedagogic system created and perfected over a number of years. This allows the architecture to work on a metaphorical level: the town as a microcosm of kindergarten life. Thus the life of the school fits the environment, and in turn the environment can be adjusted and improved to fit the evolving educational system. The analogy to the wider urban environment gives it meaning without it being over-literal in its metaphorical representations. This makes it a sort of laboratory of nursery school expertise, delivered to the children with energy, creativity and commitment, by highly trained and highly motivated staff – and with considerable financial resources.[32] However, the architecture in itself is unexceptional, particularly when viewed as a building in the landscape and compared externally, for example, to the evident architectural presence of the children's day care centre in Valency, Lausanne.

Despite its age, we should be careful not to dismiss Diane merely as a well-funded educational research project. It has profound architectural lessons, particularly on the level of its interior qualities. The apparent ease with which it strikes a balance between openness and semi-privacy is as important as the diversity of the educative activities it offers. The use of materials that are simple but nevertheless respond to the expressive rather than the functional needs of different spaces has also been touched upon. For example, bleached timber planks in the courtyards, white ceramic tiles in the 'public square' and polished beech floors in the activity areas are architectural choices rather than being merely functional or economic. They add meaning to the activities intended to be carried out.

This general attention to detail is a basic principle that is apparent in this and other less didactic projects, such as the UCLA Child Care Center in Los Angeles or Günther Behnisch's Neugereut Kindergarten in Stuttgart. Grand architectural statements are avoided; instead, the modest needs and small-scale sensibilities of young children become the main architectural preoccupations and the modest theme of the buildings.

Wouldn't it give us pleasure to see a string of meaningful details in a children's world? Things that admittedly serve trivial purposes, that stand for themselves and their function and, besides, come together in the realm of fantasy, of poetry. They could be minor details: a star of light, patterns in a wall . . . little things, showing that we have made an effort to understand the world of children; that we have overcome what stands between us – age, drawing board, cost calculations . . . ambition, architecture.'[33]

In its detail and wider administrative structure, Diane has fundamental lessons for all architects designing kindergartens. Perhaps most important, given the needs of a complex pedagogic system, is the generous amount of space available to each of the children. It is not just space for its own sake, but highly sophisticated low-key interior architecture, where every corner and vista supports the whole, and where enclosed safe space is provided as well as open-plan adventure space. Although similar on some formal levels, it is not architecturally perfect in the sense that a Miesian pavilion would claim to be: spatially neutral yet mathematically whole. Its perfection lies in the humane match between scale, touch, quality of light and function. However, it could not work without the vital ingredients already discussed – most importantly, a committed long-serving staff and a rich programme of integrated pedagogic activities that create a complete internal landscape for play. It could be said that 'its floors, ceilings, walls and all its horizontal and vertical surfaces can be seen as interactive surfaces to which the children are responding and from which they receive information and, one hopes, comfort', thus optimizing child development.[34]

Returning to the Bolles Wilson Frankfurt Kindertagesstätte, we do not suggest that its staff are any less committed than those of Reggio Emilia, merely that the architectural 'events' to be experienced in Diane were devised and invented by the *staff*, and tested over a longer period of time. Inevitably, they work in a more child-centred way. On that level, the neutral frame of Diane may not be that different from Peter Wilson's 'frame and the adjacencies' when considered ten or so years hence. A neutral architecture requires greater pedagogic commitment in order for it to succeed. Rigorous attention to basic aspects of spatial quality are also crucial, particularly in relation to the amount of space given to each child.

Inevitably, the appropriateness of adopting any architectural idea should be considered within a broader framework, relating design decisions to all members of the kindergarten community. Practical considerations are of fundamental significance when designing for children, and architects should of course get these things as right as is possible. However, a balance must be struck between functional practicalities and the need to create an architecture that has meaning to young children and therefore 'fascinates'. For example, the decision to introduce level changes (and therefore potentially hazardous steps) would be justifiable if the spatial experience is sufficiently enriched to effect an enhanced awareness for the children of their space. This would negate the hazard, and satisfy the almost insatiable need for toddlers and young children to test their walking and balancing skills, as is the case in the Honjo Kindergarten. Similarly, the use of different floor surfaces in Diane communicate so much more about how each of these spaces can be used, despite the fact that a simple vinyl floor covering throughout would have been far more cost-effective and practical.

At the beginning of this chapter we defined four categories of kindergarten, identified on the basis of the way we interpreted the distinctive style of each. In children's architecture, the meaning of the architectural idea is, in our view, primary. The use of metaphor or narrative can enrich a simple building programme without reverting to organic or technological design methods which may have only superficial meaning. An architecture that is low-key and moderate can have equal value. It is for architects to respond to the different cultural, economic and pedagogic contexts within which they are working. Through in depth consultation with carers, children and other members of the community, they can develop a form to which all parties can relate with enthusiasm and joy.

However, in the use of less didactic strategies it seems that the responsibility placed upon the architect to work closely with the pedagogic theory to create the correct architectural 'frame' is more onerous and time-consuming, implying a longer-term commitment by the design team. This is not usually possible, given the limited budgets for these small projects and, in addition, the way in which buildings are funded, mainly on a one-off basis, with very little maintenance finance built in. It is therefore difficult to allow for later adaptations and extensions to imitate the Diane design process. In view of the success of this example, it may be worth reviewing the ways kindergarten buildings are financed, to allow adaptations and changes over a longer period of time.

These debates rely of course on the veracity of general theoretical principles when in the current pluralistic climate there are few. However, the debate between the organic of Steiner set against the modernistic structuralism exemplified by the kindergarten buildings of Luscher or Bolles Wilson will continue to rage. It is likely that these arguments will gain greater significance as the spiritualistic/humanistic dichotomy becomes part of the wider architectural debate. However, the meaning of the architecture will be constantly reinterpreted and reworked in the games and imaginings of the young children who use it, if architects are open to the significance of play within their architecture. To reiterate, it is not enough to adopt functionally prescribed standards and then expect an authentic kindergarten architecture to emerge. Architects, educationalists and commissioning bodies should take their cue from the radical and imaginative quality of these featured case studies, and be less timid in their approach to kindergarten architecture. This will ensure that the enchantment of childhood is amplified, and remains as a positive and potent memory for the individual to carry throughout life.

References and notes

1. Olds, Anita Rui (1987), 'Designing Settings for Infants and Toddlers', *Spaces for Children – The Built Environment and Child Development*, in C.S. Weinstein and Thomas G. David (eds), Plenum Press, p. 117.
2. Malaguzzi, L. *et al.* (1984), *The Hundred Languages of Children*, trans. from the exhibition catalogue *I Cento Linguaggi Dei Bambini*, Dept of Education, City of Reggio Emilia, Region of Emilia Romagna, p. 16.
3. Münster, N. *et al.* (1992), 'Architecture – Child's Play. New Kindergartens in Frankfurt', *Archigrad 1*, Verlag AFW Klaus Winkler, Frankfurt, p. 2. 'Kita' is short for Kindertagesstätte, children's day care centre.
4. Clelland, D. *et al.* (1987), Neubau. 'Berlin: Origins to IBA', *Architectural Review*, April 1987, The Architectural Press, London, pp. 81–2.
5. *Ibid.*
6. Bungawitta is an Aboriginal term meaning 'a place of little possums'.
7. The miniature façades were removed three years after the school opened.
8. Blundell Jones, P. *et al.* (1991), 'Schooling', *Architectural Review*, September 1991, The Architectural Press, London, pp. 54–5.
9. Hundertwasser, F. *et al.* (1992), 'Frankfurt Heddernheim-Nord', *Archigrad, 1*, Verlag AFW Klaus Winkler, Frankfurt, p. 21.
10. Bachelard, G. (1969), *The Poetics of Space*, Toronto, Beacon Press, p. xxxiii.
11. Day, C. *et al.* (1995), 'Nant-y-Cwm Steiner Nursery School', *Caravan*, School of Architecture and Interior Design Research Journal, University of Brighton, Sussex, p. 16.
12. *Ibid.*

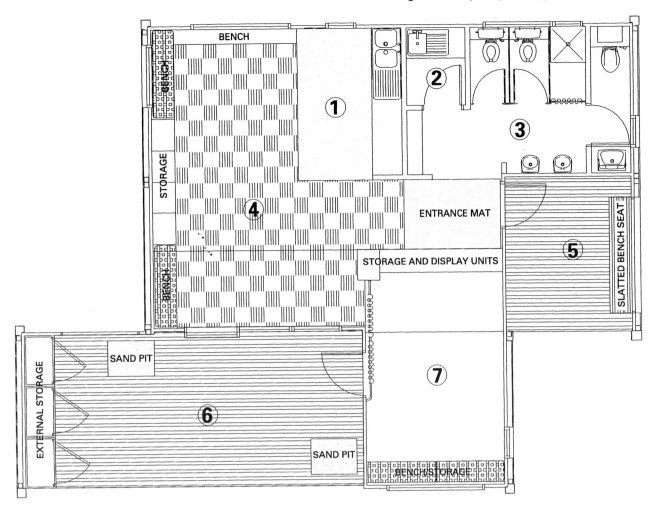

3.17

3.18

3.17 Lilliput nursery: 15 place nursery, plan.
Key:
1 wet area
2 kitchenette
3 child's toilet and shower area and staff toilet
4 playroom
5 covered entrance
6 covered outdoor play area
7 quiet room

3.18 The first Lilliput nursery was commissioned for a school in Harlow, Essex, in July 1998.

13. Veseley, D. *et al.* (1978), 'Surrealism, Myth and Modernity', *Architectural Design, Surrealism*, vol. 48, nos. 2–3, p. 94.

14. Architect James Hubbell in conversation with the author. The notion of 'beauty for beauty's sake' was further illuminated by Hubbell in the context of a Russian fable: 'In the 12th century, the Csar of Russia wanted to find a new religion, so he sent envoys to Rome, Israel and the Muslim countries. Finally, his envoy reached the mosque at Santa Sofia which, with its polyphonic music and gold tiling, combined the highest aesthetic qualities. The envoy wrote back and said, 'We have seen God', so they chose their religion on the basis of beauty.'

15. Wilson, P. *et al.* (1995), 'European Union', *Caravan*, p. 26.

16. Dietsch, D.K. (1989), 'Prefab preschool', *Architectural Record*, June 1989, pp. 126–27.

17. Geghard, D. (1971), *Schindler*, London, Thames Hudson, pp. 47–8.

18. *Ibid.*, p. 48. The external fireplace was a frequent way of extending communal family activity in the evenings.

19. Head Teacher Gaye MacDonald in conversation with the author, December 1994.

20. Blundell Jones, P. *et al.* (1991), 'Kindergarten Contrasts', *Architectural Review, Schooling*, September 1991, p. 48.

21. Dudek, M. *et al.* (1994), 'The Temple or the Cathedral', *Companion to Contemporary Architectural Thought* (eds. Farmer and Louw), London, Routledge, p. 12: 'Rather than effecting a harmonious relationship with its natural setting, Villa Savoye dominates the surrounding countryside through this deliberately unequivocal imagery. This dichotomy was of course intentional, and the new interest in psychological self-analysis at that time, and increasingly through the 20th century, further underlines the human-centred nature of the piece.'

22. Buchs, M. (1994), 'La révolution enfantine de Valency', *L'Hebdo – Le Magazine Suisse d'Information*, no. 29, 21–7 juillet 1994, p. 37.

23. Kroner, W. (1994), *Architecture for Children*, Stuttgart and Zurich, Karl Kramer Verlag, p. 15.

24. In a recent exhibition of contemporary kindergartens organized by the author at the RIBA, London, April–May 1994, the Ringrose Kindergarten proved to be the most popular of all 14 exhibits among the members of the public who visited.

25. The dimensions are nett areas and comparisons are provided for general guidance purposes. We have attempted to be as accurate as possible; however, inconsistencies are inevitable. For example, the total area of Diane includes the courtyards which are open to the elements; they are an integral part of the central activity spaces and are therefore included in the total usable area. The child ratio relating to the Frankfurt project would include *kinderhort* children, who usually attend only in the afternoons.

26. Goulet, P. *et al.* (1991), 'Wild and Uncertain Times: Team Zoo's Savoir-Faire', *Team Zoo's Buildings and Projects 1971–1990* in Manfred Speidel (ed.), London, Thames & Hudson, p. 23.

27. Vesley, D. *et al.* (1978), 'Surrealism, Myth and Modernity', *Architectural Design, Surrealism*, vol. 48, nos. 2–3, p. 94.

28. Bayes, K. (1994), *Living Architecture — Rudolf Steiner's Ideas in Practice*, Floris Books, Edinburgh, pp. 104–5.

29. Day, C. *op. cit.*: 'With organic paints internally and site-made lime-milk formulation externally, the walls can breathe. Classroom floors are beeswax–carnauba wax-finished softwood with cellulose fibre insulation on breather paper; cork tiles are laid with non-toxic adhesive. and so on.'

30. We might illustrate this idea not with a contemporary kindergarten but with the archetypal late 20th-century children's interior – MacDonalds, any street, any town, anywhere. Unfortunately, many contemporary kindergartens adopt a similar arcane language.

31. Branzi, A. *et al.*, *The Hundred Languages of Children*, *op. cit.*, p. 33.

32. Visiting study tours for educationalists from throughout the world help to finance the running of the school.

33. Behnisch und Partner, *Architekten Behnisch und Partner Arbeiten aus den Jahren 1952–1987*, exhibition catalogue, Stuttgart, München PT, p. 60.

34. Rui Olds, Anita, *The Hundred Languages of Children*, *op. cit.*, p. 118.

CHAPTER 4

Defining quality: characteristics of space within the kindergarten environment

4.1 Symbolic meanings

There are long established and broadly agreed programmatic requirements for the design of pre-school kindergartens and nursery schools. For example, Joseph Featherstone in a series of articles published in the 1960s in *The New Republic*, set out a clearly prescribed set of ideal conditions:

> storage space, including individual lockers; room dividers (the need for many small spaces); flat working surfaces (tables instead of individual desks); easels; walk-in doll's house; play store; dress-up area, with racks for adult clothes, costumes, etc.; puppet theatre; library alcove, with book shelves; display racks and copious pin-up surfaces; sinks; carpentry space, with work bench, tools, etc.; building blocks, clay, etc.; greenhouse; zoo; a classroom opening out on to the playground.[1]

The areas described in this quotation accurately summarize contemporary needs at a basic level of activity-related functions. A more recent briefing document by Nottinghamshire Education Department, relating to the economical adaptation of existing buildings, defines a number of 'essential features'. This hints at a flexible approach to nursery school layouts, enabling the staff and children to organize these activities in their own way:

> The design of the interior of the nursery is of course constrained by space, both in extensions and in adaptations, but when proper allowance has been made for the inclusion of essential features such as the quiet area, the domestic area and the utility and toilet accommodation there is a need to design the remaining space to allow for an attractive, warm, homely and stimulating environment which can be exploited by teachers and children in a variety of ways. Some parts of the nursery will be clearly defined by partitions but generally the space available should be left for the teacher to be able to organize use of space to the best effect.[2]

The need to give children enough space is important. In her survey of 60 children's day care centres in Denmark (which has one of the most confined statutory space standards in the world), Vibeke Bidsrube chose centres that all had more space than the

4.1 Centre de Vie Enfantine, Lausanne, by Rudolphe Luscher; open-plan WCs for four-year-olds.

4.2

4.2 The ostensible reason for Klaus Zillich's ceiling treatment in his Neukölln 'Kita' foyer space is to reduce reverberation; however, it is also playful and distracting – aluminium acoustic baffles in the form of 'paper darts'. External noise from busy roads or aircraft flightpaths is disturbing, especially to very young children and babies. Noise from roads can be screened out by the use of walls and the strategic location of the building as a screen. Internal noise and reverberation can be reduced by the adoption of highly faceted internal surfaces and acoustic ceilings. Music spaces and the activity spaces that generate most noise can be acoustically separated from the quieter classroom spaces.

4.3 Detail of an 'egg-crate' acoustic ceiling at the Cantalamessa baby unit, Bologna.

4.3

recommended norm. She asked the teachers and care workers what the most important benefits of these larger spaces were. Forty-six of the centres cited fewer conflicts as the key benefit. Second, children could divide into smaller groups. Other advantages related to privacy and the possibility of quiet moments, so that children could sit and be alone.[3]

Although the amount of space is crucially important, particularly in urban areas where children may be living in cramped homes, the need to understand and prioritize how those constituent elements might best fit together architecturally suggests that more precise quality criteria can be applied to the basic kindergarten programme. For example, a research study carried out in the USA by Prescott and Jones (1967) revealed that there was a clear relationship between spatial quality and child behaviour. Their environmental assessment looked at five practical aspects of physical space which were deemed to be significant factors in defining quality. They were: organization, variety of

spatial experience, complexity, amount to do (range and variety of distractions), and special areas such as the positioning of bathrooms, access to external space, sun-shading or the use of colour and planning to reduce internal and external acoustic disturbance. Their conclusions relating to the organization of space in the kindergarten are particularly worth noting: although the amount of space was undoubtedly important, clear 'pathways' were felt to be essential:

A path is the empty space on the floor or ground through which people move in getting from one place to another; it need be no different in composition from the rest of the surface. A clear path is broad, elongated and easily visible . . . If an observer looking at a play area can't answer readily the question, 'How do children get from one place to another?' Probably the children can't either; and there is no clear path.[4]

4.4, 5 Diagrammatic interpretations of the spatial organization in the Diane child care centre, Emilia Romagna.

4.4 The home-base, with a generous open-plan area at the centre and a number of rooms or zones for smaller group activities.

4.5 The school layout as a whole. Each of three home-based activity areas is linked visually to the public 'piazza'.

Figure 4.4
Key:
1 threshold
2 WC/washroom
3 cloakroom
4 open activity area
5 quiet area
6 art studio
7 music room
8 terrace
9 garden

Figure 4.5
Key:
1 entrance lobby
2 parent's notice board and waiting area
3 office
4 kitchen, accessible to children
5 communal dining room/restaurant
6 public 'piazza': communal space used by the whole school
7 home-base: three groups of three-year olds, four-year olds and five-year olds
8 WC/washrooms
9 open courtyard for group reading
10 communal art studio

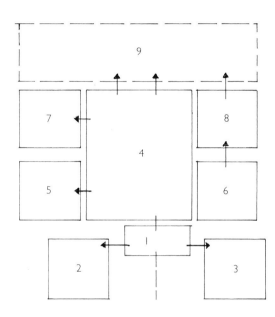

4.4

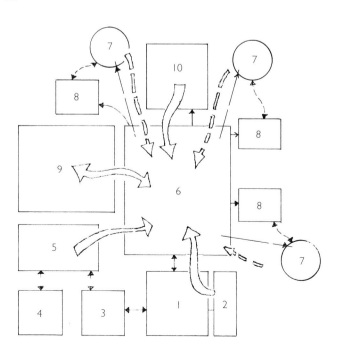

4.5

Developing this theme of movement within the pre-school environment, Anita Rui Olds discussed the importance of the environment in the development of young children's motor skills:

> The ideal environment affords infants and toddlers frequent opportunities to learn to move and to learn by moving; it should stimulate a full range of movement for body control, object control and control of self in space: sitting, swaying, crawling, bouncing, running, climbing, jumping, grasping, bending and throwing. It conceives of all surfaces, and the entire ambience, as an invitation to move in ways that give motoric capacities their fullest reign within safe and tolerable limits.[5]

While these physical activities are important, especially for toddlers and younger pre-schoolers, the overall ideal within any kindergarten environment applies: facilitating a sense of physical and psychological exploration in a clear, comprehensible way - challenging children through the environment, but not overwhelming them.

In the recently published discussion document *Quality in Services for Young Children*, the environment was mentioned as the second of ten criteria and 'aesthetics' as an important constituent element defining quality.[6] Claus Jensen, a political scientist with 20 years' experience in Danish pre-school education, set out the following points to remember when designing a kindergarten:

> changeability and the ability for children to make and adapt their own spaces (the kindergarten building is a frame within which this creativity can take place); lots of different small rooms so that, if they wish, children can feel as if they are private; view and orientation, to make the best use of sunlight and aspect; fantasy – children understand through narrative and illusion – the building and its surroundings should support this; ways of communicating with parents – through notice boards, community events and the careful consideration of entrance conditions (in nursery schools parents do not generally participate in classroom activities); elegance – aesthetics, colour, light and texture; distinctions between boys' and girls' spaces; little cupboards, niches – the room within the room.[7]

4.6 Two boys use the shelter at Neugereut, Stuttgart.

4.7 Piccolina nursery school, Bologna. The Wendy house provides a child-height space within a somewhat scaleless environment.

4.6

Comprehensive as these observations are, they tend to obscure the meanings that relate not just to 'practical objects', but to virtually every functioning aspect of a modern kindergarten environment. These range from notions such as the entrance as a symbolic 'threshold', which is a psychologically important point where parent–child separation often takes place, to the conception of children's rights, with the provision of child-only spaces which 'give even small children some power back over their lives'.[8]

Many of these activities, far from being merely use-related, have the power to socialize a young child to a certain habit or way of life. Attempting to disentangle functions from their symbolic meaning is fraught, since it implies simplistic solutions to a complex process of design. However, understanding these symbols and meanings can help in the conceptualization and communication of the design to its users.[9]

Of equal importance are behavioural aspects, which are often ignored in the design of buildings for children. For example, the use of colour to calm or stimulate activity. The psychological concerns of the growing child can be reflected in the architecture so that it begins to generate its own programme which is in tune with the more complex aspects of child development and spatiality. Thus the kindergarten can be justifiably described as a 'therapeutic environment' in that it has a holistic quality, including rather than excluding child-centred meanings, without compromising functional quality.

In this chapter we use Jensen's list as a framework to expand on some of these functionally precise areas to illustrate other important aspects of children's environments. The extended captions to the illustrations should be read in conjunction with the text.

4.7

4.2 Entrance spaces and lobbies

Perhaps the entrance to every child space should be graced by a 'torre', a Japanese arch signalling the transition from profane to sacred territory, from a realm of the spontaneous and ordinary to one of spritual and aesthetic integrity.[10]

In Italian regional legislation, guidelines for the organization of indoor and outdoor spaces are set out in child-centred statutory articles; architects must organize space on the basis of the developmental needs of the children. In practical terms, this means that one important requirement in new facilities is a common or 'public' area which acts as a focus for each facility at or close to the entrance.[11] This area must then give access to spaces for individual and group activities. The spatial requirements are described in functional terms, but these terms are flexible. For instance, a specific requirement is that the entrance hall incorporates a waiting space for parents. This should be designed to encourage conversation between them while waiting to collect their children.

A carefully considered approach to the design of the entrance enhances its symbolic significance. Not only is it important as a defining space for the child and parent as the point where they separate, it also fulfils an increasingly important security role, controlling the access of strangers. The designer should be aware of both factors. Clearly, security is of fundamental significance; however, the child's mood should be considered, and many of the featured case studies illustrate how distracting events or architectural features, positioned strategically in or just beyond the threshold space, can have a remarkably calming effect. It can be most useful to locate the head teacher's office at this point; a friendly exchange of looks at the point of separation may be enough to reassure nervous parents that their children are in safe hands.

At the UCLA campus nursery school in Los Angeles, the architects organized the form of the three pavilions in a protective U-shape within which the children's garden shelters. The administrative block is at the centre of this tripartite organization, and parents must pass through it before they reach the children's accommodation. This control of the entrance route is discreet yet foolproof; if adults are not spotted by the head teacher, they will almost certainly be seen by the office staff, who

have views out towards the corridor from their work spaces on the garden side of the plan. The sense of threshold is expressed discreetly, with a change from the external rough stone paving to a single inscribed piece of granite beneath the external canopy, before the interior is marked by the light timber floor. Once within the building, one space flows into the next, so the security 'control' is maintained within the framework of a fluid route.

4.3 Secret spaces: the house within the house, corners and dens

What special depth there is in a child's daydream! And how happy the child who really possesses his moments of solitude! It is a good thing, it is even salutary, for a child to have periods of boredom, for him to learn to know the dialectics of exaggerated play and causeless pure boredom.[12]

All children seek to explore and appropriate space as an initial response to the realization of their own independence within the safety of the kindergarten. At the age of four and even earlier, children's awareness of their own space is demonstrable; anyone who cares to observe children will notice how they are attracted to small-scale spaces, such as the Wendy house, the garden shed, the tree-house – indeed, any space that creates a sense of enclosure and has a child's scale, heightens feelings of autonomy within a public world.

The urge towards privacy and even solitude within the public milieu of the kindergarten enables children to develop their own games, either alone or with their chosen playmates, free from the inhibiting presence of adults and other young children, hence fantasy and imagination can be fully explored. The urge towards hidey-holes where children can play undisturbed was identified by the Oxford Pre-School Research Project, which demonstrated that high-quality and prolonged bouts of play most frequently occurred when two or more children played together apparently hidden from adults.[13]

Some children undoubtedly find privacy and solitude of profound therapeutic value. Explained in psychological terms this phenomenon relates to the development of an inner psyche or ego of which many pre-school children become aware when they are separated from parents. This awareness can often become a

4.8 The mature garden at the rear of the Dorothy Gardiner Centre, Westminster, one of the government's first designated Early Excellence Centres illustrates that all space is usable, particularly on confined urban sites.

4.8

source of difficulties. The conscious realization of the child's inner self, and the coming to terms with it generally, would require the child to escape into his or her own imagination. Hence the therapeutic value of kindergarten as an escape from difficult home environments, but more particularly the need for certain types of space within the kindergarten to support fully this need for retreat.

Children who have psychological problems are often characterized by their need for privacy, secrecy or the making of shelters, dens or underground hiding places. This has been described by Norwegian educationalist Ivar Selmer-Olsen of Queen Maud's College of Early Childhood Education in Oslo, as 'the world of conceptions in the child's own culture'. This statement has relevance on two levels: first, it suggests that the kindergarten should allow the child the possibility for fantasy as a kind of therapy; and secondly, that the desire for a sense of privacy and secrecy away from the adult world has crucial benefits in terms of the development of self-confidence, autonomy and ultimately learning during these difficult transformations.

Selmer-Olsen states that his admittedly 'half finished thoughts' in this area support the view that secrets and treasure have an important symbolic relevance to children in psychological therapy: 'Perhaps, in a concrete fashion, treasure is a way of gestalting the idea of the hidden, beautiful "I", of the dream or vision. Secrecy may then tell about the need for protection from abuses and suppression of grown-ups. Or, more positively, about integrity and attempts to preserve oneself.' This then is the heart of the notion of 'conceptions' within the child's own culture. And these conceptions can help the child (and adult) during the psychological trauma of individuation.

This may not only assist in conventional clinical psychology, but also in our understanding of the power of fascination in children's literature and films, and undoubtedly in architecture. Other child conceptions which Selmer-Olsen describes as 'primitive, original, archetypal' can be identified as the following:

the cottage (my own room/space), the escape (which can also be associated with laughter), the tribe, the secret association, the collection, writing (the magic constant), the hiding place, the raft, the dam, the castle, war, the dog, the (awful) animal, the mother (good and awful), the unbeliev-

able, the ball, the king, the word, and death and paradise [the Norwegian name for the game of Hopscotch].[14]

Many children, of course, do not experience the need for privacy in the context of their own development. However, children's ability to possess space within the kindergarten environment is often overlooked as being of benefit only to those who are psychologically damaged; it also enables balanced children to feel a sense of independence within the kindergarten environment, in order to explore and develop their own fantasies. In many Danish children's centres, child-only rooms are provided that are inaccessible to adults. These spaces can be totally taken over by the children; their dressing-up games take place in the clear knowledge of their own individuality and growing personal autonomy.[15] Dens, niches and child-height spaces have such profound learning benefits for young children that, no matter how difficult control may become as a result of their incorporation, such elements define the fully mature kindergarten environment.

4.4 Kitchens, storerooms, washrooms and lavatories

Functionally explicit spaces within the kindergarten, such as the kitchen, the storeroom and the WC/washroom, are often considered to have only utilitarian value. Young children are constantly mimicking the activities of their adult carers, and will be provided with play kitchens, 'home' areas, toy sweeping brushes and indoor sand-pits. Kindergarten programmes often separate service areas from children's areas. If these boundaries can be avoided, children can gain an understanding of these integral components of the real world. This is a plea for authentic kitchens with kitchen staff as integral members of the teaching team. 'Homes do not have meals delivered in uniform tinfoil packets unseen by children until they arrive at the lunch table.'[16]

For safety reasons, kitchens tend to be out of bounds to young children. However, on a symbolic level the kitchen or hearth can represent the centre, where the source of warmth and sustenance is generated. Even the aroma of cooking helps considerably in maintaining a homely caring atmosphere. Children can also gain a profound sense of their own value by being allowed to assist in the preparation of food and drink. For example, in the Diane nursery school, four- and five-year-old

4.9 Red Barnets kindergarten, Aarhuis; the entrance area has a children's kitchen.

4.10 An open kitchen lies at the centre of the Kompan Kindergarten, Copenhagen, designed by Helle Grangaard.

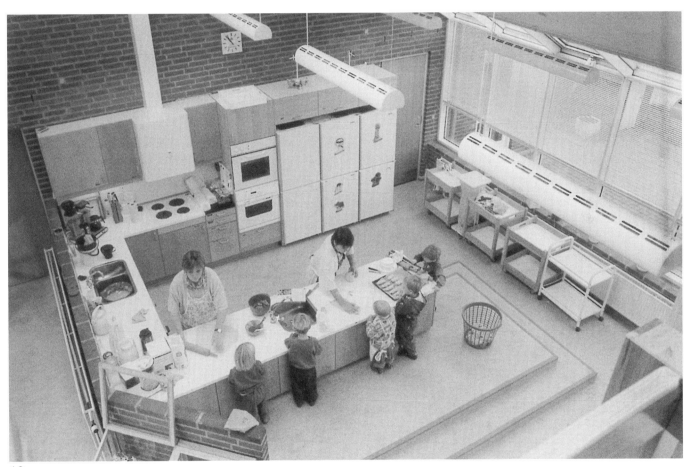

4.9

4.10

children wander freely in and out of the generously proportioned kitchen, carrying food and returning used plates and cutlery. Safety is ensured by the empowerment of kitchen staff to play a recognized pedagogic role, and hence to take responsibility for those who use their spaces.

Space that will support the child's sense of autonomy is not necessarily private space. A kitchen placed at the entrance foyer of a Danish centre enables the children to play out the role of being in their own kitchen. The fact that the kitchen is open, in an essentially public area, does not inhibit the game, or prevent the children from becoming engrossed in their role play for long concentrated periods of time. The space represents a fantasy

4.11 The Jumoke play nursery, Southwark, south London, by Matrix. The intention was to create a sequence of linked rooms that could be used by the children in a fluid way. Activity-related areas — such as the 'wet area' or 'soft play space'— have diverse spatial qualities. Steps heighten this sense of movement, and different age groups mix freely. A child-height gallery accessible by a gentle staircase enables children to withdraw and create their own activities without being disturbed by adults, although accessibility is now recognized as being a problem. First-floor plan.
Key:
1 staffroom
2 office
3 WC
4 lift
5 kitchen
6 resources space
7 sessions room
8 crèche
9 WC
Ground-floor plan (axonometric).
Key to main spaces:
1 soft playroom
2 child-height play platform
3 main play room
4 entrance hall
5 wet play
6 outdoor play area
7 kitchen

capsule, which can be as safe and hermetic a world as the 'den' or secret hiding place.

Children who are insulated from everyday events such as food preparation will tend to be more passive observers than participants. Julia Dwyer, an architect who worked with the feminist architectural practice Matrix, highlighted the implications of a complete separation between these so-called service spaces and teaching or activity spaces. She believes it is a reflection of the social and political structure and states that it is important to adopt.

a questioning approach to the usual relationships between rooms in plan, particularly between the service rooms, the kitchen and laundry and the play spaces. This is born out of a critique given to service work *versus* professional work and the expression of this in architecture. In a conventional nursery, service work is separated from child care in plan and by the division of the nursery's workers into service workers, usually women on low pay, and professional workers, [usually trained] nursery school teachers, and is not seen as relevant to children at that age. The Matrix child care buildings all explore the possibilities of using the kitchen or a part of it as a space which is used during the day as a part of the children's activities.[17]

In many Spanish nursery schools, the cook is an essential member of the pedagogic system. He or she will bring in the fresh produce in the mornings, and prepare and cook throughout the morning in the kitchen, which is open to all the children. Thus the whole sense of a social structure associated with eating is ritualized and celebrated to the point where everyone sits down to lunch in family-sized units in a café to share in this important communal activity. Not only is this an important group socializing experience, encouraging the child to structure his or her day around the lunchtime event, it also becomes clear how significant is the kitchen, fireplace or hearth in the symbolic representation of the kindergarten as home.

Nobody would suggest that toilet training should be celebrated, yet not dissimilar spatial concerns are often expressed about kindergarten lavatories and washrooms. Mary Hart, Head Teacher at a large nursery school in north London, talks about the need for space. She does not refer just to the amount of

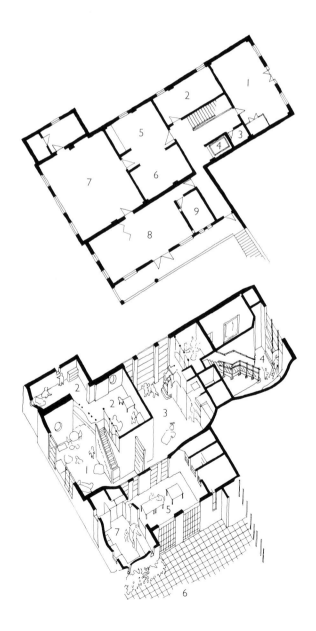

4.11

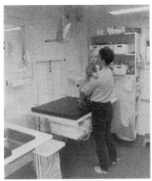

4.12

4.12 Child care centre, Amager, Copenhagen: nappy-changing facility. The purpose-made, height-adjustable soft tables are located within a quiet, private space. The surface should be at least 90cm above the ground, easily washable and close to the sink, with storage shelves. Reflective surfaces and mirrors, mobiles and ceiling graphics can help to distract babies and toddlers. A well-ventilated space for potty-training (which is not the WC) can help the transformation from nappies.

4.13 Neukölln 'Kita', Berlin. 1994, by Klaus Zillich. Glass block used along the corridor creates a bright and open relationship between toilets and activity areas.

4.14 The service wall of the Neukölln 'Kita', with circular bathroom windows hidden behind acoustic screens. The building is located close to the Berlin airport to which it makes symbolic reference with the projecting 'wing' roof – many of the parents are employed in aircraft-related jobs.

4.13

4.14

space but to the quality of space which should infuse every area. This, she feels, is particularly important in the toilet and bathroom areas. When children are learning to be independent, it is crucial that the experience of using the lavatory is a healthy, open one so that they do not get an inhibited view of the activity: 'Often the architects locate the toilet in a tiny little bit of left-over space. It is important that the lavatories are light, spacious and calming. It does not help if it is full of cubicles and cupboards. The toilet is as important a socializing space as any part of the building.'

It is generally considered to be good practice to locate lavatories and washrooms directly off the activity spaces themselves. For example, the Cantalamessa nursery school (for three- to six-year-olds), which is part of the combined infants' school at Via

Storage

4.15

4.16

4.15 Lützowstrasse Kindertagesstätte, Berlin, by Klaus Zillich. Steps up to the raised sun terrace allow storage drawers beneath the platform. These platforms provide safe, warm surfaces where children can play in their natural reclining position.

4.16 Centre de Vie Enfantine, Lausanne, by Rudolphe Luscher: cloakroom and storage areas. Storage is a constant problem: there never appears to be enough, whether it is for the safe storage of items to be kept out of the reach of children, or large toys and other materials that are accessible to the children. Each activity and each area generates its own storage needs, and if these can be anticipated and built into the scheme at design stage, the kindergarten environment will maintain its own order.

4.17 The 'lunch box' wall at Westborough Primary Westcliff on Sea, UK. A series of storage racks on the outside face of the building is protected from the rain by a protecting canopy. It provides storage for the lunch boxes and throughout most of the year ensures that the food remains fresh and cool. It also looks wonderful like an advertizing hoarding, expressing the individuality of the child and making a group collage which changes from day to day.

4.17

Kindergarten Architecture

4.18 Plan of the Vanessa Nursery School, London. The children's swimming pool is integrated into the planning of the school curriculum.

Key:
1 group activities
2 garden courtyard
3 group room (originally a store)
4 pool room
5 activity niches – science, quiet area, computers
6 head teacher
7 children's washroom/WC
8 parents/staffroom
9 plant room

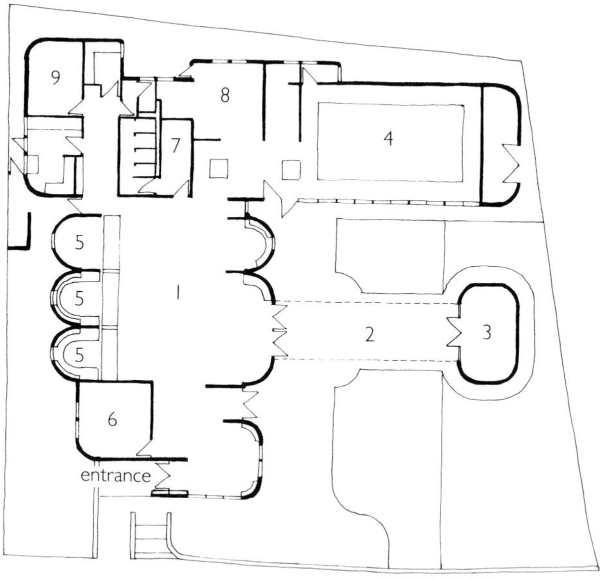

4.18

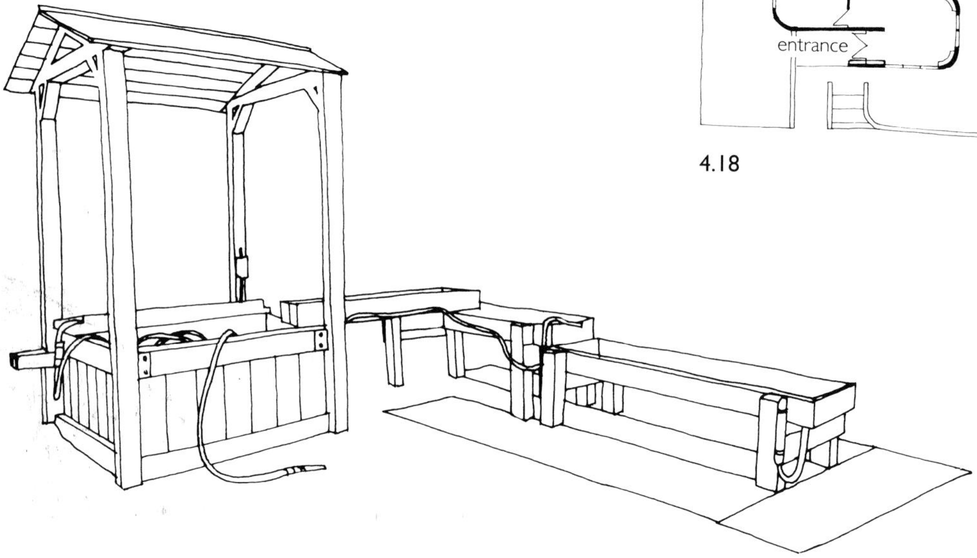

4.19

4.19 Water play apparatus in the garden of the Crocetta kindergarten, Modena.

Dello Sport in Bologna, provides approximately 12.5m² of toilet/washroom space to each class or *sezione* of 25 children, with three cubicles and a minimum of three wide and low washbasins per class. The washroom spaces are accessed directly off the activity areas, and act as a kind of lobby for the inner toilet areas. This means that the toilets are close at hand, in fact an integral and pleasurable part of the daily routine, yet separated by the washing room. It is, of course, important that these areas are properly ventilated and naturally lit.

Italian day nurseries for babies up to three have higher space standards than most other European child care systems. The Bologna example provides a single wash/toilet area of 33m², which is a ratio of almost 1m² per child. The space is well lit and naturally ventilated, with windows on three sides with views from the activity areas. However, pre-WC children require nappy-changing facilities which are more akin to the bedroom – warm, quiet and soothing.

The Neukölln 'Kita' in Berlin designed by Claus Zillich adopts the overall organizing device of a service wall that protects the activity areas from the noise and pollution of a busy road. The toilet and bathroom facilities are therefore placed in blocks with-

in this service wall. In order to use the facilities, children must make a 'journey' along or across the corridor from their home bases, where they may meet children of other ages. Thus the social purpose of the kindergarten is extended. The neutral colours and the use of glass block on the corridor side provide a bright, friendly atmosphere within the toilet areas. Contact is maintained with the other activity areas which encourages a healthy, open attitude.

The issue of developing positive attitudes to toilet training is felt to be important at this age. Indeed, Rudolphe Luscher's Centre de Vie Enfantine in Lausanne takes a radical view, consistent with the architectural philosophy of the whole school. With lavatories for three- to four-year-old children in a completely open-plan form, the children can talk and spend time rather than viewing the activity as a surreptitious chore. Low-level partitions (in a circular form) create a sense of privacy for the children when seated. When the child stands, vistas are opened beyond the lavatory spaces that add spatial dynamic and reinforce the importance of the room within the hierarchy of the whole building. This appeals to pre-school children, who are not yet inhibited in their toilet attitudes.

4.20

4.20 Penn Green Children's Centre, Corby, UK. One of the first designated Early Excellence Centres incorporates the discovery area, a sand and water play area beneath a large industrial-style canopy. The pleasure and excitement of children releasing water to flow down slides into a lagoon is testament to this particular form of play.

4.21 The Vanessa Nursery School play rooms overlook the pool.

4.21

The approach taken in this project encapsulates an attitude to kindergarten design in which spaces overlap, so that children are made aware not just of the activities of other children but also of the workings of the whole system. This is made possible by a subtle dialectic between transparency and enclosure. For children, 'curiosity is permanent, to see the laundry machinery from the stair landing, to spy the babies eating from the "big" children's dining area, to observe the cook at work in the kitchen from the entrance, to discover together between two and four years how to use the cloakroom, the wash basin and toilet'. This makes the building operate like a highly informative social puzzle. Everything, down to the water pipes, is open and revealed, provoking an understanding of the building as a microcosm of the world.[18]

4.5 The body: water play, baths and pools

Bathrooms in the home environment are usually cosy and intimate, often part of a relaxing sequence of bedtime events. In the kindergarten, the bathroom is usually part of a toilet area; the intimacy and warmth of the home equivalent is rarely transferred to the school. Water can be used as an essential route towards bodily relaxation, and also be a fundamental element in playful, imaginative games and distractions that can be integrated into the design itself.

In the Lausanne project, water valves in the cisterns were adjusted to make a distinctive whistling noise when the toilets are flushed. In the Luginsland Kindergarten, transparent rainwater downpipes are used. These effects heighten the children's awareness of the purifying properties of water, as well as amusing them. Any type of game involving water has great appeal for young children. For obvious reasons, water play is usually confined to external hard areas and gardens. If specific spaces for water activities are introduced as all-year-round pursuits within the kindergarten, they can have a tremendously positive and therapeutic effect. For example, the kindergarten in Viborg Seminariet has a shallow pool large enough for three or four children to use together. The whole room is a wet area and children can spend time enjoying the pleasure of a steamy splashing bath on a cold winter morning.

Mary Hart's Margaret McMillan Nursery School in Islington, north London, has a swimming pool adjacent to the entrance, which can be used by the young children. However, it is a little too large and public, and mainly benefits outside adult groups, but its visible presence upon entering the building for the first time is a positive distraction. Swimming itself is widely recognized as having great therapeutic value, but it is important to ensure that the scale and depth of a pool for pre-school children is right. Most importantly, the water temperature must be high and the general environment should be warm, acoustically calming, and provide a safe, protective feeling.

One of the best examples of this conjunction is at the Vanessa Nursery School located in west London. It is a 40-place facility, designed in 1973. Actress Vanessa Redgrave had the idea of building the school with a small swimming pool at its heart, following her own children's experience with teacher Jann Stevens. Stevens believed that swimming and water play have important educational and psychological benefits for young children, and suggested the unusual idea of a pool at the heart of the new school. The project was funded by the actress's own charitable trust, established to help underprivileged children.

Located on one side of a courtyard garden, but directly accessible from the main activity space, the pool room is well proportioned but small. There are gentle steps running down into the shallow end. Plain, cream-coloured non-slip ceramic tiles are used on the floor, and elegant timber-framed wall-sized windows encourage views into the adjacent play space. A generally informal attitude to changing (which takes place in the pool room

Kindergarten Architecture

4.22 The child care centre, Amager, Copenhagen: the pram store.

4.23 Bad Blanckenburg by Friedrich Froebel, 1818, garden/play area layout.
Key:
1–16 individual garden plots for the children, A–T vegetable plots, a–t flower beds for a variety of plants
17   play area
18   for visiting parents and friends of the children, B bench seats

The formal similarity between David Stow's first model infants' school of 1828 and the converted former artisans' houses of the Viborg Seminariet kindergarten, is in marked contrast to the landscape philosophy: in the former, children would respect fruit trees and plants by not touching these desirable things; through this they would show 'that moral teaching in schools would be the cheapest police'

(Stow, 1836). By comparison, 25 years later, Froebel encourages the children to tend the land and use their endeavours to grow fruit and vegetables. In a similar way, Belgian landscape architect Jacques Gustin encourages the children to tend the garden themselves and pick the fruit and flowers when ready (Markus, Thomas A., 1993, *Buildings and Power*, London, Routledge, p. 78).

4.22

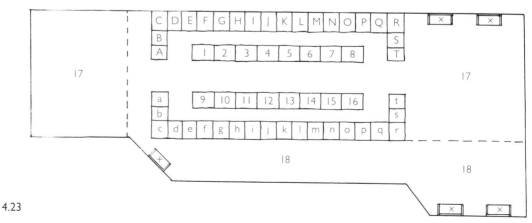

4.23

4.24 Drygate Infants' School, Glasgow, 1828. Note the participation of the schoolmaster (in top hat) expressing a new informal approach to education.

4.25 Bad Blanckenburg by Friedrich Froebel, 1818, engraving.

4.24

4.25

itself) make the space comfortable and almost cosy, with baskets of clothing ranged along the pool-side. As part of the curriculum, twice a week children can spend a blissful 20-minute period in shoulder-depth, blood-temperature water, a symbolic womb-like encounter that profoundly enriches the weekly programme of activities.[19]

The pool has become an important, but not all-embracing, part of the functioning of the kindergarten curriculum. All the teachers are required to take basic swimming proficiency courses, and all of them, including Head Teacher Evelyn Moss, take their turn with children in the pool; her statement that 'it doesn't take over the life of the whole school, it's just an unusual feature,' would appear to underestimate its benefits.[20] The positive impact can be viewed in terms of the outside community groups that use it constantly. Since it can be accessed through the garden, the school itself can remain closed and secure at weekends without restricting the use of the pool. Thus the value of this small building is spread to the wider community.

4.6 The external environment: gardens, fields, meadows

It has long been a part of the pre-school curriculum that children learn how to care for living things. It is widely believed that, by observing how plants and animals grow and change over time, young children will come to an understanding of their place within the natural world. In addition, the value of experiencing natural phenomena is frequently referred to by child psychologists who cite it as a factor in relieving stress in children and adults. What Fiske and Maddi (1961) refer to as 'difference within sameness' is the subtle variation in aural stimulation afforded by nature.[21] For example, sea breezes, aromatic flowers and plants, gently flowing rivers and streams, provide stimulation which relieves the stress often seen in urban dwellers. This implies that the natural environment should be optimized, even in the most urban of kindergarten locations. Activity areas should open on to outside space, sunlight and ventilation always be let in, and the building orientated to provide vistas towards any greenery. The garden remains the most potent element in this equation.

Mary Hart, Head Teacher at the Margaret McMillan Nursery School in north London, presides over an institution that supports the needs of 85 pre-school children. She stresses the importance and the benefits of the garden, which slopes up from the school, front to back. It enables the children to 'lose themselves', but never be far from visual contact with the kindergarten building itself. The garden, in a similar way to the activity spaces, has quiet, almost niche-like areas into which the children can withdraw and develop group games in a way that enables them to feel independent of the teachers. It can support an alternative set of activities that have great developmental value.

In schools that use the High/Scope curriculum the garden is formally recognized as a fundamental aspect of the prescribed educational system. The spaces within the garden should extend the educational experience by providing specific learning activity

4.26

4.26 Conceptual plan for Healey House Community Garden, Brixton, south London, by landscape architects Whitelaw Turkington, 1994. The older residents can sit apart from the play area, their garden being partially segregated from the children's by a sinuous beech hedge. On the far side, the children will be able to rummage about in 'the wood', a coppice planting of willow dogwood. They can dig in the earth and explore the bog, created by impeding the drainage of part of this 'ecology' garden. Stepping stones invite the children to explore beyond the bog, and disappear behind the 'dark tree', an existing conifer incorporated into the design.

areas. The 'ideal playground', defined by Steen B. Esbensen in his High/Scope Educational Foundation publication, lists a number of spaces, such as the sand-pit, the hill and the garden, and relates them to particular cognitive experiences: projective/fantasy, running and rolling, and natural elements. This structure gives positive direction to the way in which the garden is formed and appropriated by teachers on behalf of the children. However, making such clearly prescribed demands on the space may not take into account the particularity of each context in terms of orientation, views, existing vegetation, topography and, perhaps most important, the organic qualities of the wild garden which can make an ideal play space.

The child care centre on Amager, Copenhagen, creates a simple structure of modest self-contained garden spaces around the projecting eaves of the child care buildings. The comforting presence of the building's 'spreading' roof is reinforced by the way in which the gardens themselves are handled, almost as reflections of the interior plan of the building: the outside play spaces are designed like little rooms, defined by low fences and brick walls. These gardens each have a distinct sensory quality: one is sandy, one is a hard climbing space, one is a herb garden and one is a field or meadow space. Small detached storage sheds which create an interface between the architecture of the main building help to create enclaves of child-scaled space that provide safe, secure yet seemingly autonomous zones within which children can play at being grown up.

A less restricting approach to the outside play space was adopted for the kindergarten in Viborg Seminariet, Denmark. It was evident how the garden was being adapted and changed when we visited. Belgian landscape architect Jacques Gustin wanted to establish a constantly evolving informal garden. The teachers and parents were responsible for the process of developing much of it, with weekend parties of volunteer cultivists putting ideas into practice. Grassed areas reverted to sand-pits and climbing areas were planted with trees and shrubs, which changed from season to season. The garden spaces became something of a foil to the ordered, elegant clarity of the interior of the building itself.

4.27 An interpretation of a High/Scope garden, with seven areas for different types of play which relate directly to the curriculum.

Key:
1. sand with physical play structure
2. hill for running and rolling
3. swings, sand
4. seesaw, grass
5. table, playsand and water with hand pump for projective fantasy
6. rocking item, loose parts on grass – a social centre and focal point
7. painting easels, wheel toys, wood working bench for manipulative creative construction

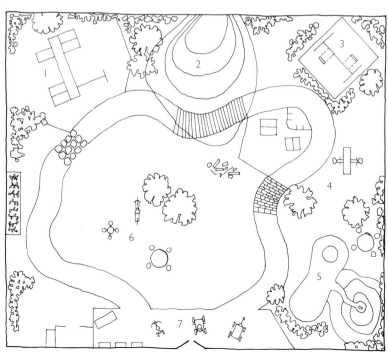

4.27

1

2

Nant-Y-Cwm Steiner Nursery, Llanycefn, Wales, by Christopher Day Associates

1 View of the school from the road, framed by the entrance gate 'carved' out of the existing hedgerow.

2 Classroom interior with alcove; note the homemade fabric-covered wall light.

Heddernheim-Nord Kindertagesstätte, Frankfurt, Germany, by Friedensreich Hundertwasser

3 Entrance colonnade 'balustrades', reminiscent of fairground architecture.

3

Jardin de Niños la Esperanza, Mexico, by James T. Hubbell

4 Conceptual painting by James Hubbell: the first idea of how the form of building would eventually appear.

5 Shell and ceramic tile sculpture. Although the parents and visitors carried out most of the sculpture, artist James Hubbell initially drew the design from his own patterns on to the 'canvas' of the building form. He also kept close control to ensure quality and evenness.

4

5

Børneinstitutioner, Amager, Copenhagen, Denmark, by Arkitekttegnestuen Virumgård

6 View from car park.

7 View from kitchen. Standard components such as these windows are used within the varied form of the buildings to keep costs low.

8 Interior of central play space. The building adopts soft colours for the interi-

or: paired purples, and blues, with complementary but more vibrant greens and blues for the exterior. In Goethe's terms, this places the colours into a harmonious rather than a conflicting relationship, and creates a calming rather than over-stimulating environment.

6

7

8

Luginsland Kindergarten, Stuttgart, Germany, by Behnisch and Partner

9 The first-floor classroom: the structural clarity is never out of control and it remains an authentic inside–outside construction, irrational yet legible. Note the window niche behind the door, a typical space in tune with children's play patterns and scale.

10 View from the playground with the prow lashed down.

The imagery is not too synthetic, since the use of conventional architectural elements is made structurally explicit.

10

Bungawitta Children's Centre, Launceston, Tasmania, Australia, by Robert Morris-Nunn

11 The garden elevation with blue timber wall curving around the activity spaces within.

12 Child-level view of the 'possum petrol station', with views of the play street.

11

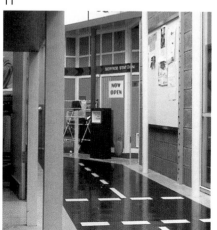

12

Ringrose Kindergarten, Subang Jaya, Selangor, Malaysia, by Akicipta Associate Architects

13 Lego building-block colours and elemental forms make this an instantly popular kindergarten image, but does it have lasting benefits for the staff and children? View from the playground.

14 The L-shaped plan around a somewhat barren playground. The section through the building encourages natural ventilation.

13

14

UCLA Child Care Center, Los Angeles, California, USA, by Charles and Elizabeth Lee

15 Activity area interior: light and texture articulate the form of the building. Glazed and translucent panels are set into a homogeneous grid, with structure and fabric exposed, but services such as water pipes hidden.

16 View from the administrative block towards the west colonnade. The gravel texture delineates the children's world, as opposed to the adults'; the newly planted hedge has now become mature and adds a further layer to this delineation.

16   15

Greisheim-Sud Kindertagestätte, Frankfurt, Germany, by Bolles Wilson and Partner

17 View up the main staircase.

18 The garden elevation, with the solid toilet block contrasting with the glazed activity area walls.

17

18

Centre de Vie Enfantine, Valency, Lausanne, Switzerland, by Rudolphe Luscher

19 Interior, showing structural clarity and integrated storage with the play of light and colour.

20 View from the park, illustrating the origination of the idea as three separate pavilions.

19

20

21

Stensby Personalbarnehage, Akerhus, Norway, by Kristin Jarmund AS

21 The four project-
ing coloured play
boxes represent the
four seasons.

22 Garden view of
'Summer' and
'Autumn'.

22

Lützowstrasse 'Kita', Tiergarten, Berlin, Germany, by Klaus Zillich

23 Storage and sliding partition within one of the activity   area 'apartments'.

Patmore Children's Centre, Wandsworth, London, UK, by the Greenhill Jenner Partnership

24 External play area with the projecting roof providing covered areas around   the perimeter of the activity areas.

23

24

Open-Air Kindergarten Annexe, Takarazuka, Japan, by Katsuhiro Miyamoto and Atelier Cinquième Architects

25 The exterior blends into the open volume of the play space, enabling the garden to become the focus of activity in all weathers.

Scuola dell' Infanzia e Asilo-nido Cantalamessa, Bologna, Italy, by Stefano Magagni/City of Bologna

26 The baby unit nestles in the trees beyond the raised Palazzo terrace.

Kindergarden, Neugereut, Stuttgart, Germany, by Behnisch and Partner

27 Individual activities take place in the class base.

4.28 Pacific Oaks Children's
School, the art studio.

When we visited on a cold autumn morning, the gardens were being used fully; children were running in and out of the building freely, and sandcastles were being made next to a bonfire. The long, low, single-storey, converted stable housing the new kindergarten relates well to the garden, protecting rather than dominating the garden spaces. One suspects that the High/Scope system would exclude the imaginative involvement of the local community in creating their own constantly changing environment. The value of the kindergarten exterior must be its evolving character, so that young children can continue to relate to their early experiences of the garden long after they have left the institution.

Landscape architect Lindsey Whitelaw has been involved in the development of a number of urban play spaces in London that attempt to engage the local community, and touch upon the symbolic meaning of the garden as a wilderness in which children can lose themselves. In her article 'A World of their Own', she alludes to the responsibility that garden designers have to children in the replication of a natural world, a central concept for the original kindergarten movement. It is, indeed, 'a weighty responsibility to have to plan for everything which children of an earlier time, despite frequent poverty, had close at hand: nature, work places, hidden corners, sheds and scrap heaps'.[22]

Whitelaw explains how they involved the local community in the development of a small community garden at Healey House, Brixton, south London. Although it was not a school garden, its terms of reference were for the creation of 'a toddler's play area, ecology garden and seating area in a small fenced space surrounded by low rise flats'. The Church Manor Tenants' Association were involved throughout the project, and included the local school children in a planting day for the ecology garden. The group are responsible for maintenance and the garden has become a meeting place for young parents. Many kindergarten gardens can have similar qualities, empowering parents and the local community to become involved.

We get used to the notion of the kindergarten as 'an extension of the classroom' to the point where the statement resonates like a meaningless cliché. Landscape architects like Whitelaw, Turkington and Jacques Gustin, working in conjunction with architects, conceive of the outside space surrounding the kindergarten as an autonomous 'wilderness'. Adult systems and metaphors that are too precise and therefore limiting to imaginative play are avoided. Instead, a flexible series of areas provides a basic structure (neces-

4.28

sary for safety reasons) which is loose enough to cope with the unpredictable and enable the children to make a garden in their own image. As Whitelaw states when describing her approach to designing for children: 'These are my terms and I would hope that in time, the children discover their own.'[23]

4.7 Art studios

Children (like poets, writers, musicians, scientists) are fervent seekers and builders of images. Images can be used to make other images: by passing through sensations, emotions, relationships, problems, passing theories, ideas about the possible and the coherent and about what seems to be impossible and incoherent. This is what Einstein meant when he said that his method of working consisted in remaining within the realm of the languages of images, postponing as long as possible the expression of these in words and actions.[24]

We have already touched upon the significance of artistic expression as a way of developing perceptions in young children. An over-emphasis on spoken language as a way of communicating at its most basic level stultifies the development of other important sensory organs (eyes, ears and hands, in particular) during these early years. Young pre-verbal children communicate in many languages, and all the senses should be stimulated

4.29

4.30

by the architecture (as well as the pedagogic system), to create a true learning environment. These 'stimulants' can range from aural experiences such as the banging of drums or the possibility of distinguishing between footsteps on different floor surfaces, to the experience of textures that have contrasting qualities.

An art studio, which is physically distinct and separate from the general teaching areas, enables flexibility and the opportunity for children to work on more ambitious projects if they are so inspired. It also reduces distractions; often in open-plan activity spaces where everything is visible children are so overwhelmed by the range of activities taking place that relatively little concentration is possible. When attention is not sustained, boredom and anxiety is often the result. The Diane kindergarten not only provides an art studio or *atelier* for each teaching group of 25 children, it has a large art studio at its centre that can be used by children from all of the three groups. There, large constructions can develop over a period of some months, and children can become engrossed in dirtier activities such as clay and collage on a large scale without adversely affecting the day-to-day activities of the other teaching areas.

The studio has large glazed doors that open on to the garden so that children can take their easels or modelling tables on to the terrace and enjoy spring and late summer sunshine. This project is widely recognized as a paradigm of pedagogic and environmental excellence in pre-school education, especially because of its art-based curriculum, supported by the art studio spaces.

The Pacific Oaks Children's School in Pasadena, California, has an outdoor art studio as a focus for its large 'campus' of mainly pre-school groups. Founded in 1945 by seven Quaker families on the basis that children should be respected and listened to as individuals, it now provides facilities for seven distinct groups of children in tree-shaded 'yards', each of which has its own turn-of-the-century timber school building. The art studio is staffed by a professional artist-in-residence: 'The program introduces art as a language, recognizing verbal and non-verbal symbols as vital to development.'[25] The art studio itself has a ramshackle quality, partly enclosed and partly covered but open to the elements. It acts as an open-air classroom, with an electric kiln and an open stage which serves as a temporary exhibition space for the creations of the children (a permanent children's school art gallery was established in 1977 on another site).

This facility has picturesque qualities that have been generated over some years in a largely ad hoc manner. As with many of the best pre-school environments, its qualities are clearly not the result of a single architectural hand. However, it is worth pointing out two admirable spatial qualities in terms of the art studio's relationship to the more general teaching areas. The climate here is mild and suited to an open arrangement. The very act of having to leave one building and walk to the art studio, making a 'journey' so to speak, is a memorable image for the children to hold – leaving one world for another world, but one which responds to more creative sensibilities. If this means umbrellas have to be used when it is raining then that becomes part of the experience. The dappled quality of sunlight filtering through an overgrown timber filigree roof, even the sound of pattering rain on the sheet roofing and the drip-drop of dew from the hanging plants, infuse the whole space and its surroundings, giving a sense of proximity to the natural elements.

The second characteristic relating to this 'journey' is the quality of the entrance into the space. Rather than being open like the rest of the campus (a symbolic representation of America itself, perhaps), the entrance into the art studio is through a confined corridor, which defines the threshold of the studio, deflecting outward views and symbolically expressing the change of mood required by the space and its more introspective activities. Here the spatial quality, linked to the pedagogic programme, calms and encourages sensitive children, providing an alternative environment to the open, often rowdy, yard activities.

4.8 Light and colour

All sensations, when they take artistic form, become immersed in the sensation of light, and therefore can only be expressed with all the colours of the prism. We will call this view: artistic expression of light – spherical expansion of light in space. In this way we will have a spherical expansion of colour in perfect accord with the spherical expansion of forms.[26]

Colour is considered to have particular relevance to kindergarten architecture, due to the way in which children perceive and develop an awareness of it at an early age. It is another language to which young children can relate. Colour is a constituent

4.29, 30 An ingenious portable store, and chairs, tables and climbing frames, designed by the Building Department of the Municipality of Bologna under the direction of Stefano Magagni. The furniture focuses on safety and adaptability; the store, for example, unfolds to provide open access to the children's drawings and painting materials.

and it cannot be isolated from texture, surface, light and form. All of these factors modify and transform it.

Debates about the best way to encourage learning through colour in the kindergarten environment range from largely discredited theories of the 1960s that young children recognize only primary colours, to the current view that 'a learning environment [should be] designed with elemental stimulus of primary forms and warm but not over-excitable colours'.[27] As the senses tend to detect changes in stimulation rather than constant inputs, they function best on the basis of gradual environmental changes which can be affected by light and colour. Stimulation must be gradual, as dramatic fluctuations can be over-stimulating to older children or, at worst, disorientating to younger children. Fiske and Maddi's notion of 'difference within sameness' is significant not just in accentuating the importance of predictability in the pre-school environment, but also in underlining the undoubted value of moderate diversity; for example if the environment is made even by the use of fluorescent lighting and white walls throughout, the value of colour and texture variations will be lost.

The notion of reducing natural colour to its primary constituents was explored when the Dutch artist Piet Mondrian argued that red, yellow and blue were the only colours, since all the others derived from them. Mondrian's colour theory influenced De Stijl designers such as Bart van der Leck, Theo van Doesburg and Gerrit Rietveld. The influence of so-called Neo-Plasticism and other modern movement colour precepts can still arguably be seen in sophisticated contemporary projects like Aldo van Eyck's Nagele School and the nursery school at Stensby Hospital, Akerhus. Colour is an identifying device, and also creates an aesthetic sensibility in a serious integrated form. For example, the Nagele School has six glazed entrance cloakroom partitions, which are painted in one of the spectral colours in the sequence red–orange–yellow–green–blue–violet. Many children's buildings and spaces use primary colour more blatantly, to stimulate a dull environment by dramatically transforming the space with highly synthetic colour 'forms'.[28]

According to architect Klaus Zillich, the Lützowstrasse 'Kita' in Berlin uses no synthetic colours, apart from a single turquoise painted wall at its entrance. Only the natural texture of the materials themselves add colour. However, the building is orientated in such a way that the sun penetrates every part of the interior, making the maximum use of reflected light even on win-

ter days. This is achieved by a rigorous north–south orientation (ignoring the orthogonal layout of the surrounding buildings): the large main hall on the east side benefits from morning sun, and the terraces of the teaching areas are orientated directly towards the south, scooping all available sun deep into the back of the classrooms, especially useful at midday on winter days when the sun shines in at a low, oblique angle. The effect of this 'solar geometry' is to accentuate the colour of the children themselves, their artwork and other objects within the spaces.

The Greisheim-Sud 'Kita' in Frankfurt by Bolles Wilson adopts a similar modernist approach, using colour, to articulate important architectural 'points' within the predominantly neutrally coloured frame of the building. Colour is applied in a painterly, purist style but it is well composed and rich. So a panel at the top of the main staircase has a vivid scarlet shape, an abstract symbol which becomes a sort of form/colour language for the children (see colour plate 17). It is all reminiscent of Corbusian concerns, with the tinting of deflected light evident in the Marseilles Unité d'Habitation, or the articulation of recess and 'thickness' in La Tourette monastery. One is also reminded of the modernist preoccupations of Wassily Kandinsky, whose concern was for the meaning of colour and form divorced from any representational aim. The intention then was the search for colour and form in painting which had the purity and expressive quality of music, yet also represented a model of organization. In projects like the Bolles Wilson 'Kita' one senses a similar search taking place. Evidently it is a language of colour to which children relate intuitively.[29]

The Ringrose Kindergarten in Malaysia adopts a non-intellectual, surface approach to colour. The architect's avowed intention was to recreate the primary colours of children's Lego bricks and communicate a joyful, almost fairground, quality. Its colour transforms the exterior of the building into a beacon for the children, which is especially relevant given the flat evenness of the sur-rounding countryside. Strangely, one feels distinctly uncomfortable with this approach, when the nature of the materials overcomes the convention of the synthetic colouring. For example, when the tiles over the projecting canopies reveal their texture and constructional patterning, this jars against the deliberately smooth covering of the surface colour, which stretches over the building like a plastic skin. Although the interior is less sombre and more naturally coloured, it also creates a similar dual-

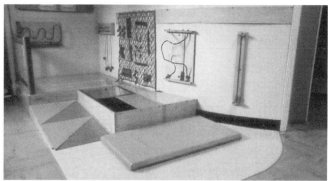

4.31

4.32

4.33

4.31 A raised floor installation in a Modena nursery school with a panel of wallmounted textures: carpet, soft mat, pebbled mat. The floor has an illuminated perspex sec-tion. According to Rudolphe Luscher, architect of Centre de Vie Enfantine, Lausanne, diverse materials and colours, when put together in a deliber-ately didactic way, can heighten their expressive appeal: 'from the roughness of concrete warmed by the vividness of a ray of sunlight, to the smoothness of a timber panel, from the radiant luminosity of painted metal to the pastel shades of a sliding screen' – all of these architec-turally contrasting effects bring quality to the learning environment and stimulate children's senses naturally.

4.32 This old wall was left deliberately exposed when the new Piccolina nursery school was built in Bologna, providing an intriguing 'memory' of the earlier building. Different mosaics, render and brickwork provide a readymade range of textures, exposed in an unusual way.

4.33 A single wall in this Viborg kindergarten acts as a gallery for the children's family and group portraits. It is framed by a single panel of domestic-style wallpaper. The whole composition changes from month to month, provid-ing a stimulating focus for the children's developing discussions on family and friendship.

4.34 This imaginative climbing installation in the garden of Kollhof and Timmerman's Tiergarten 'Kita', Frankfurt, is set in a graded range of stone-sets surrounding a sand pit, which provides a safe landing in the event of falls. The potential dangers during these years of explosive development are something the kindergarten environment should recognize. The developing child of course needs to climb, but may not yet be fully aware of his or her own capabilities. Badly designed play equipment can not only be a risk in the event of serious mishaps, but it may also dis-courage the child from explor-ing and developing if the chal-lenge is mentally or physically too great. Here, the textures help to establish in the minds of the children certain clearly identifiable 'zones', within which certain activities may be taking place.

4.34

4.35 Economical solutions to the provision of child care facilities: the Railway Carriage 'Kita', Frankfurt, a sketch proposal.

4.36 Plan.

ity or tension.

The Nant-y-Cwm Steiner Nursery in Wales by architect Christopher Day attempts to use colour in a totally organic way to the point where the process becomes more important than the final effect; external render is a soft warm earth colour to match the natural context of woods and fields, and comprises a 'site-made lime-milk formulation'. The building is used like a canvas for the artist/architect to mix his colours, in a similar but much less mechanical style to the Frankfurt project by Bolles Wilson. In the classrooms, the colour is used to manipulate the mood of the spaces (and the children): 'secure, calm, warm, activity-inducing in a gentle, dreamy way'. So the colour, a sort of pink, is described by the architect in a much more romantic way as 'thin veils of rose madder and alizarin crimson with, in selected places, vermilion and ultramarine blue: Winsor and Newton and Stockmeyer watercolours over a casein white emulsion on 4:1 plaster . . .'[30].

Ulla Poulsen and Jørgen Raun, who designed the child care centre on Amager, Copenhagen, allude to Goethe in the colour treatment of their building. This theory was developed by the late 18th-century poet and writer and further expanded upon by the theosophist Rudolf Steiner. Colour is perceived to relate to specific moods and senses. So reds, yellows and oranges are described as 'advancing' and would be characterized as positive, bright and stimulating. At the opposite end of the spectrum, blues and purples would be 'retiring' and characterized as sombre and calming. It was Goethe's contention that colour is an essential part of the totality of the forces guiding the human mind.

The analysis here must necessarily be brief; however, these ideas are important to organic kindergarten theory. Although based on scientific principles, this was a complex spiritual quest: 'We breathe soul into deaf form when, through colour, we make it living.'[31] The search for basic unity in the world of colour as a reflection of nature was recognized by Goethe in the phenomena of complementary and opposite colours. Goethe's three-part study of 1810, *Farbenlehre* [Theory of Colour], sought to show how colour, unlike light, was 'at all times specific, characteristic, significant'.[32] His colour theory was very popular during the first years of the 20th century, particularly to the German Expressionists, because of its combination of mystical and scientific themes which related well to the emerging theories of child psychology. Overlaid by Steiner's later developments, it has

remained in use, especially in Waldorf schools.[33]

The psychological debate, combined with some of Steiner's occult and spiritualist elements, had a strong effect on the later writings of Kandinsky. His interest in synaesthesia, the stimulation of several senses at the same time, led to discussions of how the use of coloured light as a form of therapy could have a particular effect on the whole body:

> Various attempts to exploit this power of colour and apply it to different nervous disorders have again noted that red light has an enlivening and stimulating effect upon the heart, while blue, on the other hand, can lead to temporary paralysis. If this sort of effect can also be observed in the case of animals, and even plants, then any explanation in terms of association completely falls down. These facts in any case prove that colour contains within itself a little studied but enormous power, which can influence the entire human body as a physical organism.[34]

Paul Klee attempted to revive the concerns of Goethe at the Bauhaus. His lectures on interior decoration, about rooms painted in tones of the complementary pairs, contained a colour theory remarkably close to Goethe's programme for his own house at Weimar, 150 years earlier. There, successive rooms were coloured in complementary, contrasting colours.

Just as naturalistic colour theory died after World War II in 'high' art, the same cultural impulse took hold in high architecture. Abstraction developed concerns for the mechanics of surface texture and other themes relating to mass production. Inevitably, this philosophy filtered down to mainstream architecture to the point where very few buildings, except children's architecture, used colour up until the mid 1980s. Today the importance of form, colour and light in children's architecture is evident in many of our featured projects, and they are used in many different ways. The theory is often personal and wilful, but the struggle to understand colour in psychological and physical terms is ongoing and serious.

If it is possible to imagine a kindergarten space that is naturally rendered without a reliance on architectural form or synthetic colour, then it is the Pacific Oaks art studio. Its form is elusive, as its 'walls' are to a certain extent defined by flowers and plants, and materials such as the timber roof structure which is used 'in

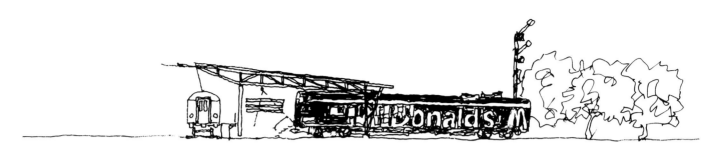

4.35

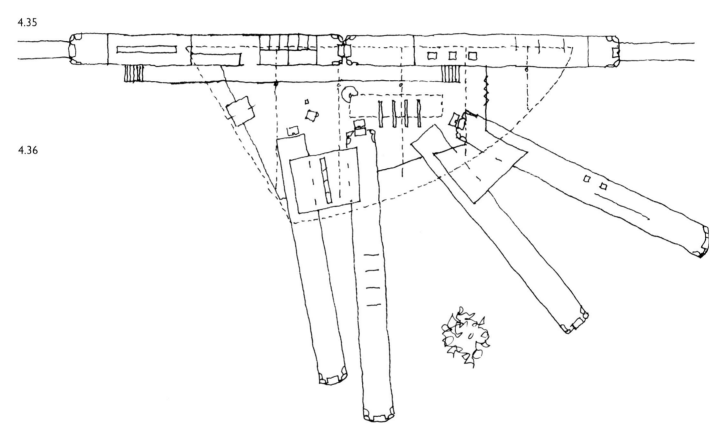

4.36

the raw'. Nevertheless, it derives its colour from these incomplete constituents that define the space, and from the children's paintings and models, and from light. Quality of light is a primary aspect of this calm, naturalistic environment. Vivid blue skies and luminous reflections from the ocean are particular to this locality, and were the reason that the film studios were first established in Hollywood. In the more northern climates of Europe, where the sun is often very low or hidden by clouds, light can be dull and even. Given such geographical variations of light quality, the use of colour in architecture has to be considered even more carefully in an international context.

4.9 Economy and cost

We have discussed kindergarten architecture, almost oblivious

to cost implications. Many of the featured centres are relatively cheap compared to other building types. However, some of the featured projects create children's environments for what many would deem a prohibitive cost. Quality in pre-school environments does not necessarily relate simply to a conventional cost per square metre criterion. The search for ideal children's environments is in the process of evolving through a variety of unusual and imaginative approaches to funding, procurement and design.

For example, Klaus Zillich's Lützowstrasse children's day care centre in Berlin was estimated to have cost in excess of £6 million. Most of the building was constructed as part of a training scheme for apprentice builders; as a result, the construction process was long and drawn out. However, this had its benefits: the architect could condemn and change those parts he felt

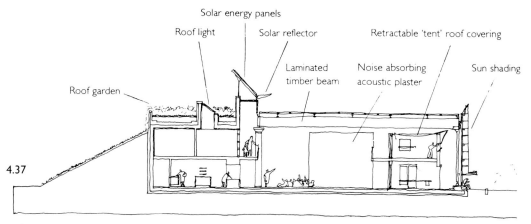

Solar energy panels

Roof light

Solar reflector

Retractable 'tent' roof covering

Laminated
timber beam

Noise absorbing
acoustic plaster

Sun shading

Roof garden

4.37

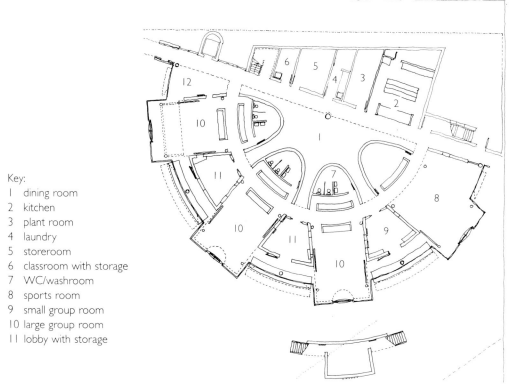

Key:
1 dining room
2 kitchen
3 plant room
4 laundry
5 storeroom
6 classroom with storage
7 WC/washroom
8 sports room
9 small group room
10 large group room
11 lobby with storage

4.38

4.37, 38 Plan and section of Frankfurt Sossenheim 'Kita' competition entry, designed by Arup Associates for low energy consumption. Here, the form is more clearly responsive to its orientation, with a solid north-facing wall covered in planted earth and, on the south, a double-skin glass wall reflecting daylight deep into the building and shielding traffic noise. This wall incorporates external daylight penetration reflectors above head height to direct daylight into the ground-floor rooms. It has internal glare-control louvres, split between high and low levels for independent control of daylight and glare.

Rectangular clear glass rooflights with sun-control louvres and night shutters are surrounded with translucent glass insulating roof. The roof incorporates internal screens to control high-summer sun-angle direct glare, but to maintain solar gain. Ventilation is supplied by a controllable variable-speed fan, linked to air-volume plant. Preheating from solar panels and the high thermal mass of the internal solar wall actively store heat, while heat recovery coils feed into the combined heat and electric power plant.

4.39

4.39, 40 Proctor Matthews's Limehouse Day Nursery, London Docklands: the external play space, and plan.

unhappy with throughout the construction process. Klaus Zillich saw it as a pilot scheme 'on producing architecture during the building process'. The end result is evidence of impeccable construction quality and attention to detail. However, the reality of financial stringency suggests that more economic approaches to producing children's architecture will be increasingly sought by public and private developers alike.

The city of Frankfurt, largely under the direction of city architect Roland Burgard, has completed 32 'Kitas' over the past ten years, with 18 more at the design stage. The 'Kita' building programme developed following the completion of a number of major new museum buildings in 1984. As they had high-quality architecture for the museums, it was felt to be equally important for the kindergarten programme: 'nothing is too expensive for our children', states Burgard. High-quality kindergartens set the standard for a child's entire life, therefore talented (but often untried) international architects were commissioned, and space standards were significantly increased. The results can be seen as some of the best examples of pre-school educational buildings in the world, and we make no excuse for featuring so many of the Frankfurt 'Kitas' here. However, the commissioning programme ground to a halt in 1993, as financial problems affected

line of play space roof

existing
play space

external play space

exist wc

base of
bell tower

exist
laundry

line of
steel truss

7.100

internal
play area

toy cupb'd

children's wc

stairs to
mezzanine
office

reception/
office

8.300

GROUND FLOOR

0   3m

N

4.40

4.41 Plan of the 'Playspace', Stratford, east London, by architects Hawkins–Brown.

Key:
1 training room
2 stationery store
3 store
4 wet play
5 crèche
6 play space
7 outline of mezzanine above
8 entrance area
9 training office
10 kitchen
11 cloakroom
12 disabled WC and baby change
13 adults' unisex WC
14 children's unisex WC
15 training library
16 store
17 office

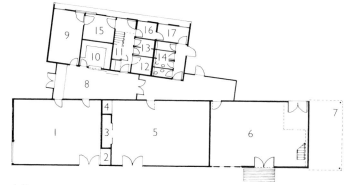

4.41

the city's spending plans.

Burgard's response is now to look towards the inventiveness of more locally based architects, who have come up with a range of economical proposals. By reducing space standards slightly, without sacrificing the complexity of the Kita programme, and adopting simple but well-built architecture, Burgard feels that quality will not be compromised too much. After the disappointing cancellation of a number of radical experimental projects, such as those by Arup Associates, Future Systems and Mecanoo, the claim sounds slightly hollow. Gimmicky proposals – such as recycled train carriages from the former East Germany, and the purchase of a ship called *Karl Marx* for £200 000, to be moored on the Main and fitted out as a child care centre – do not convince as genuine solutions to the needs of stable long-term, nursery school environments.

If necessity is the mother of invention, then British architects have to be particularly fertile in the provision of good, economical child care buildings.[35] Usually the success of these projects hinges on a number of factors: the involvement of architects themselves (usually young and committed) in all stages of the project, close consultation with the end users, and an adaptable and equally committed contractor. For example, Proctor Matthews' conversion of a railway arch in London's Docklands provides an economical extension to the existing Limehouse Day Nursery. An ingenious lightweight structural system enables minimal disturbance to the existing railway arch, as the structure is 'inserted' into it. This structure extends out and provides an architectural feature, a belltower, which becomes a focus within the secure play space. This simple and economic device links the new facility to the existing areas, and extends the range of spatial experiences available to the children, providing space for an additional 20 children at a cost of £1440 per m². The glazed Douglas fir screen enclosing the back of the arch is fixed in a deep steel lining to allow for the structural movement that occurs every time a train passes overhead. The noise and vibration is not disturbing to the children, who spend only two hours at a time there; one might take a less sanguine view if this was a full-day nursery school. Nevertheless, the use of leftover parcels of land in the commercial heart of our cities where land is at a premium not only supports working mothers, it helps to humanize our cities.

Also in east London, although on a reasonably generous site on the edge of an attractive park, architects Hawkins Brown have further developed their earlier standardized low-cost 'barn' solution at the Playcentre, Stratford.[36] The project comprises a child care training centre, a so-called 'play space' and a crèche. Although not spatially complex, the project is flexible and remarkably economical within the framework of a relaxed and elegant architectural form. Funds have been spread carefully: standardized fittings are used for lights and basins, but more money is spent on specially made doors and door handles. This the architects justified since the doors were touched and felt by the children; perhaps it was a reminder of the way in which small children value details and textures in a way that adults do not. The large play spaces utilized low-cost industrialized building techniques to create large open-plan areas, whereas a more conventional masonry construction technique was adopted for the more cellular accommodation. At a cost of approximately £600 per m² the project is clearly one that greatly benefits from this enforced economy. Similar costings were achieved by Education Design Group's more recent Roke Manor Nursery; here, a standardized steel frame is clad in timber to provide a warm, natural finish.

The two Amager projects in Copenhagen cost approximately £1 million per building. Each 'pavilion' has a total floor area of 698m²; the cost was approximately £1430 per m². The budget for one of the latest English nursery schools, Birchwood in Hatfield, Hertfordshire, is anticipated to be in the region of £600 000, providing 750m² of usable built space, at £800 per m². This economy is achieved by the adoption of a basic architectural style of pitched roofs and conventional brick/blockwork walls, ensuring that maintenance costs are minimized. It is not particularly inspiring architecturally, but it is cheap. However, by comparison, the cost of the Nant-y-Cwm Steiner Nursery by Christopher Day was tiny: it was completed for the price of between £280 and £300 per m² which even at 1988 prices is astonishing. However, the procurement process was complex and should be further explained.

The architect's commitment was essential to the realization of the building. Not only did he produce the design and oversee the works in excess of any commensurate fee, Day (whose children were attending the former school building at the time) was very much engaged in fundraising. Initially, 'gift labour' was used to excavate the foundations, and it was not until a parent lent

£1000 that it was possible to purchase the first building materials. The money went towards concrete for foundations, blocks and bricks, sand and cement. Several manufacturers offered very generous discounts on their products. Throughout the construction process there were about seven people working free of charge; on one occasion a group of 'travellers' helped. Eventually, people from at least 13 different countries donated their labour free of charge in order to complete the project.

In some months there was no money at all to buy materials; on occasion nails were removed from old planks in order to save on costs. Through the sale of crafts, handmade toys and the organization of other fundraising events, the project was kept alive during the two years of its construction. Unexpected donations from the USA, Germany and Holland helped. One donation of £1310 from an anonymous Swiss source augmented other donations ranging from £5 down to £1. The development also received a £2000 bank loan towards the end of the construction process.

Other examples of self-help projects, such as the Tijuana kindergarten and nursery school, utilize gift labour and the considerable ingenuity of the 'patron' to raise funds. The majority of Tijuana's people are young single parents, settling in the area to work in the new multinational factories. Christine Brady Kosko wanted to provide a beautiful kindergarten for this poor community living on the edge of the developed world. She rightly felt that this would benefit not only the children but also their mothers, who deserved to feel special after years of poverty and abuse.

James Hubbell, her chosen architect, was initially reluctant to take on the job, understandably perhaps since the budget was a meagre $80 000, and Hubbell's approach to architecture can be expensive. Having realized the significance of the project to the wellbeing of the community of Colonia Esperanza, however, he agreed to waive his fee and he regularly donated building materials at his own expense. Rather than an act of exploitation, the use of gift labour was organized in such a way that work on the project had something of a therapeutic healing effect: it re-engaged the mothers back into meaningful community activity, and ensured that their endeavours were creative and fulfilling.

Hubbell is not a trained architect. He studied painting and sculpture at Cranbrook, but has been involved in many building projects of a particular environmental quality. The sense that a piece of architecture can have innate beauty is always important in Hubbell's buildings. Recognition that the expressive, idiosyncratic quality of the architecture has an instant visual appeal – perhaps similar to that of the baroque for the uneducated peoples of 18th-century southern Germany – is of primary importance. This is not just because the local people associate with it so strongly, but also for very practical reasons: the main financial catalyst for the project, Christine Brady Kosko, who raises development finance from private individuals and groups from the USA through her 'Americas Foundation', admits that the peculiarly strong architectural statement gives identity to the community outside the Colonia. The power of art and architecture (combined with the sentimental appeal of very impoverished children), attracts sponsorship that would probably have failed to emerge for a lower-profile form of architecture.

Hubbell frequently adopts a self-build technique, working with people from the local community to decorate his buildings. However, as many as 1000 outsiders have come to Jardin de Niños la Esperanza over the years, working for periods of three to four days under the direction of Hubbell and Kosko. This, he believes, is an involvement which enriches their lives, too; it is the aesthetic quality of the experience, the involvement with craft-based creativity, that keeps these 'pilgrims' coming.

This spirit is reminiscent of the original aims and ideals of the kindergarten movements in the 19th and early 20th centuries, established by benevolent groups and individuals as a response to industrialization. Unlike those early initiatives, which were largely devoid of specific architectural value, the Jardin de Niños la Esperanza is an example of a similar benevolent process that holds at its core the idea that architecture can in itself contribute towards the social and spiritual improvement of young children, and also have financial benefits in the area of charitable fundraising – surely a commitment that should be welcomed with open arms. To make architecture cheap is one thing, to make it beautiful is truly miraculous!

Western economies should not be driven wholly by short-term financial considerations in choices as to how scarce resources are distributed.[37] Economy in pre-school care has a place, but not at the expense of high-quality environments. Full-day nursery education demands to be well resourced, and must command a solid, serious architectural response that does not float on a sea of whimsy or nostalgia. Whether it is in an organic

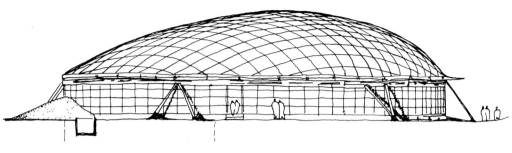

4.42

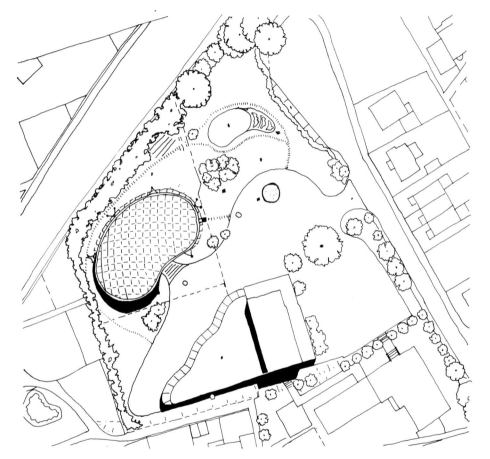

4.43

4.42, 43 South-west elevation and site plan of Frankfurt Sossenheim 'Kita' competition entry, designed by Future Systems, 1991. Unbuilt. The aim was to minimize the use of primary energy in the construction process and achieve a low level of operational energy. The organic form is a foil to the formality of the existing primary school, and creates a 'greenhouse' within which enclosed classrooms provide more cellular accommodation.

The wrapping consists of a roof with clear double-glazing to the south inclined at 60° to optimize the use of solar energy for light and heat, and insulated glazing to the north. During temperature extremes, a retractable fabric screen protects the occupants from both solar radiation and down draughts. On sunny days, a reservoir of hot air forms at high level, which is then circulated by a single fan, drawing hot air down through a number of flues to the classrooms. The 'stack effect' would dispose of surplus summer heat out through vents at the apex of the roof. The fan does not run under these conditions and external fabric blinds would control glare as required. During summer nights, the fan would run constantly, drawing cool night air through the cavity floor to pre-cool the high thermal mass of the concrete floor slabs.

or modernist style is a choice that can bond individuals into the decision-making process. Contextual variations enrich that process, and the immense long-term financial benfits to society have been well documented.

4.10 The 'green' nursery school: orientation

To complete this chapter we summarize environmental criteria which should lead to the creation of a 'green' nursery school. As with many aspects already discussed, low-energy design should be common to all new architecture. However, environmental considerations are particularly appropriate to the needs of young children on a number of levels: it is necessary to keep them warm and healthy at all times, in well-ventilated environments avoiding the use of hazardous or pollutant materials.[38] Acoustic considerations should be applied both internally and externally. Direct access to the garden from the activity areas is required, as are full-height windows through which small children can see. Rooflights are also valuable for variable daylight penetration and ventilation. A building which is physically open to the elements, yet remains warm and secure throughout the year, is the somewhat contradictory aspiration.

A 'green' nursery should be energy-efficient as well as healthy and safe. Passive solar design, with its romantic notion of natural-

4.44 Competition-winning entry for a low-energy Kindertagesstätte in Frankfurt Sossenheim by Mecanoo Architekten, Delft: adopts a fragmented, expressive architectural style, which is inherently low cost.

4.44

4.45

ism and holistically balanced environments, is particularly appropriate. Although more active environmental strategies have been explored, in the passive approach the intention is to maximize the use of the sun's energy for lighting and heating without resorting to elaborate mechanical equipment. The basic requirement to orientate activity areas directly onto the garden, with carefully considered sight lines and pathways, can be complemented by considering solar and daylighting factors. For example, windows will lose heat in winter and gain during the summer, unless double glazed with a 12mm or 25mm gap between the panes; low emissivity glass should be specified.

In Britain and other northern climates the optimum orienta-

4.45 The terrace at the UCLA Campus Child Care Center benefits from the warm Californian weather, extending the kindergarten space from classrooms out into the garden. Kindergartens in Denmark, Sweden and even the most northern parts of Norway use their gardens, almost oblivious of the weather. Suitable outdoor clothing is usually located in cloakrooms adjacent to the garden doors, so that children can move in and out easily. Surprisingly, this freedom is less evident in Britain, Germany and Italy, where access to gardens tended to be limited to short periods of time. This is a cultural difference, relating perhaps to the premium placed on light in the Scandinavian countries.

4.46

4.47

4.46 A more relaxed attitude to the external spaces prevails in many of the Italian and Spanish examples, where the climate and culture encourage protection from the sun, hence the need to stay indoors. However, an imaginatively designed covered terrace extends the shading out into the garden at the Crocetta nursery school in Modena.

4.47 This ivy-covered terrace dissipates the effect of the service rear of the kitchen in the Diane kindergarten at Reggio Emilia.

tion is generally one that allows sunlight both to external play areas and to the activity areas within the building. By orientating the main window areas to the south (plus or minus 30°) and avoiding overshadowing by other buildings, optimum solar penetration can be achieved. With a south orientation, windows should be a minimum of 30% and a maximum of 60% (although these figures should be adjusted to match regional requirements more precisely). With a higher percentage of glazing (from 50% upwards), it is necessary to provide shading, preferably externally, which should be designed in such a way that useful winter solar gains are not blocked out. Overheating is a particular problem

with glazing in west façades, when the time of peak solar radiation coincides with peak temperatures on midsummer afternoons. However, if full-size doors and windows on to the garden can be opened the effects of overheating can be neutralized. Glare from low-lying intense sun can also be a problem, and is more difficult to shade because the sun is at such a low altitude.

Internal overheating can be avoided by reducing solar gain through the roof, which can be achieved by good insulation and light, reflective surface colours. Windows can be shaded with roof overhangs, canopies, blinds and louvres, and the adoption of a high-thermal mass construction that will tend to soak up the

4.48 This Barcelona kindergarten, Escola Bressol La Mar, has a sun terrace on the first floor, elevated above the road, giving views to the sea.

4.48

heat rather than transmit it to the internal environment, as is the case with more lightweight constructions. This explains why it is so difficult to make lightweight pre-fabricated nurseries environmentally neutral. Through ventilation can be increased by the use of the stack effect, which entails the provision of higher outlets within the volume of the building; hot air rising will then force air upwards, where it can be expelled naturally. This is particularly useful where a deeper plan is adopted. With shallow-plan rooms, windows that can be locked open at nighttime provide a good natural summer cooling system.

Most energy-efficient measures can be installed economically if they are designed in at the start. An early dialogue between the needs of the staff and what is possible within the framework of the budget and building programme is vital. Sensible planning can achieve this. For example, sun spaces, atria and conservatories are very useful in extending and varying the environmental quality of space within the kindergarten. Small open courtyards contained within the plan of the buildiing can provide intimate space, which is sheltered and therefore usable on warm windy days. The 'hole' also provides light and ventilation in deep plan forms, and its proximity to the main activity areas enables it to be incorporated into the curriculum activities.

Daylight (as opposed to sunlight) comes from all directions of the compass; in overcast conditions it is strongest from the zenith. Rooflights can provide good daylight quality, particularly when mixed with window lighting. This combination can negate excessive contrast beween light and dark areas. Choice of interior colour will also effect light penetration, as well as the perception of contrast. However, rooflights can be a potential source of both cold draughts and overheating, unless they are well designed and provided with some form of external shading.

4.11 Heating

Enclosed atria can be beneficial by reducing heat loss from surrounding rooms, but energy-users if heated to the same temperature as the rest of the building. The best configuration for atria, as for internal courtyards, is for them to be within the form of the building rather than simply attached, and to be either unheated or background heated.

The selection of an efficient heating system is as important as built form in determining the building's energy costs and carbon

dioxide emissions. In kindergartens, heating systems need to be responsive to changes in external temperature and, most importantly, the heat emitters must be safe. Low-temperature radiators should be specified if they are exposed, and these should not have sharp metal plate edges. Hot pipes should be concealed or located above head height. Often conventional convector radiators can be used if they are concealed. For example, the Frankfurt Tiergarten 'Kita' uses an elegant boxed form around the ground-level window radiators, designed so that children can use them as sitting or playing benches. Wet central heating systems with condensing gas boilers that are temperature compensated would also be suitable. Although these will be more expensive than conventional boilers within three to five years, savings made on running costs will have repaid the difference. The heating supply to each space should be separately controlled, with full zone control and thermostats in each room with lockable radiator controls. It is important to provide variable heating output within different types of activity space, with higher temperatures for quiet activities and lower temperatures in more physical activity areas.

Warm air systems have been used with mixed results. In spaces that are used for more physical activities, they can be effective in quickly warming the air temperature; however, for more normal floor-play activities, advanced underfloor systems (often criticised in Britain as being unresponsive) are being successfully incorporated into new state-of-the-art German kindergartens. The technology now provides an ideal radiant heating source which, when combined with good ventilation, can provide an environment particularly suitable for younger babies and toddlers. Ideal environmental conditions can be achieved if underfloor heating is combined with a conventional convector system, although this should be designed carefully to provide a balanced, responsive and well-ventilated environment. Hot water may be provided either by point of use direct electricity, or by way of a storage tank powered by the central heating boiler. Both types require thermostatic mixers to ensure that hot water is not delivered above 40°.

4.12 Lighting

Lighting is particularly important in full-day facilities where children and teachers may be confined indoors during the winter

Activity areas

4.49 Sliding folding partitions and varnished ash wall panelling to a height of 2.5 metres provide pin-up space in this Frankfurt 'Kita'.

4.50 By comparison with Figures 51–53, this more conventional classroom has big windows that access directly on to the garden, and a sliding partition enabling the space to be divided. Table and floor activities are possible, and toys and materials are accessible to the children. However, the space is not too cluttered.

4.51 Plan of the Crocetta nursery school.

4.52 Intimate 'soft' areas in the Crocetta nursery school, Modena. The activity area or classroom is the secure base for the children, where their relationship with the smaller group and with individual teachers can develop without undue distraction. Ideally, the classroom should relate less to the needs of children for physical activity, and more to small group activities. This makes it important that the classroom is only one part of a larger children's environment, and that the activity areas do not exclude rumbustious, excitable play. Here, the converted stable block has been broken up by the insertion of low-level and full-height curved partitions.

4.53 The diverse range of spaces include those specially for physical activity.

4.49

4.52

4.50

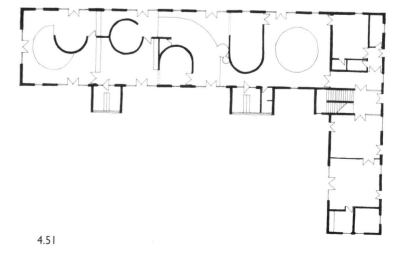

4.51

4.53

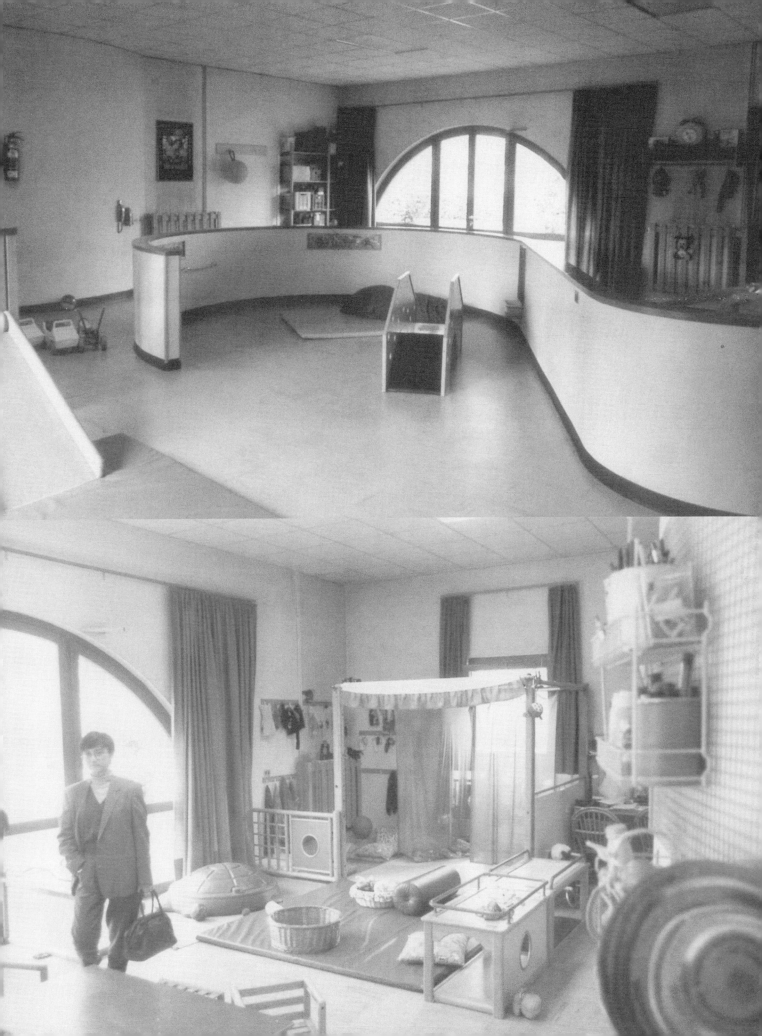

4.54 A timber pergola modifies the quality of light within a traditional urban playground at the Larminia First School, Hammersmith, London.

4.54

months. Lighting should be considered in domestic terms, avoiding simple unilateral approaches. For example, the effects on health of flicker from conventional fluorescent sources are now widely known. Given the soft, intimate atmosphere desirable in many of the kindergarten spaces, bare fluorescent lighting tubes would be unsuitable.

Today's domestic lighting is sophisticated and has a considerable effect on our perceptions of space. A combination of downward and lateral lighting to create a gentle ambient level of 50 lux minimum, providing modelling to spaces, can be achieved in a variety of ways. High-frequency low-energy compact fluorescent fittings, when enclosed in a lampshade or holder, use 80% less power than the tungsten equivalent but are virtually indistinguishable in their effect. In play areas higher levels of illumination, of around 150 lux, will be necessary. Since activities such as painting and reading would require task lighting in the home setting, a safe representation of this is also required within the modern nursery school. The selection of two types of lighting is desirable, so lateral light can be projected from wall lights and ceiling-mounted spotlights, or indirectly from wall and ceiling 'washers'.

While a minimum level of lighting is needed for all areas, total uniformity is undesirable. Particular walls can be highlighted with focused task lighting. In a refurbishment with high ceilings, suspended downlighters can be used to reduce the apparant height of the space. Sparkle and brilliance can be provided to highlight an entrance area or to light a display, with the use of low-voltage tungsten halogen lamps. More efficient than tungsten lights, these have a whiter, brighter appearance. They are used extensively in the UCLA campus nursery, and architect Elizabeth Lee believes they are much more gentle as a source because they 'glow' or 'hum' in a soothing way. A child care centre in Bologna uses halogen lights externally, which reflect back into the central space through the rooflights. However, it is generally felt that these should not be used exclusively as they will tend to be too bright and visually cold; also they give off a lot of heat.

All nurseries should have lighting that is controllable and allows for different options. Lighting can provide surprising spatial variety, and teachers can adjust it to the changing moods of the children to create a cosy warmth for sleeping or quieter activities, or more vibrant, higher levels for periods of physical activity. Low-energy lights, high-frequency fluorescents and low-voltage tungsten can all be dimmed. At the relatively low levels of illumina-

tion required for kindergartens, lamps with a warm appearance feel most comfortable. In the Nant-y-Cwm Steiner Nursery, artificial light has been designed to be as playful as the rest of the building. Each room has a central pendulum lamp with a single white pear shade, supplemented with wall-mounted lanterns. These are standard fittings modified by purpose-made shades, constructed of timber sticks lashed together with pink or yellow material hand sewn in soft, billowing shapes. They provide customized lighting, which is warm, cosy and cheap, yet in harmony with the setting and architectural philosophy of the building.

Anita Rui Olds draws analogies to nature, suggesting the use of full-spectrum bulbs to approximate the range of wavelengths provided by sunshine. These, she states, should replace standard fluorescent and tungsten bulbs, and should be balanced, washing light up and down the walls and reflecting it from the ceiling planes: 'a means of stimulating the experience in nature of being surrounded by light'.[39]

4.13 Summary

Jørgen Raun who, together with Ulla Poulsen, designed the award-winning child care centre in Amager, Copenhagen, is happy to return to the building a year after it was opened to discuss design problems with parents and teachers. He feels this consultation not only helps him as a designer to avoid mistakes in future kindergarten projects, but also enables problems to be rectified within the framework of the existing building. However, the architect's idea or overall conception should not be compromised. As Raun states, 'The primary gift architects have is that they have a horizontal as well as a vertical perspective. You don't get that from non-architects.'

Where experiments have been carried out that involved parents and teachers in the actual design process, the end result has not been wholly convincing. For example, experiments in staff-planned layouts during the early 1980s in Sweden resulted in a number of built projects of extremely limited architectural quality. Rather than benefiting from the imaginative potential of untrained architects, the limitations of the systems necessary for the communication of architectural ideas brought about badly proportioned rooms of a poor spatial quality, lacking any real sense of volume, scale or light. The projects were one-dimensional, concentrating the minds of the participating designers on purely functional or organizational issues.

The 'hands on' child-centred experience of teachers, care workers and educational theorists certainly holds important lessons, which should not be ignored by the designers of pre-school buildings. Their experiences can help to prevent practical mistakes during the development of the design, while producing a less didactic form of architecture. More importantly, through

consultation and the gradual adaptation of the building fabric, sometimes over a period of some years, architectural quality can emerge which suits the needs of children more precisely. This process can validate the use of less architecturally extreme forms, but requires the ongoing commitment of teachers and flexible financial structures to enable on-going change to be built into the funding process.

One must therefore support a degree of professional élitism in the design of kindergartens On balance, it is not a good thing to try to design the kindergarten through the end users. Further evidence of this can be empirically deduced from discussions with many of those architects who have projects featured in this volume. The design process has not primarily been one of close consultation, rather the adoption of a strong architectural philosophy from the outset which was subsequently tailored to the practical and pedagogic needs of the teachers and children. The inherently radical nature of designing for children supports this view, and it is the flexibilty of the architecture, the possibility for its later adaptation and change, that is often a key factor in its long-term success.

The best kindergarten architecture has been produced by largely strong, independent architectural concepts. Of course, functional issues are important, and it is required that architects 'get it right'. This implies that the architect–client relationship must be supported by a city or regional authority, which respects the design intentions of the architect, but can also guide and direct the designer in basic areas of safety and functionality. For example, Ulla Poulsen states that the Copenhagen Municipal Architects' Department gave invaluable practical expertise, but they also had the experience to respect the architect's creative process. The end result was a radical building, with very few practical faults.

Our modern, adult-orientated world is punctuated by overt time structures which are meaningless to young children. The way in which time passes is the most important issue. Kindergarten time is structured by activity: if a range of activities supported by a stimulating environment do not sustain the child's fascination or attention, then boredom may make the day interminable. While some passages of boredom are inevitable, the child's developing ability to engage in new interests will be encouraged by games or fantasies that can be sustained. The oft-quoted cliché, that it is not duration but quality that structures the life of the young child, is echoed by the Danish theorist Torben Hangard Rasmussen when he states that:

> where the child is bored, is missing a parent, is teased, or interrupted in exciting play, then time appears from nowhere. Then time is suddenly a mood or feeling that takes over the child. A bored child feels a time that is barren of possibility. The empty moments announce their presence waiting to be filled.[40]

Our terms of reference within this section have been deliberately eclectic, drawing from functional and philosophical sources to illustrate that designing for children can never be rationalized down to a few simple criteria. Each context requires a different and particular response which is aimed at the replication of complexities within the real world. We have summarized a number of factors we believe to be important in raising the quality of life for children in all-day kindergartens. Spaces like art studios and water play areas; environmental and aesthetic factors, like light and colour; moral or social lessons, which can be enhanced by architecture, such as the group meal (cooked and prepared on the premises from fresh ingredients); lessons from radical 'green architecture', or special spaces for children like niches and dens — all of these can help to prevent distraction and aid concentration to make an authentic architecture for children.

References and notes

1. Schmitt, Peter (1995), 'A Prolegomenon to Designing a Learning Environment', *Caravan*, no. 2, March 1995, section 2, p. 9.
2. 'Nurseries by Adaptation', paper presented to Nottinghamshire Education Department, 9 July 1992, ref. no. D40R01, p. 1.
3. Bidsrube, Vibeke (1993), *Children and Square Metres*, Copenhagen, Paedagogisk Bogklub. It is worth noting that miserly space standards in Danish kindergartens have long been a source of general concern, which this study helped to reinforce in a somewhat preconceived way.
4. Kritchevsky, S. and Prescott, E. *et al.* (1969), *Physical Space: Planning Environments for Young Children*, Washington, DC, National Association for the Education of Young Children, p. 15.
5. Rui Olds, A. *et al.* (1987), 'Designing Settings for Infants and Toddlers', in C.S. Wein-stein and T.G. David (eds.), *Spaces for Children — The Built Environment and Child Development*, Plenum Press, p. 120.
6. European Commission Childcare Network, 'Quality in Services for Young Children'.
7. Claus Jensen presented a paper at a seminar entitled 'Two Views of Quality in Early Childhood Services' at the Institute of Education, University of London, 12 September 1994. They have been slightly reorganized here, but accurately reflect his view.
8. Morris-Nunn, Robert (1994), 'Building Magical Realism', paper presented at the Royal Institute of Australian Architects' bi-annual conferenc, Hobart.
9. This section is paraphrased from Csikszentmihalyi, Mihaly and Rochberg-Halton, Eugene (1981), *The Meaning of Things: Domestic Symbols and the Self*, Cambridge University Press, p. 21.
10. *Spaces for Children, op. cit.*, p. 137.
11. The space is within the kindergarten building and is 'public' to all the children, but not to others from the outside world.
12. Bachelard, Gaston (1969), *The Poetics of Space*, Boston MA, Beacon Press, p. 16.
13. Curtis, Audrey (1964), *A Curriculum for the Pre-school Child*, NFER–Nelson, p. 120.
14. Selmer-Olsen, Ivar (1993), 'Children's Culture and Adult Presentation of this Culture', *International Play Journal*, vol. 1, no. 3, September 1993, p. 201.
15. An example of a child-only space can be found in 'the blue room' in Børnehuset Herluf Trollesgade 23, 8200 Aarhuis N., Denmark, which was featured on the European Childcare Network video, 'Can You Feel the Colour?', March 1994.
16. Prescott, E. *et al.* (1987), 'Environment as Organiser in Child Care Settings', in Rui Olds, *op. cit.*, p. 85.
17. Dwyer, Julia (1995), 'Giancarlo and Matrix', *Caravan*, no. 2, March 1995, section 3, p. 3.
18. From a briefing document written by architect Rudolphe Luscher
19. It is important to maintain a generally higher temperature for children's swimming pools than for adult ones.
20. 'Reva Klein Visits the Vanessa Nursery, Founded 21 Years Ago by the Actress Who Gave it its Name', *Times Educational Supplement*, London, 7 October, 1994, p. 6.
21. Fiske, D.W. and Maddi, S.R. (1961), *Functions of Varied Experience*, Homewood IL, Dorsey.
22. Noren-Bjorn, Eva (1982), *Why? The Impossible Playground*, vol. 1: *A Trilogy of Play*, New York, Leisure Press p. 32; quoted in Whitelaw, Lindsey (1995), 'A World of their Own', *Caravan*, no. 2, March 1995, section 1, p. 11.
23. Whitelaw, Lindsey (1995), 'A World of Their Own', *op. cit.*, p. 13.
24. Malaguzzi, Loris (1987), *I Cento Linguaggi dei Bambini* [The Hundred Languages of Children], narrative of the possible: proposals and intuitions of children from the infant and toddler centres and pre-schools of the city of Reggio Emilia, exhibition catalogue by the City of Reggio Emilia Dept of Education, Modena, p. 23.
25. From the Pacific Oaks Children's School prospectus, 714 West California Boulevard, Pasadena, California 91105.
26. Severini, Gino, quoted in Hertzberger, Herman, van Roijen-Wortmann, Addie and Strauven, Francis (1982), *Aldo Van Eyck*, Amsterdam, Stichting Wonen/Van Loghum Slaterus, p. 89. Reference to van Eyck's Nagele School is on p. 80.
27. Schmitt, Peter, *op. cit.*, p. 12.

28. The analogy between painting and music was something of an obsession for intellectuals in the late 19th and early 20th centuries. Today, similar analogies are frequently drawn between music and modern architecture. See Vergo, Peter (1980), 'Music and Abstract Painting', in *Towards a New Art*, London.

29. Austin, David (1972), 'The Moral Effect of Colour in Space and Form', dissertation presented to Brighton Polytechnic School of Architecture and Interior Design, July 1972; colour analysis from Appendix 1.

30. All quotations in this paragraph are taken from a paper by Christopher Day and kindly reproduced in *Caravan,* June 1995, section 1, p. 17.

31. Austin, David, *op. cit.*

32. Gage, John (1993), 'Colours of the Mind: Goethe's Legacy', in *Colour and Culture – Practice and Meaning from Antiquity to Abstraction*, London, Thames & Hudson, p. 203.

33. Steiner, Rudolf, 'Ways to a New Style in Architecture', quoted in Austin, David, *op. cit.*, p. 4.

34. Kandinsky, Wassily, quoted in Gage, John, *op. cit.*, p. 207, and see p. 293, n. 107. Also see Gage, John (1980), 'The Psychological Background to Early Modern Colour', in *Towards a New Art, op. cit.*

35. Playgroups, crèches and workplace nurseries are defined as being part of the private and voluntary sector in Britain. A playgroup is controlled by the local authority but does not usually provide structured educational curricula. Its typical context is a non-specific building, such as the local community centre or the home of a parent or care worker; as such it is a form that is physically incapable of providing an adequate service to the young child in full-time nursery education.

36. 'Child's Play at Newham', *Architect's Journal*, 6 February 1991, pp. 22–5, 41–3.

37. We make an unashamedly political point here. The Lloyds Insurance Company invested £120 million in the construction of their new headquarters in the City of London in 1981. Each one of the toilet pods reputedly cost £35 000. As the Lloyds insurance market continues to lose billions annually – money that is presumably coming from within the British economy – Nottinghamshire Local Education Authority boasted about their ability to provide a single converted nursery unit for 50 children for the same sum as the aforementioned toilet pod.

38. Young children are susceptible to emissions of indoor pollutants such as volatile organic chemicals. Timber products, medium dense fibreboard, chipboard and plywood all contain the most common indoor pollutant formaldehyde. Water-based or organic paints should be specified.

39. *Spaces for Children, op. cit.*, p. 123.

40. Selmer-Olsen, *op. cit.*, p. 193.

The Projects

The Projects

Organic/metaphorical

Nant-y-Cwm Steiner Nursery, Llanycefn, Wales:
Christopher Day Associates

Heddernheim-Nord Kindertagesstätte, Frankfurt, Germany:
Friedensreich Hundertwasser

Jardin de Niños la Esperanza, Tijuana, Mexico:
James T. Hubbell

Børneinstitutioner, Amager, Copenhagen, Denmark:
Arkitekttegnestuen Virumgård

Luginsland Kindergarten, Stuttgart, Germany:
Behnisch and Partner

Bungawitta Children's Centre, Launceston, Tasmania, Australia:
Robert Morris-Nunn

Bornehaven 'De Fire Arstider:
Helle Grangaard

Late modern

Corning Child Development Center:
Mack Scogin and Merrill Elam

UCLA Child Care Center, Los Angeles, California:
Charles and Elizabeth Lee

Eckenheim-Sud Kindertagesstätte, Frankfurt, Germany:
Toyo Ito and Associates

Greisheim-Sud Kindertagesstätte, Frankfurt, Germany:
Bolles Wilson and Partner

Centre de Vie Enfantine, Lausanne, Switzerland:
Rudolphe Luscher

Stensby Personalbarnehage, Akerhus, Norway:
Kristin Jarmund AS

Lützowstrasse 'Kita', Tiergarten, Berlin, Germany:
Klaus Zillich

Contextual

Gross-Ziethener Chausee Kindertagesstätte, Berlin, Germany:
Duebtzer and König

Open-Air Kindergarten Annexe, Takarazuka, Japan:
Katsuhiro Miyamoto and Atelier Cinquième Architects

Scuola dell' Infanzia Diane, Reggio Emilia, Italy:
Loris Malaguzzi / Municipal Architects' Dept, Reggio Emilia

Børnehus, Viborg Seminariet, Denmark:
Petersen and Aaris

Scuola dell' Infanzia e Asilo-nido Cantalamessa, Bologna, Italy:
Stefano Magagni / City of Bologna

Neugereut Kindergarten, Stuttgart, Germany:
Behnisch and Partner

Introduction

Our selection criteria for these projects is that they are contemporary, having been largely designed and built over the last five years (with a few important exceptions), and that they exhibit design excellence – for us this means that they are innovative, either in social or technical terms; exhibit what we consider to be radical stylistic tendencies, or are particularly responsive to the needs of the pre-school educational curriculum. The following examples are organized in categories relating to architectural/educational themes rather than on the basis of their geographical location.

For example, two projects designed by the same architect, Günther Behnisch, and located in the same city, Stuttgart, are featured in different categories. Their importance in the context of this publication lies not in any regional significance (which they undoubtedly exhibit), but as exemplars of a particular theoretical approach to kindergarten architecture.

We celebrate here diversity and imagination rather than predetermined rules and regulations. This rich diversity can be best illustrated in the section on organic projects which are all to some degree influenced by early romantic notions primarily associated with Froebel. However, of the six projects illustrated in that section, only two are Steiner schools. The other four may show to varying degrees the value of a strong personal architectural and pedagogic philosophy. We believe that this encourages functional and spatial comparisons. Ultimately, the pleasure of this lies in the rich architectural diversity exhibited within the framework of a distinctive new building type: the contemporary kindergarten.

The examples are organized in the following categories:

- organic/metaphorical: naturalistic or spiritualistic concerns, exemplified by the Steiner schools, or those using less extreme symbolic or metaphorical forms that are nevertheless expressionistic.
- late modern: technologically advanced, functionally explicit or predominantly concerned with Modern Movement ideas relating to social or health aspirations.
- contextual: buildings that develop primarily from their integration into a particular urban context, whether that is a physical or a programmatic integration. This includes conversions and extensions to existing buildings, which may adopt any of the above styles within the framework of an existing building or context.

There is inevitably a degree of overlap between the categories defined above. Area analysis is as accurate as possible and indicated as nett usable area. Storage areas are measured as fixed rooms or cupboards occupying part of the floor plan rather than moveable cupboards or open-plan cloakroom areas, which form part of the larger environment. 'Activity area' analysis relates to measured areas of class-based enclosed rooms, as opposed to open-plan play spaces. Garden areas relate to usable play space. Area per child figures take the total nett floor area of each facility, including administration areas, and divide this by the maximum number of children who may be in attendance at any one time. An architects' statement is included where the author feels it is appropriate, and any particularly significant features illustrating a strong educational–architectural convergence are noted at the end of the text.

The Nant-y-Cwm Steiner Nursery, Llanycefn, Wales

Architect: Christopher Day Associates, Crymych, Wales.

Client: a cooperative group of parents from the original Steiner playgroup.

Occupancy: 30 children in two groups of 14 (class A) and 16 (class B), part-time attending for morning and afternoon sessions, four- to six-year-olds.

Construction cost: £300 per m², approximately £36,000. Note: the contract was carried out using self-build techniques and gift labour.

Construction: rendered cavity blockwork walls, timber roof structure with 'breathing' turf roof cover.

Completed: September 1991.

Classrooms: 56m². Storage: 8m². Total area: 102.5m², 6.8m² per child (15 children). Garden area: approx. 0.25ha.

Parking: none, but parking available 75m away with the main school building.

Children's play is no luxurious indulgence. It is an outward manifestation of of how they feel, of the inner processes they are going through. We can prohibit aggressive or anti-social play but, unless we can transform it, we are only suppressing disharmonies within the child and risking thereby a growth of a psychological or physiological disturbance. An underlying requirement for any building for small children is, then, that it is as magical and full of reverent wonder as an ancient fairy tale.[1] *Christopher Day*

Nant-y-Cwm Nursery is located five miles south of the village of Llanycefn on the edge of a woodland overlooking a swift-flowing river. The architect adopted a clear philosophical approach, which is wholly in tune with the ideas of Rudolf Steiner. The building sits on the edge of a hedgerow facing on to a clear part of the wooded site. It was important to avoid the removal of any existing vegetation and retain almost untouched the considerable charms of the site. So the building blends into this natural topography, with warm earth-coloured walls and a rustic, overgrown turf roof.

Because of its integration into the landscape, the scale of the building is at first sight deceptive, appearing to be much smaller from the outside than it is. Entering the site from the country road through a low latch-gate 'carved' out of the existing hedgerow, a level play area opens up, to the right of which sits the building. This is a sort of threshold, prior to the more rugged landscape beyond. The idea of establishing a series of threshold conditions was an important generating principle. The notion of departing from the noisy synthetic outside world and entering a much more harmonious and organic environment is reinforced by the overgrown gateway, then by the slightly flattened courtyard within and finally by the entrance to the building itself. Thus the porch is set asymmetrically, recessed into the wall and forming its own inviting shelter.

Once within, the scale of the building appears to enlarge as if by magic. The colours – light yellows, ochres and crimsons – enhance the curving forms. It is reminiscent of the image of a child's cave – cosy, warm and moulded to human contours. Despite the rather small window openings, it is surprisingly well lit. To the immediate left of the entrance is a room originally intended to be the staffroom, but now used as a coat room; with the heating boiler, it is like a breathing heart where the chil-

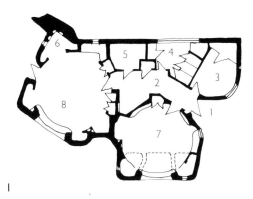

1 Plan.
Key:
1 entrance
2 lobby
3 staff/cloaks
4 toilets
5 store
6 alcove
7 classroom a
8 classroom b

2 Interior view of classroom b, showing the large alcove.

3 Section.

4 South-west elevation.

1

2

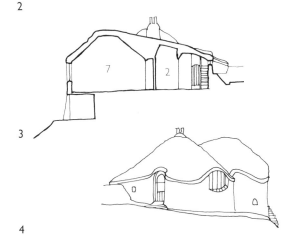

3

4

dren discard their external coats and shoes and change into a more appropriate reflective mood, for indoor creative activities. Along the walls of the entrance corridor are small shelves and niches, and a parents' noticeboard.

The Steiner principle emphasizes that toys and other synthetic distractions should be minimized; instead, children should play through their own creative endeavours. Both classrooms are circular, and designed to enhance sociable games. However, they are not complete circles, but rather circles with corners and alcoves which, according to Day, give the space a more humane quality than the geometrical purity of the simple circle. It is a subtle but profoundly important distinction. Similar subtlety can be seen in the way in which the rough, rendered walls have been painted. After whitewashing they are given gossamer-

The Nant-y-Cwm Steiner Nursery, Llanycefn, Wales

5 Detailed cutaway isometric drawing, showing the earth roof construction with the insulated wall.

Key:
1 topsoil
2 old hay stuffed twine
3 scrap carpet on steep slopes for moisture retention and to avoid slippage
4 palpropylene twine at 200mm CRS
5 100mm long round wooden pegs
6 12mm dia bar in 150 ×150mm concrete kurb
7 225 × 25mm treated sw fascia board
8 10mm ventilation slot
9 double glazed window units
10 2 layers natural slate with neat cement fill sitting on 1:4 motar
11 1:1:5 render coated with limed-based vells combined with earth colours
12 undersheet: polyester reinforced bituminous felt with bituminous mastic 100mm sealed laps, all fixed with galvanised clout nails at 150mm CRS along top edges
13 topsheet pitch elastomer membrane clout nails at 150mm CRS and 50mm CRS along top edges
14 old hay
15 galv EMI
16 220mm upstand
17 32mm dia vent holes
18 1200mm dia apex disc
19 100mm × 75mm sw members
20 rafters in compression on apex disc
21 18mm sheathing plywood

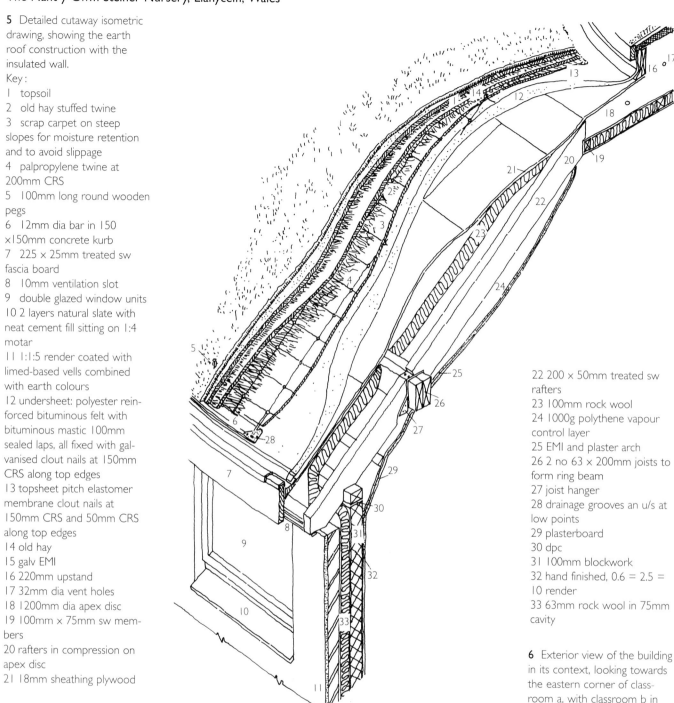

22 200 × 50mm treated sw rafters
23 100mm rock wool
24 1000g polythene vapour control layer
25 EMI and plaster arch
26 2 no 63 × 200mm joists to form ring beam
27 joist hanger
28 drainage grooves an u/s at low points
29 plasterboard
30 dpc
31 100mm blockwork
32 hand finished, 0.6 = 2.5 = 10 render
33 63mm rock wool in 75mm cavity

6 Exterior view of the building in its context, looking towards the eastern corner of classroom a, with classroom b in the foreground.

5

thin layers of pink pigment applied with a 'lazure' technique, veils so thin that they are barely visible. This layering creates a subtle, glowing effect.

The structure and fabric of the building, like its form, were intended to be as natural and ecologically sound as possible. The masonry walls are heavily insulated to provide an average 'U' value of 0.35 (walls and roof) The external render is a 1:1:6 mix, coated with veils (washes) of a lime–milk formulation intended to allow the fabric to 'breathe'. The architect was determined to match the walls with a roof structure that would

be equally organic, and it is covered in earth. Because the roof pitch is as steep as 39°, a twine net is incorporated to discourage soil slumping. An edge kerb helps further to keep the turf in place, and the drainage gutter is formed against this edge upstand. Wild flowers were planted on the roof to complete the detail design of a building wholly in tune with its natural setting and, as Christopher Day would have us believe, with the educational needs of pre-school children.

Special significance: it is the archetypal Steiner kindergarten.

Heddernheim-Nord Kindertagesstätte, Frankfurt

Architect: Friedensreich Hundertwasser, Vienna, with Ursula Gandoura and Beck, Gravert, Schneider, Frankfurt (construction architects).

Client: City of Frankfurt.

Occupancy: 60 pre-school (three- to six-year-olds) and afternoon study spaces for 40 schoolchildren (Kinderhort).

Construction: brick/blockwork walls rendered and tiled with a cast concrete structural frame, a flat and sloping earth-covered roof with zinc cupolas.

Completed: 1994.

Classroom/activity areas: 360m². Storage: 8m². Total area: 780m², 7.8m² per child. Garden area: not known.

Parking: none.

Study the plans of this 'Kita' and try to locate the entrance. Draw an axonometric (a three-dimensional plan projection to scale) and you have a disconnected collage of columns, stairs and windows that seem to float indeterminably. Attempts to represent this building in the language of contemporary architectural theory is very difficult. It disregards conventional rules and adopts an extremely playful, almost naive form.

This, one suspects, is neither a surprise nor a matter of regret to environmental artist Friedensreich Hundertwasser, who designed this building in 1989. Indeed, he would probably be pleased to hear the indignant response of most architects (including this critic) and other building professionals, who find it irrational, wilful – almost absurd. Especially so when considering

1

2

1 North-facing entrance, elevation: an unfinished collage of eccentric forms which challenge adult perceptions of architecture.

2 View from the street, with turf-covered roof moulded gently into the meadowlands.

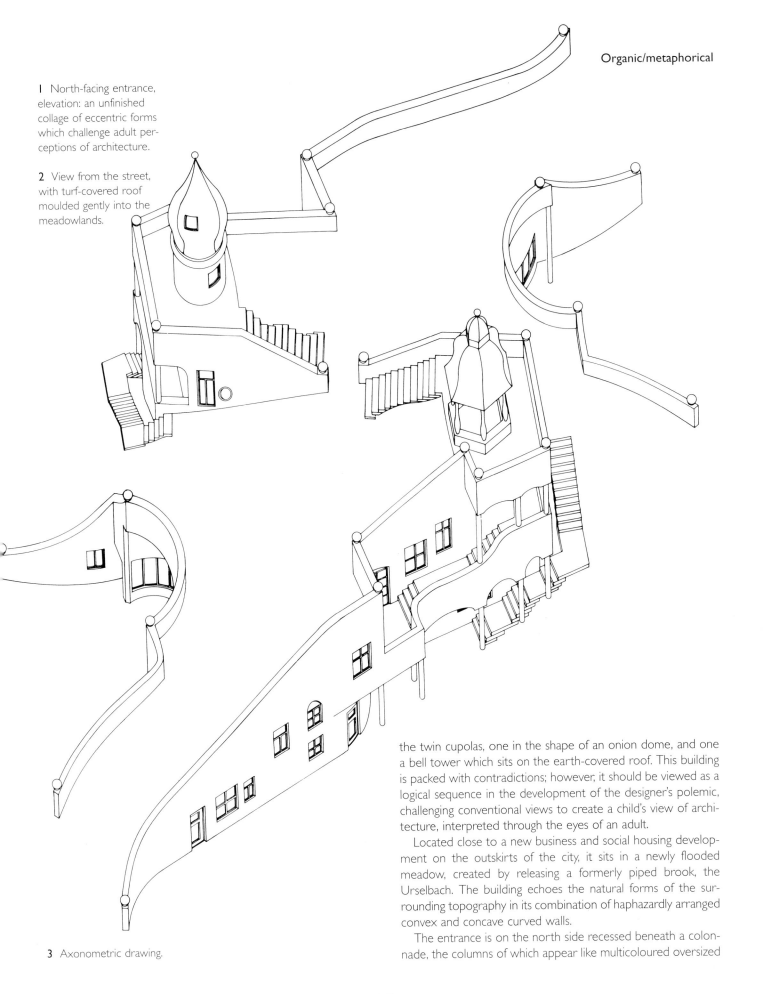

3 Axonometric drawing.

the twin cupolas, one in the shape of an onion dome, and one a bell tower which sits on the earth-covered roof. This building is packed with contradictions; however, it should be viewed as a logical sequence in the development of the designer's polemic, challenging conventional views to create a child's view of architecture, interpreted through the eyes of an adult.

Located close to a new business and social housing development on the outskirts of the city, it sits in a newly flooded meadow, created by releasing a formerly piped brook, the Urselbach. The building echoes the natural forms of the surrounding topography in its combination of haphazardly arranged convex and concave curved walls.

The entrance is on the north side recessed beneath a colonnade, the columns of which appear like multicoloured oversized

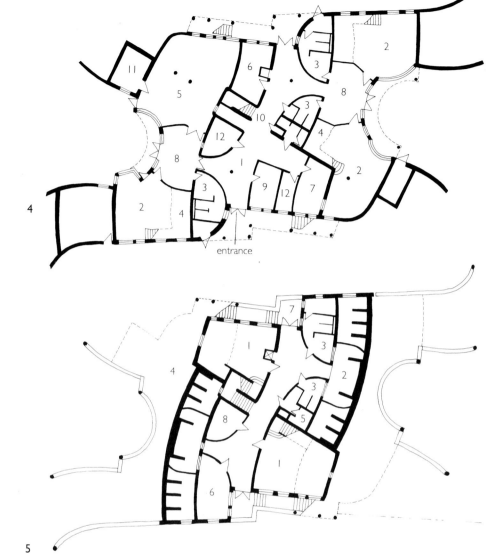

4 Plan, ground-floor/basement.
Key:
1 entrance hall
2 activity area/group room
3 washroom/WC
4 ground floor gallery areas
5 multipurpose room
6 kitchen with lift
7 head teacher's room
8 cloakroom/lobby
9 staffroom
10 stair to first floor
11 plant room/heating
12 storage

5 Plan, first-floor (Kinderhort).
Key:
1 activity area/group room
2 cloakroom
3 washroom/WC
4 external terrace
5 storeroom
6 workroom/kitchen
7 access to roof terrace
8 storage

6 Entrance elevation.

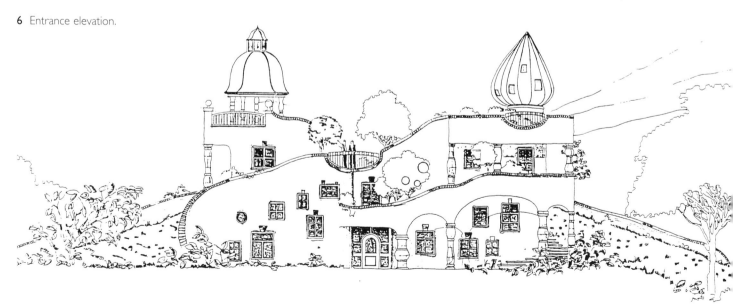

7

balustrades. Virtually every window in this chaotic elevation is different, with circular, square and rectangular shapes. Doors and windows have keystone shapes painted onto the exposed concrete walls, while brickwork appears on the second-floor parapet. White flashes of mosaic tiling run across the brown concrete of the walls; it has an incompleteness which suggests that the original intention was to cover the whole wall surface with these mosaics.

Once inside the entrance colonnade, a meandering internal corridor links the accommodation from north to south. In front of each of the kindergarten activity areas is a cloakroom lobby space which overlooks an external terrace. This terrace is formed by a deeply scalloped cut into the side of the form. The activity spaces themselves all have a first-floor gallery, accessed by a staircase decorated with a frieze of blue and black ceramic tiles.

There are three 'group rooms' and an additional multipurpose space on the ground floor. An internal staircase leads up to the first-floor Kinderhort (afternoon study spaces for older children), where there are two more group rooms with terrace links out on to the grassed roof. Here, there are two separate study spaces located beneath the cupolas, with views out over the surrounding countryside.

Some of the interior spaces seem quite dark, due to the depth of the plan and the relatively small window-to-wall ratio. However, with its thick turf roof and massive construction, the building is highly insulated and economical. In addition, some of the external walls are ill-defined, with exposed concrete retaining walls of an unfinished quality. Although nature tends to repair its damaged parts, this building is yet to sink back into the landscape in the way its designer intended. As we write, the project is yet to be inhabited, as there are problems of site soil contamination.

Clearly, time will tell whether or not this is a successful environment for children. However, one has to admire the choice of the City of Frankfurt in building this design. It is a radical example of children's architecture that attempts to reassert the importance of nature, touching upon Froebel's and Steiner's philosophies. It is a timely, if experimental, restatement of those romantic child-centred values in which, it might be said, architecture no longer stands apart from nature.

8 Section through multipurpose hall.

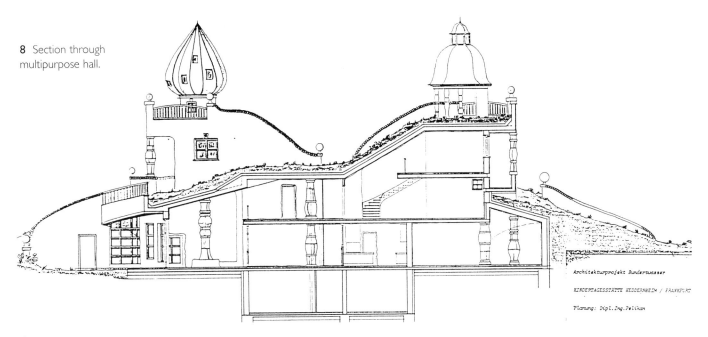

8

Jardin de Niños la Esperanza, Tijuana

Architect: James T. Hubbell, San Diego, California.

Client: The Americas Foundation [Fundacion de Las Americas], charitable foundation.

Occupancy: 120 children in two sessions, 20 children in each of three classrooms for three- and four-year-olds.

Construction cost: approximately $53 000. Note: gift labour involved parents in the beautifying process.

Construction: in situ concrete shell cast on to steel mesh reinforcements, decorated with ceramic tiles.

Completed: June 1992.

Classrooms: 85m² (including covered loggia). Storage: 13m². Total area: 140m², 2.3m² per child. Courtyard area: 240m².

Parking: none.

This kindergarten for the impoverished children of Tijuana has involved over 1000 helpers during the course of its construction. It sits within the decayed urban landscape of this Mexican border town like a small jewel, projecting positive feelings for the children, their mothers and the wider community (many of whom assisted in its decoration). The plan of the building is simple. The square site is bounded by a high wall. Within it the architect/artist orientated the new building diagonally across the site with classroom windows facing towards the southeast. An existing building, the south wing, was incorporated into the structure, providing accommodation for the third classroom, a doctor's office and a community kitchen for parents and visitors.

The heat of the midday sun is tempered by a deep colonnade which sweeps elegantly down towards the ground from the heavy concrete roof. The form appears like a pristine white frog, squat yet lithe and dynamic. The scallop-shaped roof collects water during the rainy season and channels it down where it can be collected or left to run off and irrigate the courtyard planting. The new structure is practical and elegant.

The building focuses on the courtyard, at the heart of which is a so-called 'story tree'. When this has grown further, it will provide additional shading; however, it also forms a focus for the external classroom, a symbolic natural reference in this arid,

1

2

1 Classroom three, with more formal 'lessons' taking place than would normally be the case for young pre-school children in the USA and Europe. Note the homemade light shade.

2 View of Tijuana from the site.

3 View of the new building nearing completion; the story tree has just been planted in the centre.

3

4 Ground-floor plan.
Key:
1 classroom one
2 classroom two
3 classroom three
4 doctor
5 community kitchen
6 outdoor play area and barbecue
7 story tree
8 office
9 storage
10 toilet
11 outdoor classroom

entrance

4

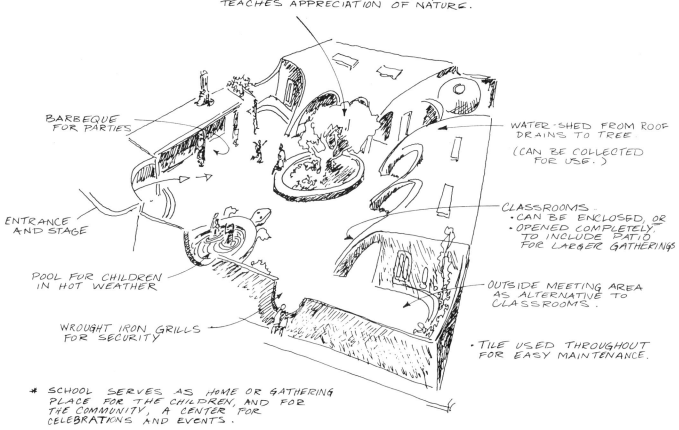

STORY TREE - CENTRAL ELEMENT OF SITE,
- BUILDING RADIATES FROM TREE

* FOCUSES ATTENTION TO TREE, AND TEACHES APPRECIATION OF NATURE.

BARBEQUE FOR PARTIES

WATER-SHED FROM ROOF DRAINS TO TREE. (CAN BE COLLECTED FOR USE.)

ENTRANCE AND STAGE

CLASSROOMS.
· CAN BE ENCLOSED, OR
· OPENED COMPLETELY, TO INCLUDE PATIO FOR LARGER GATHERINGS

POOL FOR CHILDREN IN HOT WEATHER

OUTSIDE MEETING AREA AS ALTERNATIVE TO CLASSROOMS.

WROUGHT IRON GRILLS FOR SECURITY

· TILE USED THROUGHOUT FOR EASY MAINTENANCE.

* SCHOOL SERVES AS HOME OR GATHERING PLACE FOR THE CHILDREN, AND FOR THE COMMUNITY, A CENTER FOR CELEBRATIONS AND EVENTS.

5

5 Architect's conceptual sketch.

6 Structural section with detail.

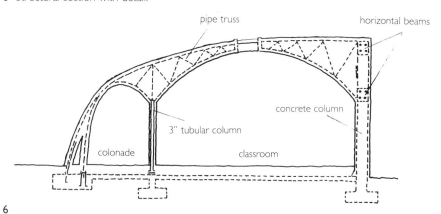

pipe truss

horizontal beams

concrete column

3" tubular column

colonade

classroom

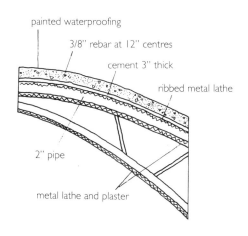

painted waterproofing

3/8" rebar at 12" centres

cement 3" thick

ribbed metal lathe

2" pipe

metal lathe and plaster

6

7

dusty landscape. Teachers can take groups of their children out and sit beneath the tree as an alternative to the cool classroom interiors. In addition, there is a decorated pool in the courtyard, complete with a frog-shaped head. During the hottest days the pool fills up with happy splashing children, who are safe and secure within the courtyard. Finally, there is an 'outdoor class-room' area with shading from a timber pergola, which extends the activity spaces further. The open courtyard is very much part of the teaching area.

The interior of the new building comprises two classrooms, a head teacher's office, a storage room and separate girls' and boys' toilets. The organically shaped toilets, considered some-thing of a luxury in themselves, are further enhanced with exot-ic ceramic tiling, decorated with tree and fish forms. Likewise the interior of the classrooms provide the context for swirling playful patterns that lighten the environment, giving the children a sense of their own worth as well as providing a cool, low-maintenance finish.

The school serves as a home or gathering place for the chil-dren and also for the wider community, the courtyard in partic-ular acting as a centre for celebrations and weekend events; there is a barbecue area running along the south wall of the open courtyard. In a transitory landscape where mothers must move to find work, this project is a beacon of hope and stabili-ty. James Hubbell (not a trained architect but an artist) has produced a building of immense beauty in a most unlikely con-text – an example of architecture that has developed from the perceived psychological needs of small children and their mothers.

Special significance: gift labour was used involving parents in the beautifying process.

Børneinstitutioner, Amager, Copenhagen

Architect: Arkitekttegnestuen Virumgård, Copenhagen, designed by Ulla Poulsen and Jørgen Raun.

Client: City of Copenhagen.

Occupancy: 220 pre-school children between the ages of one and six, 110 children in each 'pavilion'. Within each building there are five group rooms containing groups of 22 three- to six-year-olds or 11 one- to three-year-olds.

Construction cost: £2 million (£1 million for each of two identical pavilions).

Construction: concrete frame with fir cladding rain-screen, internal blockwork, zinc roof.

Completed: June 1993–June 1994.

Classrooms/activity areas: five groups each 44m², plus one 65m² common room, 285m² in total. Storage: 18m², plus 10m² outside the building in connection with the garden. Total area: 698m² (each pavilion), 6.3m² per child. Garden area: 1200m².

Parking: spaces for five cars (ten spaces in total).

The location of these twin child care 'pavilions' is the island of Amager, reclaimed land close to Copenhagen's airport. From the outset, the architects believed that the new centre should be in tune with contemporary thinking relating child psychology to the environment, and some of Steiner's philosophical ideas have been adopted. Although this is a working-class district, the architects felt that the parents, generally enlightened regarding the kindergarten idea, would understand this philosophy.

The site is close to the Christiania community, established in 1968 by rebellious intellectuals whose once-anarchistic views are now part of a mature political system in the form of enlightened social liberalism. As well as the Steiner ethos, the architectural concept also echoes the *ad hoc* nature of the Christiania developments, as opposed to the more conventional high-rise social housing of the immediate surroundings. The concept was never intended to be a 'home from home', rather a stimulating and thought-provoking 'alternative' environment.

The form of the two identical buildings is slightly organic; classrooms and quiet spaces seem to grow like leaves from the centre of the plan. The 'branch' holds staffrooms and the central common playroom which rises in a two-storey volume above the single-storey classrooms. Although the plan is orthogonal, corners are splayed both in plan and in section, so that ultimately no two spaces or corners appear to be the same. The

1　Section.

3　Detail of entrance porch.

2　The rear garden with storage sheds and upturned eaves.

4　Central communal space.

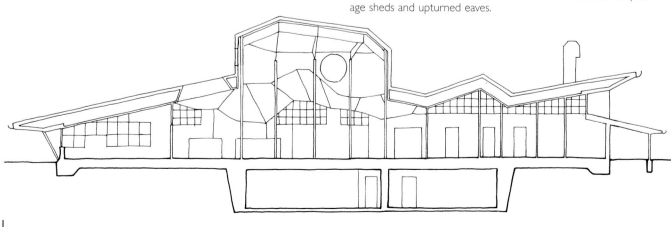

1

2

3

4

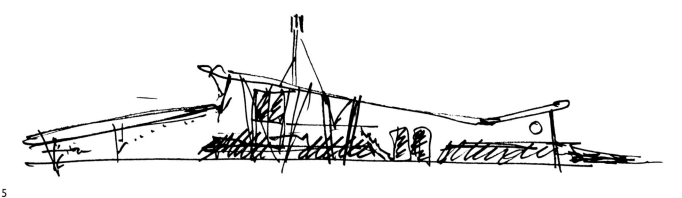

5

low exaggerated eaves of the building that wrap all the way round the rambling outer walls create safe sheltered niches. Thus the internal form of the building makes interesting external space. Similarly, the internal areas appear enclosing, intimate and varied.

The building provides spatial diversity within which children can feel safe and secure. They can shelter in their own enclosed activity areas or, when feeling more adventurous, play in the pub-

lic hall or in the little garden compounds around the outside of the building. Some of Goethe's colour theory is used both internally and externally, creating a building that is engaging but never whimsical. The architects express their concern for the children in a gentle, mild form of organic expressionism, which is not only appropriate for its setting but also in tune with the times.

Special significance: it uses Goethe's colour theory.

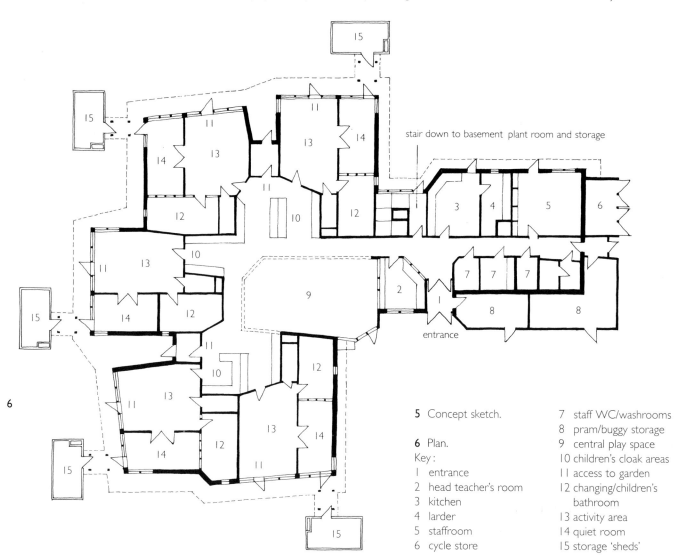

6

stair down to basement plant room and storage

entrance

5 Concept sketch.

6 Plan.
Key:
1 entrance
2 head teacher's room
3 kitchen
4 larder
5 staffroom
6 cycle store

7 staff WC/washrooms
8 pram/buggy storage
9 central play space
10 children's cloak areas
11 access to garden
12 changing/children's
   bathroom
13 activity area
14 quiet room
15 storage 'sheds'

7

7 Entrance canopy with newly planted flower garden.

8 Site plan.
Key :
1 parking
2 meadow garden
3 herb garden
4 sand yard
5 hard play space
6 sand pit
7 storage sheds

8

Luginsland Kindergarten, Stuttgart

1 Section.

2 Sketch drawing by the architect.

3 The first-floor classroom: the structural clarity is never out of control and it remains an authentic inside–outside construction, irrational yet legible. Note the window niche behind the door, a typical space in tune with children's play patterns and scale.

Architect: Behnisch and Partner, Stuttgart, with project architect, Sibylle Käppel-Klieber.

Client: City of Stuttgart.

Occupancy: 56 pre-school children in two groups which are then subdivided.

Construction cost: 1.7 million DM.

Construction: timber and steel structural frame with a mixture of timber and currugated metal cladding.

Completed: October 1990.

Classrooms/activity areas: 150m². Storage: 8m². Total area: 317m², 5.6m² per child. Garden area: 1350m².

Parking: spaces for three cars.

The Luginsland Kindergarten is located on the outskirts of Stuttgart on a steep hillside within the Neckar valley. State-funded by 10% above the normal cost of similar facilities, the add-on value manifests itself in two ways: first, Stuttgart gains a distinctive symbol of civic pride, underlining the importance placed on children in the city; secondly, the children have a building that immediately challenges their conventional view of architecture.

On the face of it, spatially eccentric and obsessively assymetrical, the organization is simple and legible to its users. The entrance is from the north-facing street side across a 'gangplank' bridge, signifying a symbolic transition from one world to another, more secure, child-orientated way of being. Once inside, there is a large multifunctional space with views *down* to the first floor. The slope of the site is accommodated within the building rather than outside, which is another pleasurable distraction for the children. So the first floor is the entrance-level lobby, with the head teacher's room to the right and the first of two activity areas to the left. The space takes discreet top and side light, which dramatically enhances the exposed timber structure, accentuating its natural warm textures.

Looking down the generously proportioned, child-friendly staircase, one becomes aware how the building is intended to be experienced – moving rather than static, almost like an 18th-century baroque interior. Because the spaces are not square, one can best appreciate the building this way (by moving through it); it is almost like being within the interior of a living organism, with every element laid bare. The structure encour-

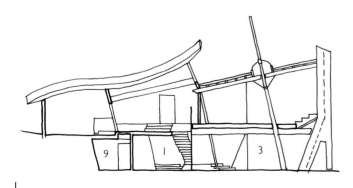

4 Ground-floor plan.
Key to ground floor and section:
1 hall
2 landing and route up
3 classroom one
4 small group space
5 washroom/WC
6 shower
7 utility room
8 staff WC
9 store
10 plant room

5 First-floor plan.
Key:
1 landing and entrance from street via bridge
2 hall
3 classroom
4 small group space
5 materials store
6 store
7 washroom/WC
8 store
9 head teacher's office

1

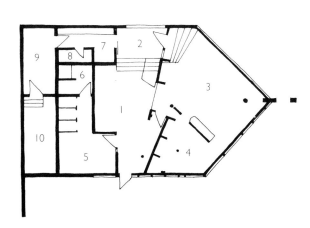

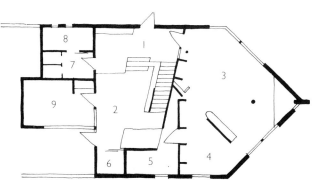

3

4   5

6 View from the 'deck',
unfortunately not accessible
to childen.

7 Site plan.

ages movement and exploration, rather than focusing the children on enclosed, conventional classrooms.

At the bottom of the stair-route in the lower hall, the second classroom is visible beneath the stair. Each of these bases for the children's daily explorations is accommodated within the 'prow' of the ship form and divided functionally in two, with open classroom areas and a quieter so-called 'small group room'. Again, the emphasis is on flexibility (of play) rather than too prescriptive a set of predefined play spaces, as one might find in a more overt metaphor, such as a fairground boat. What the architecture encourages is not only a sense of exploration within the children, but also a diverse range of different play spaces within the activity areas. All those strange angles and corners and oddly positioned windows have clearly been rigorously thought out, with the needs of children's play at the forefront. For example, rather than having all the windows at adult height, some are nearer the ground, where young children play more naturally. In questioning the logic of such a radical approach to children's architecture, one need only witness the joyful confidence of the children as they use the building on a daily basis:

One could simply build a house of the kind that have been built in the vicinity . . . one could also build something that did not actually exist in the world the children have lived in up to now; something that could not possibly originate in the adult world, the world that we tend to explain rationally; perhaps something which, at first, one would not expect to find there, something that 'doesn't add up'.[2] *Günter Behnisch*

The overt boat metaphor makes this one of the most memorable kindergarten projects featured, and it is described by the architect in the language of Froebelian romanticism. It is a small building compared to many of the other featured projects; however, it remains in the imagination as a fairytale remains from childhood. It is contentious, yet it speaks an understandable architectural language which is organic and highly playful, a flight from the uniform rationality of an over-ordered adult world. If anyone finds this building difficult, it is the adults rather than the children!

Special significance: use of a strong, playful metaphor.

5

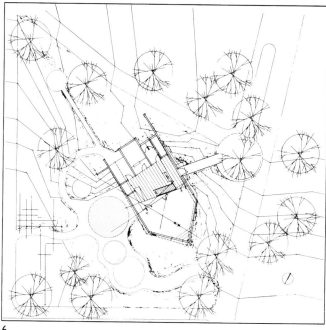

6

The Bungawitta Children's Centre, Launceston, Tasmania

Architect: Robert Morris-Nunn, Tasmania, Australia.
Client: East Tamar Child Care Association.
Occupancy: 50 children in four groups comprising babies, one- to two-year-olds, two- to three-year-olds and three- to five-year-olds.
Construction cost: A$300 000.
Construction: steel portal and stud-framed structure with block-work screen wall, slightly pitched tile roof.
Completed: 1985.
Classrooms/activity areas: 184m^2. Storage: 15m^2. Total area: 390m^2, 7.8m^2 per child. Garden area: 500m^2.
Parking: none.

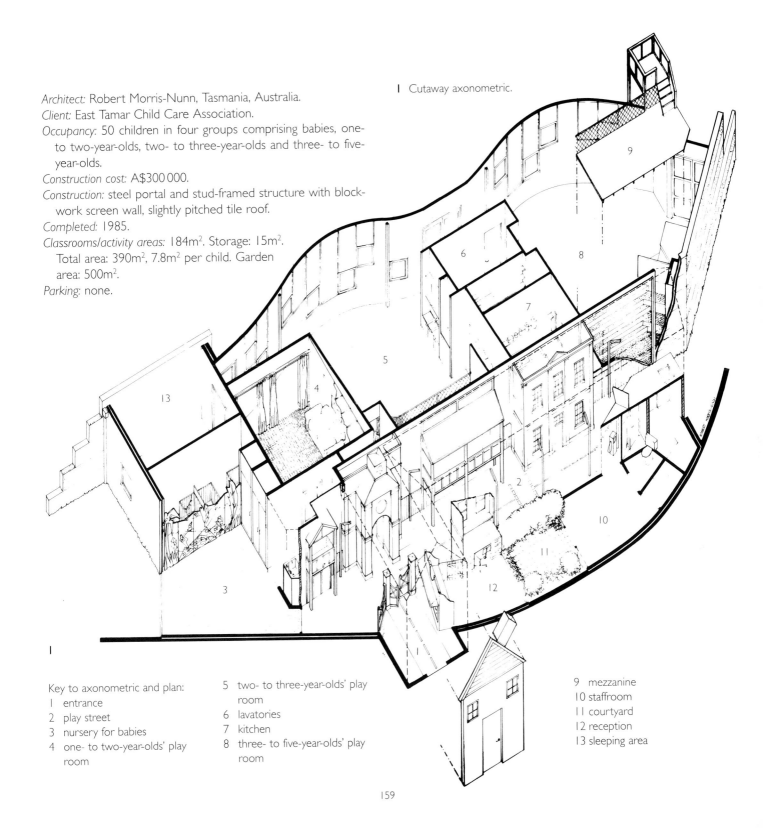

1 Cutaway axonometric.

Key to axonometric and plan:
1 entrance
2 play street
3 nursery for babies
4 one- to two-year-olds' play room
5 two- to three-year-olds' play room
6 lavatories
7 kitchen
8 three- to five-year-olds' play room
9 mezzanine
10 staffroom
11 courtyard
12 reception
13 sleeping area

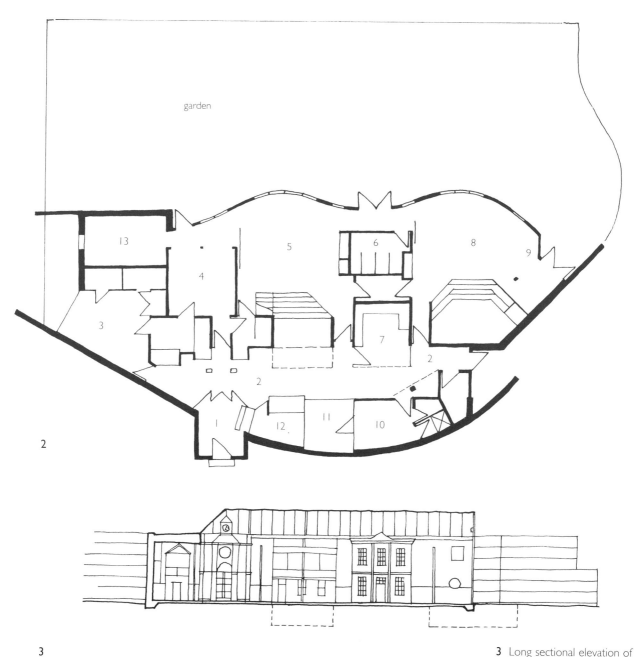

2

3

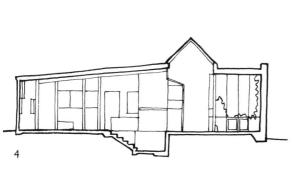

4

2 Plan.
Key:
1 entrance
2 play street
3 nursery
4 one–two-year-olds' playroom
5 two–three-year-olds' playroom
6 lavatories
7 litchen
8 three–five-year-old's play room
9 mezzanine
10 staffroom
11 courtyard
12 reception
13 sleeping area

3 Long sectional elevation of the internal street.

4 Cross-section through the glazed roof and staff courtyard.

5 Elements of a children's world: safety within a building which is top-lit, with toy buildings for enhanced play.

6 The 'post office'.

7 Entrance wall and children's house.

5

6

7

My search for an architecture which has a deeper spiritual meaning has led me to projects which relate to people who for whatever reason come to be part of an institution. Why? Because I feel for such people whose desire to find meaning in their lives is often as great as their opportunities to find it are restricted, and need more than most of us buildings that speak not of authority and its miserly currency of supervision, timetabling routine, discipline and punishment, but instead buildings that speak of the possibilities of personal and social liberation, of connection to place, past and community.[3] *Robert Morris-Nunn*

This small kindergarten illustrates an extreme form of children's architecture, which takes the imaginative needs of children's play very literally, creating a Lilliputian distortion as a major part of its architectural representation. One's first sight of the building is a banded, curving wall within which is set a small gabled projection. This is the entrance and, as one might expect a four-year-old child to represent his or her image of a house, it has the familiar Georgian anthropomorphic composition with a triangular gable, four-square paned window 'eyes', a red eccentrically proportioned door in the centre, and an authentically skewed chimney block. When comparing it to a child's drawing of home, 'all that is missing from the common image is a looping scribble of smoke'.[4] This, then, is a metaphor that sets the tone for the interior of the building.

Once within the front wall, the miniature main street of an Australian country town is revealed. This is complete with garage, post office, bank and Georgian town-house and, an even more surprising sight, the street lamps work and road markings are delineated in coloured vinyl. This theatrical illusion is perfectly practical, as the street acts as a circulation spine, providing a link to all of the inner activity spaces. Yet, rather than being a leftover neutral corridor territory as is so frequently the case, it is in fact a positive area for arrival, daytime play and a waiting space for parents. It maximizes the potential of the building for imaginative play, and is strategically placed to create a vital distraction at a point where children are leaving one type of experience, the secure world of parental protection, to their own more autonomous being.

Although the planning of this building appears complex, it is a simple series of layers comprising three basic parts: the front

wall with staff spaces, which includes a small open courtyard located immediately behind; a spine of utility spaces running down the centre containing kitchens, lavatories and quiet areas; and the activity areas themselves, orientated out towards the north-facing sunny garden. There are special rooms for each age group, which run west to east in the following sequence. First, there is a nursery for the youngest group which has its own courtyard; it is almost insulated from the rest of the building, part of the institution but an element that has its own self-contained environment, quiet calm and soothing. Second is a pair of spaces for the one- to two-year-olds and the two- to three-year-olds. They can share time together, but the younger ones have a more sheltered, homely space which is delineated by a sliding partition. These spaces are separated from the final activity room by a kitchen and toilet/washroom block, which shows how the architect's sense of spatial organization is working positively to separate different age groups without compromising the aesthetic quality of the overall architectural idea. This final play space for three- to five-year-olds is the largest; it has a raised theatrical stage and a mezzanine 'crow's nest' that overlooks the garden.

The three activity areas for the one- to five-year-old children are linked externally by a sinuous timber-and-glass wall, a lightweight counterpoint to the the heavy wall on the street front. Contrasting with the ordered orthogonal inner walls, these two elements unite the whole rich composition.

There are doubts about this highly prescriptive approach to children's architecture, as in a number of the other organic projects. These are concerns that relate to adult perceptions of how children should be, rather than any functional shortcomings. However, there is no easy conclusion to the veracity of this experiment in designing 'magical realism'. Clearly, the whole building could operate without the miniature buildings. Yet the pre-school child's perceptions are in tune to this form of stimulation, and the fine detail of the streetscape shows that Morris-Nunn's understanding and affection for the fragile beauty of Launceston's historic buildings is genuine and well understood. If nothing else, the internalizing effect of the city's streets and squares will provide the children with a similar appreciation of the real city environment — a valuable lesson that, sadly, may already be lost to future generations since a head teacher has recently removed all the child-scaled buildings.

Bornehaven 'De Fire Arstider, Copenhagen

Architect: Helle Grangaard.

Client: The Kompan Company.

Occupancy: 40 pre-school children aged three to six years with approximately five adult carers. There are no groups allocated to specific parts of the building, rather children utilize the whole environment as they wish and groupings develop organically.

Construction cost: 2.2 million Danish Kroner or 8000 Kr per m². The building was designed as a modular unit build construction to be sold as a complete 'kit', therefore the price quoted does not include the cost of construction. However, implicit in the design is a self-build ethos.

Construction: The building is entirely of timber with untreated cedar externally (with an asphalt roof), Iroko floors and play decks and linoleum for the wet areas. The main structure is of Danish pine. The internal walls are treated with a white pigment to provide a smooth stain resistant surface.

Completed: September 1996

Classrooms/activity areas: Main 'core' activity space 75.5m² (kitchen area 8.8 m²), entrance cloak room area 22.5m², art studio 44.5m², lobby to WC 3.6m², children's bathroom 8.6m², staff WC 6.2m², boiler room 7.6m², staff room/office 9.0m².

Total area: 8m² per child.

Parking: There is no dedicated parking. However, the Kompan Factory benefits from its own large workers' car park.

This small workplace nursery was designed as a prototype for the Kompan Company, which specializes in the manufacture of children's playground equipment. Architect Helle Grangaard worked closely with the company to develop a concept which was in tune with its modular construction; the building can be manufactured in just eight weeks and assembled within two to three days on pre-built foundations. However, unlike many similar pre-assembled units, this building was designed from a strong child-orientated perspective which transcends the machine aesthetic, providing an environment that is sensitive to its natural setting, and in tune with the kindergarten ethos.

The very earliest conceptual diagrams show a concern for the needs of young children to experience developing independence. The central core activity area provides an enclosed area that is autonomous from the outside. This provides the warm shelter essential for young vulnerable children when they first attend the centre. It responds to the outside, with a large window and fireplace orientated towards the forest, a Danish symbol of great significance, yet the space retains its sense of solid, secure enclosure. There is an open kitchen or hearth at its heart, where the aromas of cooking help to create a warm, homely atmosphere. Cooking and eating inform the pedagogic process in the most fundamental way.

From this core space, an outer layer of accommodation forms the interface beween the inside and outside spaces. The 'wrap' comprises of three mini buildings which radiate out from the central core. One contains the wet bathroom areas, one the entrance lobby with cloakroom and one an art studio which is also used as a sleeping area after lunch. The latter is glazed and fulfils the need for a winter garden space implied in the original conceptual diagram. These houses enclose outside spaces which are dedicated to three specific gardens; one adjacent to the open kitchen for the cultivation of herbs and fruit; a rough, hard garden adjacent to the studio for making and constructing activities; and a flower garden orientated towards the south-west, for more quiet contemplative activities.

The radial plan relates to the movement of the sun, and encourages a similar fluidity among the children. Activities develop around the natural life of the building, so that as lunch is prepared in the central kitchen, children assist or play on the floor around the edges of the core space. Afternoons are generally orientated towards the outside spaces, with the winter garden encouraging more out-going activities as the sun moves around the building. Sitting within a large 2000m² site, the building constructs safe pathways within which children can explore the environment at their own pace.

This highly symbolic building combines modern technological methods of construction with an almost primordial response to the needs of young children. The whole plan is predicated on the central 'tree trunk', spreading out across the site, to provide an educational framework which children appear to understand intuitively. This care for the environment is also reflected in the use of different timbers, which articulate a subtle solid and void within the overall radial planning. As yet only two of these modular buildings have been constructed, however, the overall success illustrates how this approach can be utilized to provide high-quality, economical kindergarten accommodation where play and activity transform in tune with the seasons.

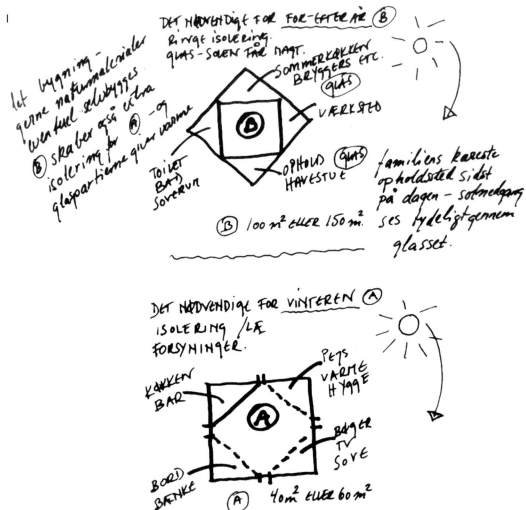

I The upper diagram shows the concept of the inner core [b] which is wrapped by potentially more outgoing activities. The lower diagram shows the potential for an inner core [a] to be more open and transparant.

2

2.2

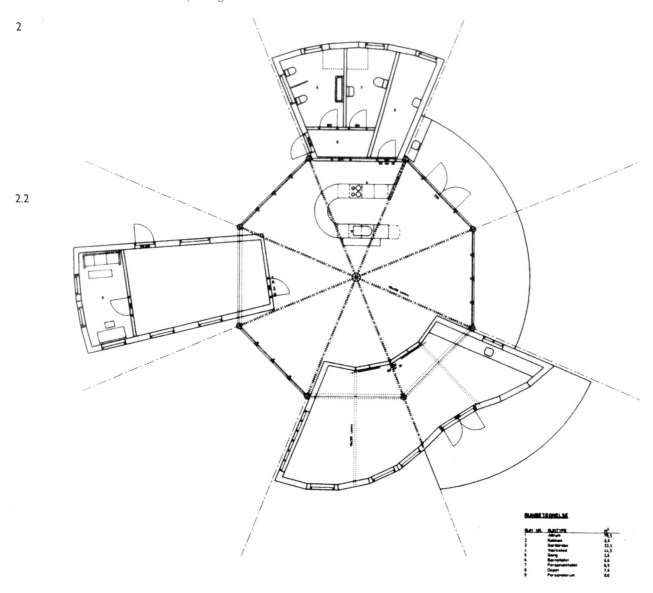

2 The open access kitchen with the hearth and beyond, the trees framed by a large window suggesting that this is a highly site specific approach.

3 The bathroom combines activities to encourage a healthy attitude, which is nevertheless private.

4

5

6

7

4 The open access kitchen in use.

5 External decks ranged around the outside of the building extend activities to encourage an awareness of important spatial relationships. Note the fabric canopies.

6 Development model.

7 A general view of the centre from the flower garden.

Corning Child Development Center, New York

Architects: Mack Scogin and Merrill Elam.

Client: Corning Incorporated (Glass Manufacturers).

Occupancy: 144 children organized into three groups, aged six weeks up to pre-kindergarten age of five years. The programme develops around the idea of family groups with age-specific classrooms grouped together so that children across a range of ages have exposure to each other and interact naturally.

Construction cost: $1.2 million.

Construction: The building has a concrete frame and slab construction with an integral (underfloor) heating system. The walls are constructed on a timber and steel framework with steel truss members. Natural and stained timber cladding is used externally with high-performance insulated glazing units in aluminium frames; elastomeric membrane roofing and inside, painted gypsum wall board, carpet, vinyl composition tile and sealed plywood and painted metal trim.

Completed: March 1994.

Classrooms/activity areas: 420m². storage: 25m². Total area: 1100m², 8.5m² per child. Garden area: 1300m².

Parking: There are 25 dedicated parking places plus a generous drop-off point for cars and buses.

Many day care centres focus on the security and control of children at the expense of fantasy and imagination. The architecture is conceived as a neutral backdrop for staff and children to decorate themselves. Here architects Mack Scogin and Merrill Elam set out to create an environment that would be rich and act as a positive extension of the toys and distractions that are used to amuse and educate. They also saw the building as a powerful tool with potential to aid carers and children in their educational development and environmental awareness: 'The overall spatial experience teaches about light, sound and spatial progression.'[5]

This approach becomes apparent from the threshold, with separate adult- and child-height doors which lead into a two-storey space, an entrance atrium that lies at the heart of the building's fractured tripartite plan. Here the scale of the experience must be awe-inspiring for young children since the volume of this space is further accentuated by its multi-faceted

1

shape. High above sits a translucent skylight tower in the shape of a slightly twisted cone. On sunny days, luminous dappled light filters down into the spaces below, lighting the route of a gently spiralling staircase which rises up towards the light. Beyond the staircase there is a voluminous eating area with its own open-access kitchen. In a corner there is a staircase which leads to nowhere suggesting a magical spot good for hiding or for story telling on cold winter days.

The plan is organized loosely around three play corridors which splay out to the west, north and east; the main entrance is orientated to the south from a large car park and formal gardens. The corridors are developed as play spaces, with

2

3

1 The entrance elevation: a playful collision of competing forms.

2 The garden elevations are full of incident; the bay windows form intimate small group reading areas inside the play spaces.

3 Corner detail looking towards the garden.

4 Corner detail showing timber cladding, with quirky window forms and checkerboard water tank.

5 Communal 'drop-in' centre with kitchen and play gallery above. The entrance foyer and reception desk are visible beyond.

4

niches and activity benches. They are the interface between the three activity areas within each wing, providing an area where the age mix of infants, toddlers and pre-schoolers may come together at certain times of the day.

The windows are of different size and type and relate to a particular height or a particular shape. This hierarchy is summarized by the architects as being high, low or irregular. However, in reality there is a more composed aesthetic working, with each window framing a particular view, or providing a certain quality of light. These range from the purposeful square bay window, used for story telling with small intimate groups, to an eccentrically skewed crescent shape, which focuses on to an area for rumbustious floor play. It is an evocative contrast to the horizontal linearity of the façade's timber boarding.

The profile of the building ranges from the low, single-storey activity room to the 6.1m high observation tower. It is a mediating form between the residential neighbourhood of two-storey timber-frame houses and the larger corporate headquarters buildings. This mediating quality can be adopted as the metaphor to describe the building as a social mediator, between the privacy of the home and the more challenging spaces of the public institution. Its complexity reflects the nature of life beyond the home, encouraging children to go out and explore, while protecting more vulnerable members of the community within safe, secure family rooms. It is an environment crafted to reflect society's needs.

5

Corning Child Development Center – New York

2a Lower-level plan.
Key:
1. lobby
2. entrance/reception
3. Head Teacher's office and staff meeting area
4. access corridor
5. kitchen
6. communal space and drop-in centre
7. play corridor: infants
8. sleep and quiet area for babies
9. infants' activity space
10. play corridor: toddlers
11. activity areas
12. quiet areas
13. play corridor: pre schoolers
14. activity areas
15. quiet area
16. staff area
17. staff washrooms

2b Upper-level plan.
Key:
1. mechanical/storage room
2. observation walkway
3. observation/play area
(A, B, C and D are section lines, see figures 2d and 2e)

2a

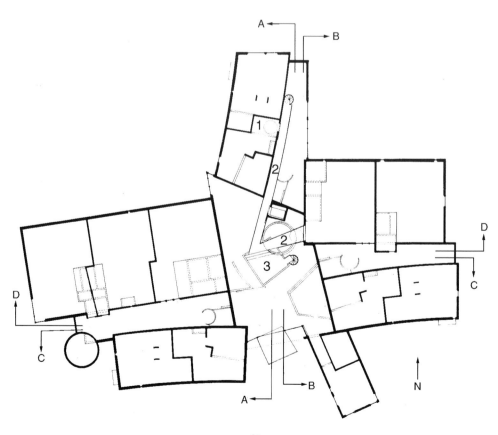

2b

2c Site Plan.
  a: car park and entrance
  b: secure garden

2d Section C-C and
Section D-D

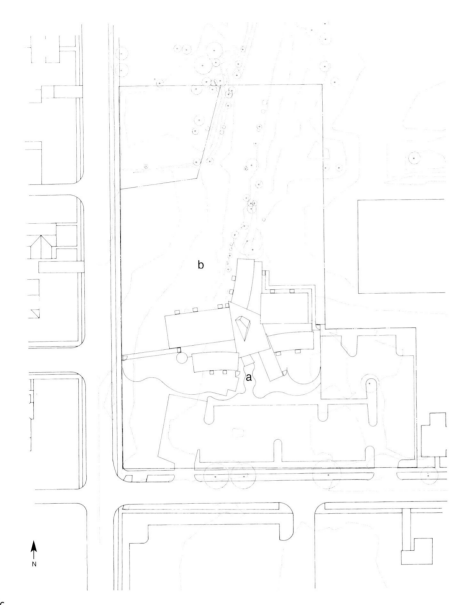

b

a

N

2c

Section C-C

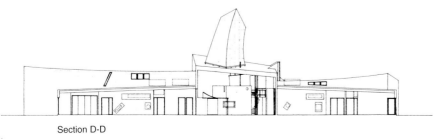

Section D-D

2d

Corning Child Development Center - New York

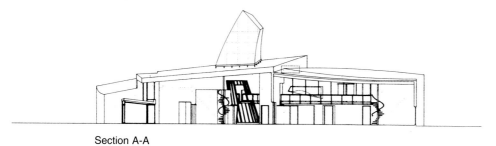

Section A-A

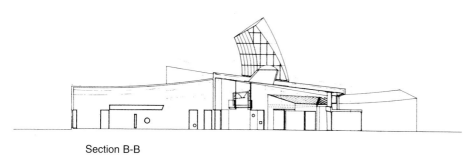

Section B-B

2e

2e Section A-A and Section B-B.

2f West elevation and east elevation.

2g South elevation and north elevation

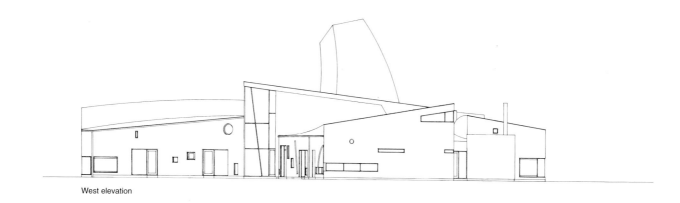

West elevation

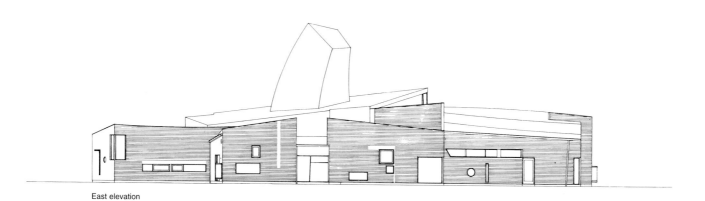

East elevation

2f

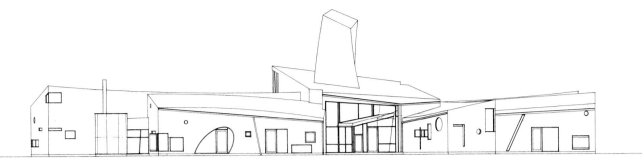

South elevation

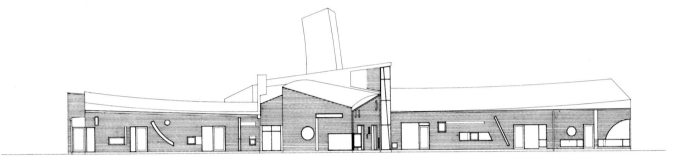

North elevation

2g

UCLA Child Care Centre, Los Angeles, California

Architect: Charles and Elizabeth Lee, Los Angeles.

Client: University College of Los Angeles.

Occupancy: 80 pre-school children, consisting of two groups of 25 (three- to four-year-olds), 18 toddlers (one-and-a-half- to two-and-a-half-year-olds) and ten babies.

Construction cost: US$5 million.

Construction: prefabricated steel frame with flat asphalt roofs, and insulated panels in glass, fibreglass and timber.

Completed: June 1991.

Activity areas: 3030ft^2/280m^2 (not including external covered loggias). Storage: no specific allocation. Total area: 10000ft^2/ 929m^2, 11.6m^2 per child. Garden area/play space: 14000ft^2/ 1300m^2.

Parking: spaces for 18 cars.

Nestled in a former orchard at the north-west corner of the university campus, the facility provides full-day care for four separate groups of children from the university staff and student population. The architects organized the building simply, in three linked pavilions, arranged in a slightly splayed U-shape orientated towards the north. The entrance is from the south-facing carpark through the central administrative pavilion, beyond which the inside of the U reveals the two play pavilions on either side of a secure internal garden. The two garden pavilions contain the children's activity areas in four separate classrooms, each sharing part of a wide, communal, colonnaded space.

The colonnade is in fact an essential focus for the life of the institution, the architects were well briefed by Director of Child Care Services June Sale, who wanted the kindergarten to be

1

2

1 The garden courtyard, with the setting sun casting deep shadows across the now divided courtyard and loggias.

2 Activity area interior with glazed and translucent fibreglass panels set into a homogeneous grid with structure and fabric exposed; but services such as electrical conduits and water pipes hidden.

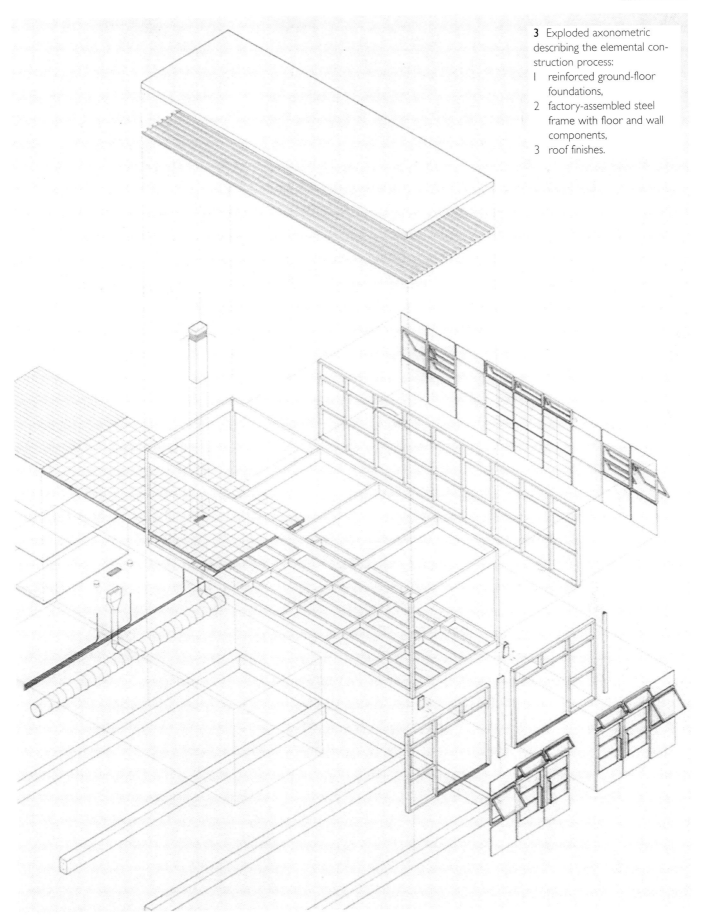

3 Exploded axonometric describing the elemental construction process:
1 reinforced ground-floor foundations,
2 factory-assembled steel frame with floor and wall components,
3 roof finishes.

UCLA Child Care Centre, Los Angeles, California

4 Site plan of the centre, adjoining the UCLA campus.

5 Ground-floor plan.
Key: a covered links between pavilions, b courtyard garden, c covered loggias
1 sleep/quiet room
2 activity room
3 entrance lobby
4 administrative offices
5 sick room
6 therapy room

7 meeting room
8 staffroom
9 head teacher's office
10 kitchen
11 staff restroom
12 therapy room lobby

6 Rear elevation. The 1994 earthquake left the building virtually unscathed.

7 View from the car park, showing how the building merges into its mature setting.

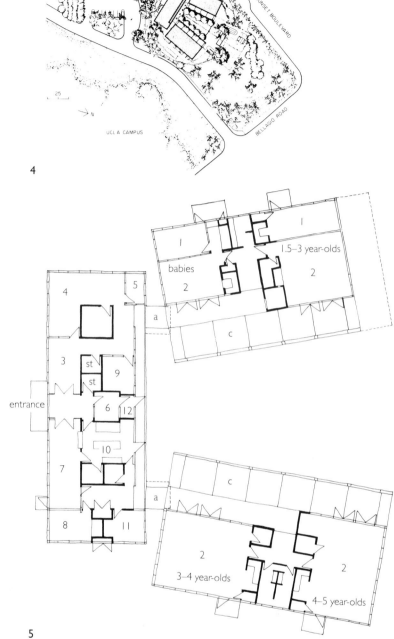

4

5

structured around a philosophy based on the family. In the archetypal pre-television Los Angeles residence, the courtyard was the focus of family life; this strong idea structured the architects' thinking from the outset. Another essential influence was the designers' interest in the spirituality of minimalist Japanese architecture and their experience of working with Charles and Ray Eames. The ordered, steely elegance of the building's aesthetic and the crisp Miesian detailing throughout is evidence of this.

The philosophy of UCLA Child Care Services is based on the belief that parents and staff can plan and implement a comprehensive program for children that reflects and meets the needs of the multi-cultural and multi-racial backgrounds of the children of our community. We believe that this may best be done by providing children a variety of age-appropriate play activities and experiences in a comfortable and non-competitive environment. *From briefing document, philosophy statement by UCLA Child Care Services*

The architects have clearly taken this guidance seriously in designing a building that is neither quirky nor too serious. It is the archetypal open, yet discreetly secure, environment that allows the children much autonomy within a reassuring framework. The notion of 'non-competitive' environments further emphasizes the appropriateness of this neutral form of architecture, yet it is nevertheless sophisticated and allows the children to 'discover' the innerworkings of the architecture.[6]

The technology is particularly significant. The architects were given a short four-month programme, not only for detail design but also for the construction. Harnessing the expertise of structural engineers Ove Arup and Partners, and utilizing their earlier experiences with Norman Foster in Hong Kong, the pair developed a largely prefabricated building. Although the services and the ground floor slab were cast *in situ*, the frame of the building – comprising U-shaped steel sections, welded together in 4 × 12 × 3 metre-high factory-made modules to fit on a lorry – was sturdy enough to avoid the temporary, lightweight feeling of many prefabricated buildings. It also proved to be highly practical, remaining largely unscathed during the recent earthquake.

The infill panelling is a mixture of double-skin glass, both clear and frosted, fibreglass ('Kowall') and some solid painted timber ply panels. With its light timber flooring and flat cream painted

ceilings, the effect is an internal environment that is calm and texturally rich, all within a strong modular framework. As with most of the best examples of pre-school building, window openings are carefully chosen and selective. Rudolph Schindler's studio house is a declared precedent with external corners in clear glass, extending vistas out across the landscape rather than straight towards the boundary fences. The subtlety within this seemingly simple building provides a suitable framework for the explorations of the children, giving a sense of permanance within a largely light-weight prefabricated structure

Special significance: prefabricated, yet permanent, relating specifically to its regional context.

6

7

Eckenheim-Sud Kindergagesstätte, Frankfurt

1

Architect: Toyo Ito & Associates, Tokyo; Schemer & Warschauer Frankfurt (construction architects).
Client: City of Frankfurt Architects' Department.
Occupancy: 60 pre-school places (three- to six-year-olds) and afternoon study spaces for 40 schoolchildren (kinderhort).
Construction cost: 2.9 million DM.
Construction: brick/blockwork walls rendered with a cast concrete retaining wall, steel and timber roof structure with zinc and asphalt roof covering.
Completed: June 1993.
Classrooms/activity areas: 264m². Storage: 50m². Total area: 1020m², 10.2m² per child. Garden area: 1918m².
Parking: spaces for two cars.

Eckenheim is a new residential quarter for working-class and immigrant families housed mainly in medium-rise blocks of flats that surround the new school. This context suggested to Japanese architect Toyo Ito that the form of the building should be low and horizontal. He wished to create an inward-looking form, presenting a strong 'back' to the road. After passing through the narrow, partly buried entrance, a safe, secure 'Alice in Wonderland' world opens up to the children. Where the street elevation is solid, comprising a concrete wall with banked earth, the building's southwest facing garden facade is fragmented, with parts of the building bulging out into the garden. An ash-clad octagonal tower appears to have completely detached itself from the main building. It stands isolated within the garden, linked only

2

4

1 Propped cantilevered roof with the octagonal tower sitting within the garden.

2 Activity corridor.

3 View looking down from the tower room.

4 Site plan.

3

by a light, ladder-like stair; it contains the art studio workshop and a first-floor meeting space. This fragmented quality is held together architecturally by a strong horizontal 'folding' roof form, which tilts up and over the classrooms creating covered terraces on the garden side. Stone granite setts radiate from the covered terrace areas, gradually degrading as the vegetation within the garden takes over.

On entering the building from the street, roughly at the centre of the plan, there is a communal space which is used freely by the children as a dining room or, on rainy days, an art room. The functional programme divides the accommodation in two with the kindergarten on one side of the entrance hall and the kinderhort on the other side; however, the overall spirit of the

building is open and informal. Self-contained teaching spaces, classrooms for the younger children, are located along an internal corridor on one side of the plan. The kindergarten classrooms are each subdivided into an area for open play and an area for quiet play. Each has its own toilet block accessed from the corridor. The toilets, although internal, are ventilated with circular rooflights – a theme echoed in the internal corridor which takes light through a series of circular coloured rooflights. The corridor curves gently round to its end where there is a special quiet space overlooking the garden.

A circular multipurpose hall is located immediately to the left of the entrance where parents can meet staff and collect children; this is accessible at weekends when the rest of the school

Eckenheim-Sud Kindergagesstätte, Frankfurt

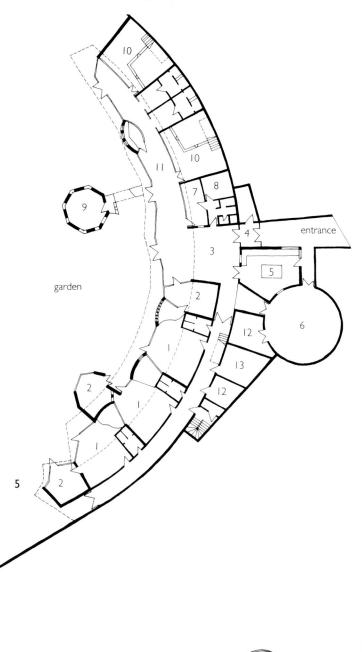

5 **Ground-floor plan.**
Key :
1   activity rooms
2   special activity rooms: library.
    quiet reading room, boys'
    play space
3   entrance/dining space
4   entrance
5   kitchen
6   multipurpose hall
7   head teacher's offce
5   staff area
9   tower with art studio and
    meeting space
10 kinderhort spaces

11 activity corridor
12 storeroom
13 plant room

6 **Section through multipurpose hall and activity rooms.**

7 **'Eye-glass' windows in one of
the activity areas.**

8 **Internal garden, with sand pit
in the foreground. The ash-clad
octagonal tower contains the
art studio and a first-floor
meeting room.**

7

8

6

is closed. The kinderhort is linked to the entrance hall by a broad gallery space running along the open garden side of the plan. It was the architect's original intention that the kinderhort activity areas would be completely open to this corridor but building regulations meant that the rooms had to be enclosed, and glazed windows borrow light from the garden space. The two kinderhort study spaces also have first-floor study rooms,

the only spaces that appear above the main roof. Visible from the street, their separation suggests the growing autonomy of the older children, looking out towards the challenges facing them in the outside world. The building is a pluralistic synthesis of a number of different Japanese architectural themes, yet it forms a relaxed, child-centred community wholly appropriate to its context.

Greisheim-Sud Kindertagesstätte, Frankfurt

Architect: Bolles Wilson and Partner, Münster.
Client: City of Frankfurt.
Occupancy: 60 pre-school (three- to six-year-olds) and afternoon study spaces for 40 schoolchildren (kinderhort).
Construction cost: 2.9 million DM.
Construction: concrete frame with rendered brick/block walls and flat asphalt roofs.
Completed: June 1992.
Classrooms/activity areas: 470m². Storage: 8m². Total area: 682m², 11.3m² per child. Garden area: 300m².
Parking: spaces for two cars.

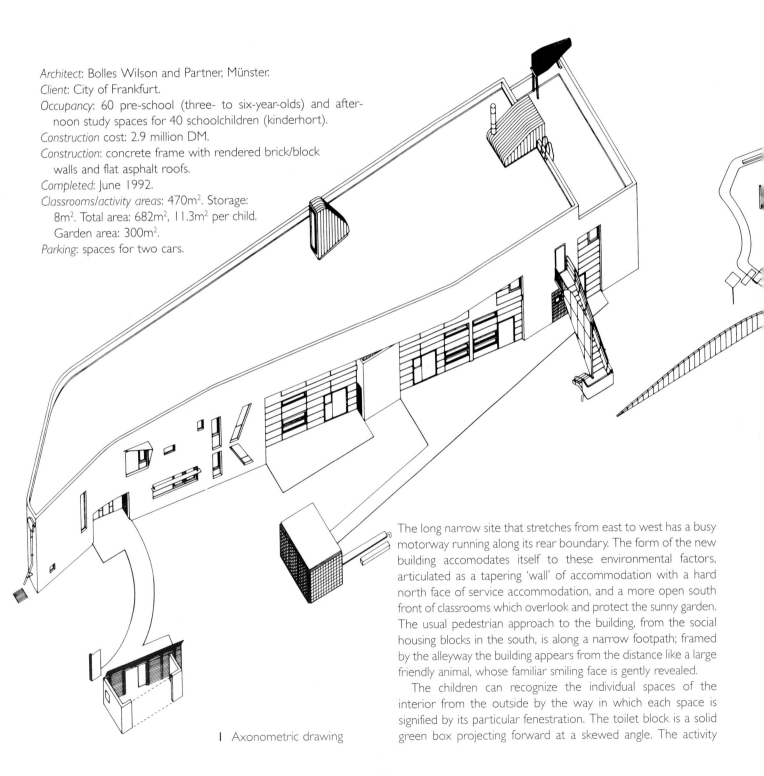

l Axonometric drawing

The long narrow site that stretches from east to west has a busy motorway running along its rear boundary. The form of the new building accomodates itself to these environmental factors, articulated as a tapering 'wall' of accommodation with a hard north face of service accommodation, and a more open south front of classrooms which overlook and protect the sunny garden. The usual pedestrian approach to the building, from the social housing blocks in the south, is along a narrow footpath; framed by the alleyway the building appears from the distance like a large friendly animal, whose familiar smiling face is gently revealed.

The children can recognize the individual spaces of the interior from the outside by the way in which each space is signified by its particular fenestration. The toilet block is a solid green box projecting forward at a skewed angle. The activity

2 View along the first-floor corridor showing niche seating detail.

3 Ground-floor plan.
Key:
1 head teacher's offce
2 activity area for three-year-olds
3 kitchen
4 activity area for pre-school children
5 multiqurpose hall
6 storage
7 play corridor
8 plant room
9 lavatories
10 stair up
11 garden store

4 First-floor plan.
Key:
1 staff area
2 lavatories
3 quiet room
4 void
5 multipurpose hall
6 stair to roof and bridge to children's kitchen
7 children's kitchen

5

6

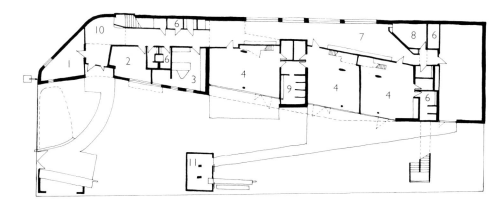

3

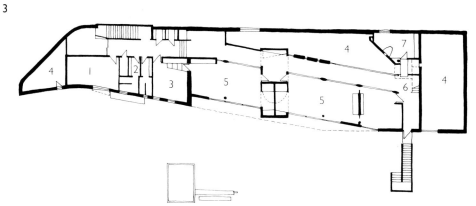

4

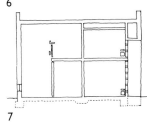

7

5 Detail of front elevation showing the external wall of the toilet block projects forward of the main line of fenestration

6 The sharp end the building, looking into the children's garden with anthropomorphic hopper heads.

7 Section.

8 Constructivist details within the activity area.

8

areas them selves are totally glazed, yet the fenestration is slightly odd, horizontals and verticals set against each other like a Mondrian painting or a complicated children's puzzle. The kitchen itself is identified more readily by windows that form a large letter K.

This playful detailing extends even to the rainwater pipe by the entrance which has a hopper shaped like an Indian head carving. This is one of a series of little architectural jokes, which are liberally scattered throughout the building. The main entrance, at the west end, is recessed into the wall and comprises two doors, one adult-sized and one child-sized. Once inside, the underside of the ceiling slopes, creating a distorted perspective within the entrance hall. Light comes in through upper-level windows between the balcony and the classrooms and, at the lower level, through long low slit windows set at toddlers' height.

The interior is organized as a linear sequence of rooms on two levels with the kinderhort on the first floor. All the rooms are accessible by a two-storey play corridor, which aids communication between the levels. The activity spaces each have their own lavatory and washroom. The size of the rooms appears to grow as the building expands along its plan; the youngest children use the smallest room closest to the entrance, and graduate further along the building as they themselves grow. A large, double-height play space at the end of the corridor terminates this expansion. It has one wall comprising full-height walk-in cupboards, a theatrical illusion that is both practical and intriguing. The whole building can be interpreted in many different ways, an imaginative exploration of playfulness and naivety in an elegant, modernist architectural form.

Centre de Vie Enfantine, Valency, Lausanne

Architect: Rudolphe Luscher, Lausanne.

Client: town of Lausanne, Department of Schools.

Occupancy: 66 children, consisting of ten babies (up to two), 24 young children (two- to four-year-olds) and 32 afternoon study places for primary school children (five- to ten-year-olds).

Construction costs: SFr 4.995 million.

Construction: concrete stabilizing walls with steel frames clad with titanium-coated zinc cladding panels.

Completed: August 1989.

Classrooms/activity areas: 318m². Storage. 6m². Total area: 1076m², 16m² per child. Garden area: 300m².

Parking: none.

This facility takes a radical approach to children's architecture; rather than providing a series of fully enclosed cellular spaces, the architect has adopted a more polemical strategy. Separate class bases are clearly identified within the plan; however, the spaces are open to the circulation routes so that views across and into each activity space are encouraged. Within the two- to four-year-old play spaces even the lavatory/washroom is open, engendering a healthy attitude to toilet training during these formative years.

The kitchen, which is open to the entrance, provides a warm, homely feeling on crossing the threshold of this 'children's house'. However, this is not a straightforwardly open-plan building. By establishing a clear structural rhythm with solid walls

1

2

3

punctuating the openness, intimacy is possible and children can make their own spaces within the recesses provided by the natural forms of the building. Indeed, sliding folding partitions and ingenious integrated storage facilities provide a flexible, continuously transforming environment, which is intriguing for young and junior school children alike.

The centre is located within a park; however, rather than seeking an integration with nature, it stands apart from it. Clad in shiny metal and sitting on a slightly raised concrete base, from the outside its function might be some sort of industrial process – a small-scale chemical plant, perhaps. With yellow window frames and green steel frames projecting in non-orthogonal

1 View towards the entrance from the park

2 Rear view, approaching the building from the street.

3 Spatial openness and exposed services characterize the interior a playful game for young children to puzzle out the source of their drinking water.

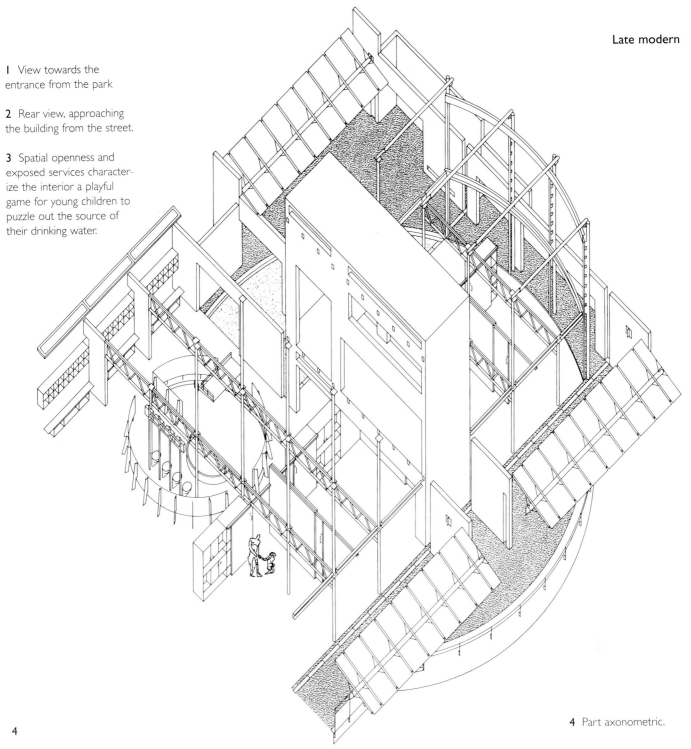

4

4 Part axonometric.

directions, it bristles with mechanistic purpose. This is mainly derived from the structural clarity. Its expression is partly to do with the design process: having first established the structure, the architect then attempts to dissolve that clarity by adding other structural and architectonic events. The children are presented with something that is fragmented, yet not too much so.

In the play of specific incidents set against the rhythm of a universal structural order, Le Corbusier's *plan libre* is brought to mind. A universal 2.7m grid reinforces this reference, a proportioning system that sets the scale for the whole building. A reduced version of Le Corbusier's module is the clearly stated intention behind the proportions, and again this establishes a

clarity in the overall composition. This becomes more apparent from the outside, where the 16-bay grid is translated into an ABAB rhythm, with projecting bays consisting of three grid widths, further disentangling the inherently complex functional layering.

Peter Blundell Jones states in his critique of the building that it is like 'a highly structured piece of music, such as a Bach fugue', with a strong identity yet with individual nuances playing against that clarity. However, one must add that while this is one of the most interesting children's buildings viewed, it is not without its critics. While a sociological study has been carried out which revealed that the children can understand its structure and

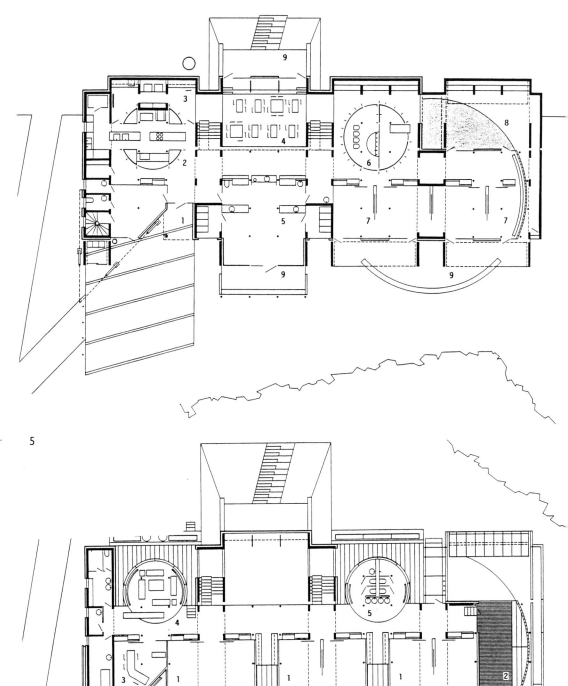

5 Ground-floor plan.
Key:
1 entrance
2 open-plan kitchen
3 laundry
4 foyer/dining area
5 day nursery
6 open-plan toilet/washroom
7 play area for two- to four year-olds
8 external play courtyard
9 terrace

6 First-floor plan.
Key:
1 infants' area for one- to ten-year-olds
2 roof terrace
3 director's office
4 staff meeting room
5 lavatories

7 Second floor/attic level plan. Attic play galleries.

8 Long secton.

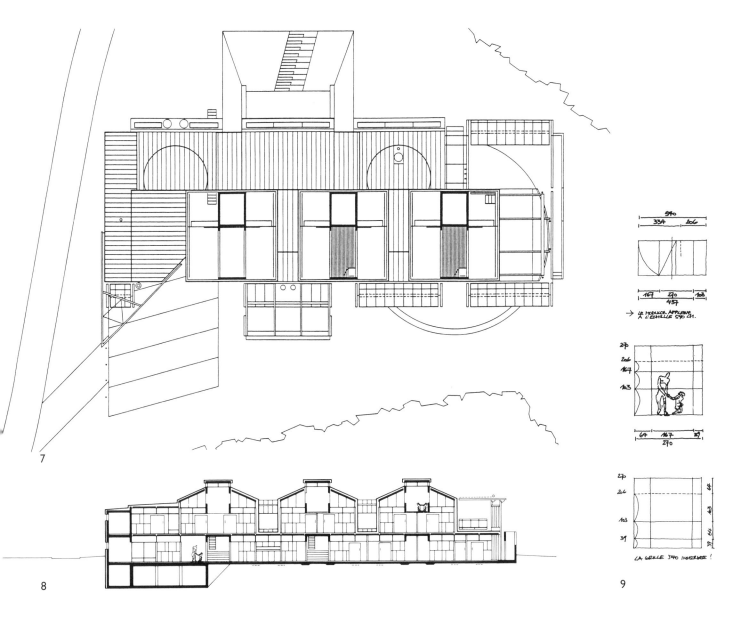

9 Modular child-scale drawing.

10 Corner construction detail.

indeed relate well to it, nevertheless some of the teachers find it extremely difficult to understand, mainly because of its openness and stylistic eccentricity. From the outset, the children used the building much more effectively than some of the adults, adapting to its technical transparency (all the services are exposed), and using it as a vehicle for their own development. As the Principal remarked, 'It is they [the children] who have taught us how to use the building'.[7]

Special significance: it combines both closed classroom forms with an open-plan arrangement to create a new hybrid form of pre-school.

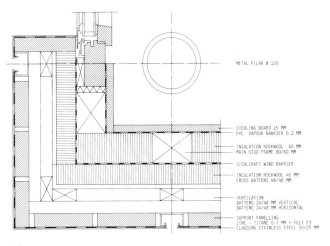

METAL PILAR ø 120

STERLING BOARD 15 MM
PVC VAPOUR BARRIER 0.2 MM

INSULATION ROCKWOOL 60 MM
MAIN STUD FRAME 80/60 MM

SISALCRAFT WIND BARRIER

INSULATION ROCKWOOL 40 MM
CROSS BATTENS 48/48 MM

VENTILATION
BATTENS 24/48 MM VERTICAL
BATTENS 24/48 MM HORIZONTAL

SUPPORT PANELLING
ZINC - TITANE 0.7 MM + FELT F3
CLADDING STAINLESS STEEL 50/25 MM

10

Stensby Personalbarnehage, Akerhus

Architect: Kristin Jarmund AS Arkitekter MNAL, Oslo. Designed by Kristin Jarmund, chief architect. Design team: Ola Helle, Gro Eileraas. Client project manager: Akerhus Fylkeskommune by Ingrid Hildrum.

Client: Stensby Hospital.

Occupancy: 60 pre-school children (up to six) in four 15-child 'departments'.

Construction cost: 6.1 million NKr.

Construction: load-bearing lightweight blockwork rendered with timber superstructure, blue asphalt roofing felt.

Completed: July 1993.

Classrooms/activity areas: 320m^2. Storage: 10m^2. Total area: 445m^2, 7.4m^2 per child. Garden area: 9600m^2 (play area 3400m^2).

Parking: spaces for five cars, to complement existing hospital parking.

The architects felt it essential to give this new nursery, located within the site of a large modern hospital, a distinctive form and scale. This manifests itself as a sequence of walls through which the children must pass before entering the south-facing activity areas. The first of these is a long, curved external wall orientated towards the north-east. Punctured and penetrated along its length by a number of architectonic 'events' such as the semi-circular 'fairytale cage', the wall discreetly suggests that there is something very interesting taking place behind.

An entrance pavilion straddles and projects beyond this external wall and once through it a children's world begins to open up. The second internal 'wall' is a service spine of wash-rooms and WCs, kitchens and storage rooms, and a quiet waiting area for parents. A corridor links all the spaces running between both walls. It takes north light from high-level clerestory windows and provides a calm, tranquil atmosphere prior to entering the play areas.

Passing through the service spine into the activity areas, the building takes on a lighter, more whimsical quality. Where the north face of the building is closed and heavy, the south face is

1 The south face of the building opens up to the sunny garden and views towards the forest beyond.

2 The internal face of the curved wall contrasts with the hospital face in a warm terra-cotta colour. The wall extends beyond the building and is used as a play sculpture with stairs, windows and a slide.

3 Site plan.

2

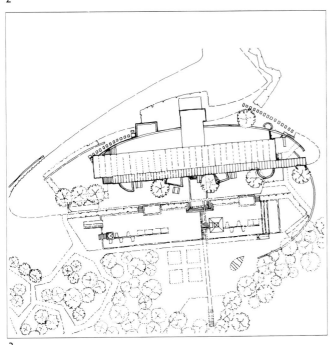

3

glassy and fragmented, with low sun pouring in through the large windows, affording views towards the forest beyond. The group rooms consist of three spaces. A quiet room and an activity area are both contained within the enclosure of the building. The third space is a so-called 'play box', a self-contained element that penetrates the external glass wall, extending the area into the garden beyond. Each box has its own distinct form and colour appearing as a small building in its own right. These host different types of play, and can be closed off as required to give children privacy within an otherwise open-plan building.

The colours of the four boxes symbolically represent the four seasons – a colour language repeated throughout the building, to provide a coding that enables the children to understand where they belong whichever part of the building they find themselves. The staff areas are located around the entrance lobby at first-floor level, symbolically separated from the nursery and connected by a staircase and bridge which pass over the entrance lobby. Every part of the building appears to be in balance, providing a constant reminder to the children of their own individuality refected in an architecture that is 'holistic', modern and user-friendly. The architectural language relies on a

Stensby Personalbarnehage, Akerhus

4

4 North-facing entrance elevation, showing the curved wall
encircling the nursery like a
protective arm. To the left of
the two-storey entrance pavilion, the children's secret fairytale cage is exposed.

5 Ground-floor plan.
Key:
1 entrance
2 lobby with stairs to first-
   floor staff room
3 staff changing rooms
4 waiting area and link to
   garden
5 open kitchen
6 laundry
7 play rooms
8 play 'boxes'
9 reading areas
10 children's cloakrooms
11 WC/washroom for children
12 staff WC
13 store
14 fairytale cage
15 plant room/heating

5

6 First-floor plan.
Key:
1 WC
2 office
3 stair
4 staff room

6

contrast between openness and enclosure, between small
dimensions and larger scales, using the wall as an architectural
device to encourage visual and physical play. Children feel safe
and comfortable, yet stimulated by the sophisticated synthesis
of form and colour.

Special significance: it creates clear boundaries with the use of
colour, and also provides internal wet rooms that can be
messed-up then easily cleaned.

7 Cross-section

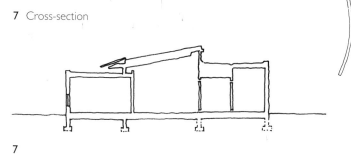

7

188

Lützowstrasse Kindertagesstätte, Berlin

Architect: Prof. Klaus Zillich with Prof. Jasper Halfmann, Berlin.

Client: Bezirksamt Tiergarten von Berlin, represented by the Senat Department for Building and Housing.

Occupancy: 75 pre-school children in three mixed age groups, for babies and children up to six with a creche/drop-in centre.

Construction cost: approximately 5 million DM.

Construction: concrete frame with part load-bearing brickwork, slightly pitched asphalt roof, double glazed 'winter garden' supported by curved timber laminated beams.

Completed: August 1993.

Activity areas: 220m^2. Storage: 8m^2. Total area: 751m^2, 10m^2 per child. Garden area: 1109m^2.

Parking: none.

This day care centre is one of the final projects of Berlin's International Building Exhibition (IBA) and is one of the most unusual. Instead of using the recommended IBA planning approach, the perimeter block, the architects have ignored the site edges and straddled the new building across the site in a diagonal, slightly off-centre position. At first sight it appears to be quite arbitrary, reinforcing the fragmented nature of the area as yet unrepaired from wartime bombing. The narrow end of the building is set at an angle to the street, stepping up in section towards the back party wall of the adjacent building. While this opens up the interior of the block, the general effect of incompleteness is considered by some to be anti-urban.

However, despite the seemingly wilful disregard for Berlin's planning laws, the building is extremely pragmatic in serving the needs of the children for sun and fresh air almost as if it was in the middle of the country. The building adopts an odd angle on its site due to its strict east–west orientation. Architect Klaus Zillich explains this as architecture based on 'solar geometry'. All the children's activity areas with their external play terraces at the front are orientated to catch the sun. Indeed, the stepped form of the building is rigorously designed to draw the lowest angles of the winter sun into the depths of the plan. The large glazed hall or 'winter garden' is placed on the east side of the building to catch the morning sun, while the large play bay windows in the group rooms take the afternoon sun. Children play

1

2

1 View of winter garden and access doors to morning play space.

2 External view of winter garden.

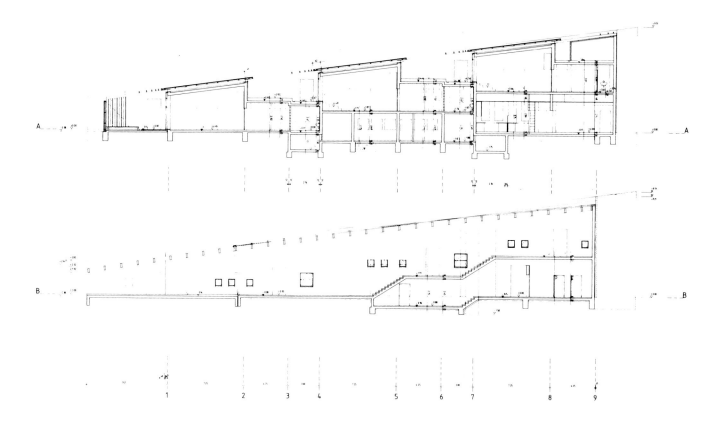

3

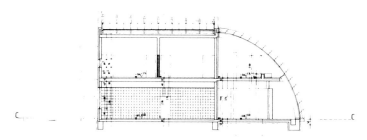

3 Long section through the sun terraces and activity areas.

4 Cross-section through the entrance.

5 West elevation.

4

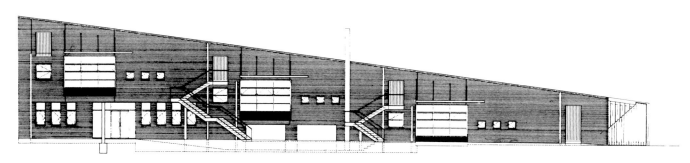

5

6

6 Upper level of the winter garden, used as an inside–outside classroom.

8 First- and second-floor split-level plan, showing two apartments with gallery access.
Key:
1   apartment two
2   apartment three
3   external sun terrace
4   upper level within the glazed winter garden

in the west-facing garden in the afternoon, closest to the point where their parents arrive to collect them. There is also a separate crèche facility beneath the building, orientated towards this garden.

Providing full-day care for 75 children up to the age of six, the school divides them into mixed age groups of 25 children in each. They are accommodated in spacious 'apartments', similar to their own home environments. The clear pedagogic implication was that each apartment should have the same condition, and this has been achieved by the adoption of a clever stepped section, which gives each of the three children's 'apartments' its own sun terrace, its own large west-facing bay window and its own front door These are accessible off the winter garden, a sloping conical curved form which not only provides access to

all parts of the building, but is large enough to host social activities such as weekend parent meetings and Christmas fairs, to provide the kindergarten with a much wider social purpose. Although prone to overheating problems on the hottest summer days, its scale and form provide a memorable counterpoint to the largely cellular spaces inhabited by the children at home and in their kindergarten apartments. From front to back this quarter barrel vault sinks gently into the ground, to create a diminishing perspective which makes the space seem even more elongated than it is.

Special significance: its use of 'solar geometry', and its apartment organization combining mixed age pre-schoolers from babies up to six-year-olds.

7 Ground-floor plan.
Key:
1   corridor
2   head teacher
3   store WC
4   kitchen
5   staffroom
6   winter garden
7   access to upper levels
8   plant room/garden service areas
9   storage
10 WC/washroom
11 entrance to apartment one
12 bay window play space
13 three-zone activity area
14 'stage' area with storage under
15 sun terrace
16 external loggia, access to east-facing morning garden
17 access from apartment two to the west-facing parents' garden

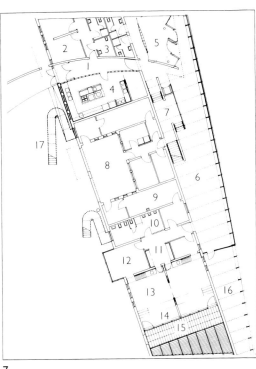

7

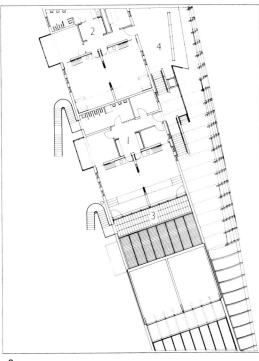

8

Gross-Ziethener Chaussee Kindertagesstätte, Neukölln, Berlin

Architect: Hannelore Deubzer and Jürgen König, Berlin.

Client: Senat Department for Building and Housing.

Occupancy: 36 small children (babies up to three), 60 kindergarten children (four- to six-year-olds), kinderhort study spaces for 80 afternoon schoolchildren.

Construction cost: 8 million DM.

Construction: concrete frame structure, rendered sand–lime masonry walls and zinc roofs.

Completed: June 1994.

Classrooms/activity areas: 1236m^2. Storage: 14m^2. Total area: 2234m^2, 12.6m^2 per child. Garden area: approximately 900m^2.

Parking: none.

1 Site plan.

2 View down from the nest into the lower part of the activity area.

3 The clearly articulated structure of the interior.

The patterns and memories of childhood . . . compel us to look back at the past and recall our own pictures, rooms, sense of wellbeing and familiar smells. Our intention is to provide children with rooms that allow them more freedom than they would otherwise enjoy at home, compensating for the familiar surroundings that they have left behind. *Architects' statement*

This children's centre is located in the very south of the city of Berlin, close to open countryside beyond the site of the former Wall. Whereas the Lützowstrasse 'Kita' responded to its site in Berlin by completely ignoring it, the form of this building is initially generated by its context. In the three house shapes of the group rooms and its low horizontal form, the suburban references are explicit.

The area is socially mixed, with middle- and working-class predominantly low-rise housing. Open from 7am, the facility serves the needs of working parents, particularly single mothers; however, the institution also caters for 80 school-age children who arrive in the afternoons. The intention was to create a building that would provide contained, private spaces for the pre-school children but could also be used by all the children as well as parents and even outside evening class groups. From the outset, this was intended to be much more than a kindergarten: it was to be a social condenser. The architecture successfully reflects this, without compromising its primary role as a kindergarten.

The commission was won in a limited competition, and is a vivid, strong architecture reminiscent of the American master Louis Kahn. The interior provides a sense of openness with long

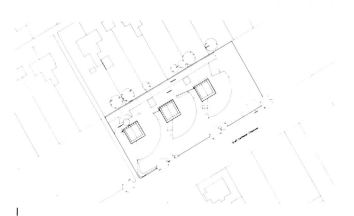

1

2

Gross-Ziethener Chaussee Kindertagesstätte, Neukölln, Berlin

4 Ground-floor plan.
Key:
1 entrance and pram store
2 refuse
3 head teacher's office
4 staff WC and kitchen
5 courtyard
6 staff meeting room (may be hired out)
7 lift
8 additional meeting room
9 classrooms for babies and children up to the age of three
10 multi-use double-height space with children's gallery
11 kindergarten classrooms and play/action room
12 music and movement space
13 kinderhort games space
14 kinderhort activity rooms
15 WCs/washrooms

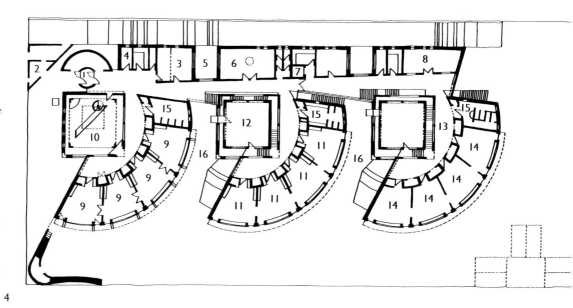

4

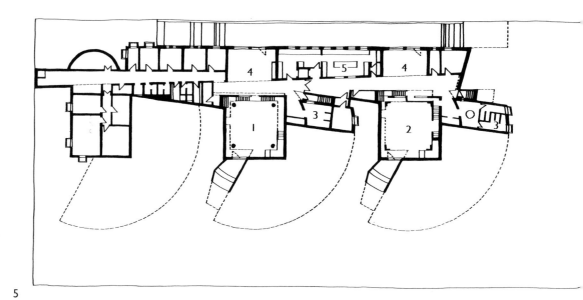

5 Basement plan.
Key:
1 dancing/movement space
2 music room
3 WC
4 open dining areas
5 open-plan kitchen

5

vistas, but without sacrificing a sense of stability and weight in the expression of the architecture. This subtle balance is achieved by two organizing principles. First, the programme naturally separates the accommodation into three parts, with a washroom and four classrooms in each. These rooms are each organized in a crescent shape, with radiating views out into the garden and, more interestingly, internally into a semi-open-plan activity space. The second organizing device is a long circulation 'spine', which links the three activity parts and contains service rooms and offices. Within the clarity of this planning, a complicated cross-section connects all the levels of the building, with discreet views across, in and down into each of the activity spaces. These open activity spaces are wrapped by a double skin wall, which contains gentle staircases down, with monumental cut-outs framing the views.

6 Interior of activity area with children's nest.

6

7

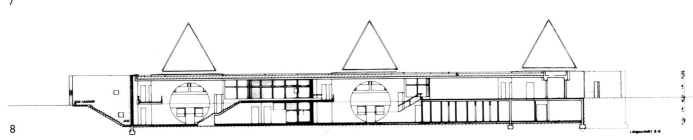

8

Each of the activity spaces is described in the following sequence: a multi-use gym space, a play and action room, and a music space. The semi-openness of the architecture encourages the natural enquiring spirit of children to explore what is taking place in other parts of the building. Music drifts unobtrusively along the open-plan spine, just as the gaze of children is extended beyond their own classroom areas to other parts of the community. It is all beautifully lit by a mixture of top and sidewindows to promote dramatic shadows and diverse qualities of light, especially on sunny days. Even on the dullest of days the building remains bright without the need for artificial lighting. Each of the activity areas is topped by an archetypal child's symbol, a little house roof, identifying the children's areas from the street outside. The children can explore the full extent of the building and identify with the whole as well as their own special areas.

7 View from the external play area towards the central activity 'house', with classrooms curving into the recess of the building with a recently planted children's herb garden.

8 Long section.

9 Cross-section through the central activity space.

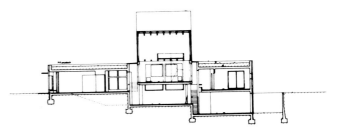

9

Open-Air Kindergarten Annexe, Takarazuka, Japan

Architect: Katsuhiro Miyamoto and Atelier Cinquième Architects, Takarazuka.

Client: Takarazuka Mukoyama Kindergarten.

Occupancy: 100 pre-school children in a number of part-time groups – 15 three-year-olds in one class; 20 four-year-olds in two classes; 20 five-year-olds in two classes. Each group uses the kindergarten and garden at different times of the day. Mothers' group meet in the basement.

Construction cost: 39.78 million yen (annexe only).

Construction: steel frame and reinforced concrete with stoneware tiles and Japanese cyprus timber fittings.

Completed: October 1992.

Classrooms/activity areas: total building: playrooms 118.2m², classrooms 215m², meeting rooms 47.5m². Storage: 36m². Total: 381m². Total built area: 575m², 5.76m² per child. Garden: 406m². Site area: 1067m². Annexe only: playrooms 40m², meeting rooms 24.8m². Storage: 5.9m². Total: 64.9m². Total built area: 72.8m², 4.5m² per child.

Parking: none.

Designed as an annexe to the main school, this small kindergarten provides a mothers' meeting room and a new ground-floor play space at the far end of the site, furthest away from the existing school buildings. Different groups of children use the facility at different times, making the 'journey' from their more conventional enclosed classrooms to this unusual open-air environment.

The original brief was to provide a garden shelter in commemoration of the 40th anniversary of the opening of the original kindergarten, a natural extension of the school's play facilities in Takarazuka's hot, humid climate. The architect has taken this idea to its logical conclusion by creating a building that opens up completely to the external environment: the two garden façades lift up and over on gas springs, to provide unobstructed access between the play space and the existing garden. Yet the environment is controlled, and can therefore be used throughout the year.

The fully retractable window walls are ingeniously supported by a part-cantilevered roof, which negates the need for column supports around the perimeter walls on the two garden sides. Minimalist translucent panels add to the effect of a roof which seems to float above the ground, creating a subtle distinction between the more formal playroom space and the garden itself. This creates a freedom of movement between inside and outside which is of great therapeutic benefit, particularly for the youngest children who may initially feel oppressed by the more formal enclosed teaching spaces of the main school building. Here, the dynamism of the architecture clearly makes a major

1 Site plan.
Key:
1 garden
2 main school buildings
3 open-air kindergarten

2 Playroom interior: natural timber floors complement the lightness of the walls.

3 Lighting is important: tungsten halogen transforms the facility into a stage set for public meetings during long humid summer evenings.

1

2

3

Open-Air Kindergarten Annexe, Takarazuka, Japan

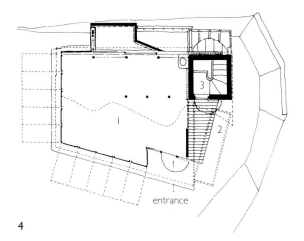

4

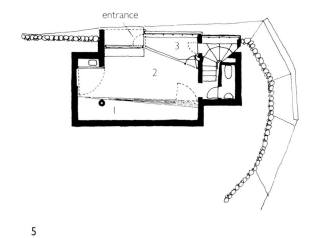

entrance

5

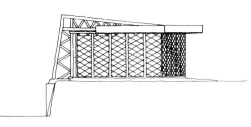

6

7

8

4 Ground-floor plan.
Key:
1 play room
2 open verandah
3 staircase

5 Basement plan.
Key:
1 storage
2 mothers' club
3 Tsuboniwa garden

6 North elevation showing the openable wall/window in closed position.

7 East–west section.

8 Structural columns are set back, and much of the roof support comes from a steel cantilevered truss that minimizes obstruction around the two opening perimeter walls.

9 North-west view from the children's play-yard with the wall/windows closed.

10 Mothers' basement room, a safe 'hideaway' with its own rear entrance.

contribution to the children's behaviour, encouraging their desire for exploration between the protection of the teachers' classroom groups and the autonomy of their own outside activities.

The complex asymmetrical form of the building is texturally rich, combining a broad range of contrasting materials including steel, glass, rustic stone and natural wood. However, the atmosphere remains calm and informal. Certainly, the children in each group view their time in the annexe as a particular treat!

Special significance: an alternative play-space which provides an extra dimension within the framework of a conventional school environment.

9

10

Scuola dell' Infanzia Diane, Reggio Emilia

Architect: Municipal Architects' Dept, Reggio Emilia, under the direction of Loris Malaguzzi.

Client: City of Reggio Emilia, Child Care Services.

Occupancy: 75 pre-school children from three to five, in three single-age groups.

Annual maintenance costs: £15, 000.

Construction: concrete frame, timber frame window/door infill panels with brick, slightly pitched asphalt roof.

Completed: 1971, frequently adapted with furniture and finishes built or specified by teachers and parents.

Classrooms/activity areas: 260m². Storage: no specific allocation. Total area: 800m², 10.67m² per child. Garden area: 1600m².

Parking: spaces for two to three cars.

It has been said that the environment should act as a kind of aquarium which reflects the ideas, ethics, attitudes and lifestyles of the people who live in it. We have been working along these lines.[8] *Loris Malaguzzi*

Architecturally this is a modest building; however, in many respects it illustrates the way in which the educational needs of children, when understood and translated into building, can generate superb and harmonious interior architecture. The structure of this 25-year-old building comprises a simple concrete frame, with bays spanning five metres across and seven metres deep. Within this framework the activity spaces are organized asymmetrically around the entrance hall or 'piazza'. Beyond this hall is an art studio separated by a gridded glazed screen, which is modulated to the height of the children. The three activity areas are accessed off

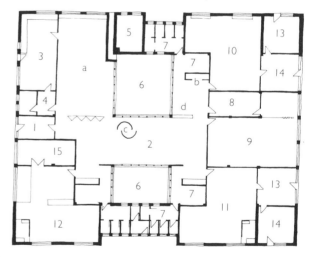

1

1   Plan.
Key :
1   entrance hall with notice boards
2   'piazza', containing (a) dining room, (b) puppet theatre, (c) cloakroom for dressing up, (d) shop
3   kitchen
4   larder

5   plant room
6   courtyard or 'little garden'
7   washrooms/lavatories
8   office
9   central art room
10 classroom for five-year-olds
11 classroom for four-year-olds
12 classroom for three-year-olds
13 music room
14 small art room

2

3

this central space. Each self-contained *sezione* is subdivided into social play areas, quiet spaces and music spaces, to create an internalized representation of the ideal city's social structure. Within this architecturally neutral form, the staff have devised a number of focal points or little events that relate closely to the educational curriculum and complement the interior architecture.

Immediately on entering the building within the lobby there is a noticeboard which provides contact between the school and the parents. Activities are explained, timetable changes and weekend events advertised. Moving through into the piazza, there is a large two-metre-high drum form which contains coats and dressing-up clothes, the first of a series of 'events' that punctuate the large open-plan piazza. A shop, a puppet theatre and other activity areas litter the space. The context or background for this is bright

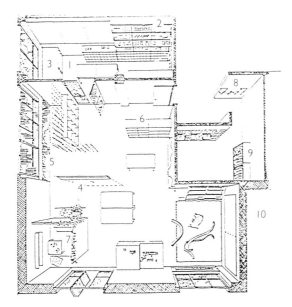

4

2 The garden elevation.

3 The garden tunnel and sand play area.

4 Axonometric view of classroom for three-year-olds, indicating main activities.
Key:
1 small art room

2 materials store
3 paper rack
4 roller blind
5 large mirror
6 individual storage area
7 little 'house'
8 programme of events
9 cloakroom
10 atrium

and airy, with a floor surface of light blue ceramic tiles and generous daylighting which appears to enter from all directions – an effect achieved by the use of little courtyards placed strategically within the centre of the deep plan. The walls are decorated with the children's art, and a profusion of green planting drapes down the sides of windows and walls, a strong factor in establishing a warm, fresh environment – a children's greenhouse which is cool and well ventilated. Within the open-plan piazza is the dining area, a communal zone where all the children can meet and eat together in a single sitting. This is considered to be a crucially important socializing point in the middle of the day.

Beyond the piazza the inner activity areas are visible through partly glazed partitions. The illusion of privacy within an open environment is a balance achieved by the subtle definition of different areas and spaces. Slightly dropped ceilings, and floor surfaces that change from hard ceramic tile, used in the piazza, to warm smooth timber in the activity areas, create subtle definitions between each space. Thus the sense of freedom of movement between the different areas of the kindergarten is maintained, yet at the same time children are made aware of what is and what is not their own territory. Access from the activity areas into the garden is provided through large glazed doors, which open during the summer months as a practical extension to the activity areas.

The staff, who have worked in the same building for many years, believe that children perceive space quickly and that the environment is important to them. Consequently, they spend a great deal of time ensuring that exhibitions change frequently to provide personality within the interior. The well-proportioned simplicity of the form ensures that the children are always confident about their surroundings, understanding what is temporary and what is permanent. Diane is an experiment in creating children's spaces by trial and error through a precise understanding of the pedagogic system, and its reflection as aesthetically harmonious interior architecture. This is achieved within the context of a clear form, treating the architecture as background to the children and their activities. It is spacious, elegant and decorated in a restrained manner so that the architectural simplicity is never overwhelmed by the artwork or the activities that take place within. It is a fascinating environment for children, providing a balance between social and private spaces in a coherent architectural style.

Special significance: it employs an open and advanced curriculum within a neutral architectural form.

Børnehus, Viborg Seminariet

Architect: Petersen and Aaris, Viborg, Denmark, designed by Svend Erik Petersen.

Client: Viborg College of Education for Pre-school and Child Care Teachers.

Occupancy: 50–60 children from two to six.

Construction cost: 2.3 million Danish kroner.

Construction: former artisans' terraced cottages converted laterally; painted, rendered masonry walls and red tiled roof.

Completed: 1989.

Activity areas: (including corridor and open-plan kitchen – no classrooms): 160m². Storage (including external storage sheds): 40m². Total area: 360m², 6m² per child. Garden area: 1520m².

Parking: spaces for seven cars.

This former terrace of artisans' houses has been laterally converted to provide a full-day kindergarten facility. Although funded as part of the town's educational system, it is used extensively by the adjacent teacher-training facility and has developed a sophisticated relationship between the pre-school environment and the pre-school educational curriculum. Local architect Svend Petersen has retained the external form of the building, reversing the former eight entrances from the street to make instead two main entrances into the building from the garden at the rear. The only evidence of a new building from the street is the white timber storesheds and cloakroom/WC appendages adjacent to either entrance.

However, once inside the building, the traditional form of cross party walls has been disregarded and a long, open corridor spine runs the length of the building.

The visitor is made immediately aware of the openness of the facility with vistas into all parts. There are a number of cellular rooms into which children can withdraw; however, the overwhelming sense is of a building which is open-plan and spatially fluid. Wherever possible the architect has exposed the roof structure. White partitions, integrated fixed furniture and services enhance the elegant simplicity; however, the most effective intervention is the timber floor, which runs throughout the building, a light warm surface which makes the once-cellular

1 Site plan showing garden.
Key :
1 theatre
2 adventure playground
3 wild gardens
4 bicycles
5 shed
6 sand pit
7 barn
8 trough
9 bonfire site
10 planter

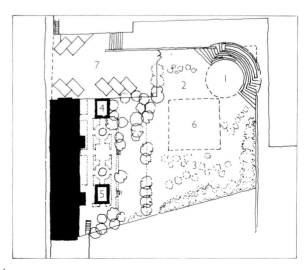

1

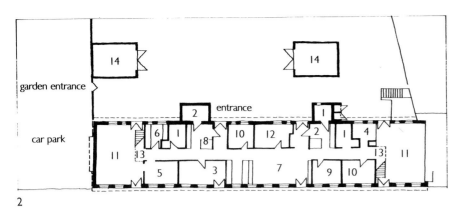

2 Ground-floor plan.
Key :
1 toilet/WC
2 cloakroom
3 office
4 bench
5 paddling pool
6 reading or rest room
7 kitchen or commonroom

8 store
9 staff room
10 enclosed room
11 activity areas
12 sliding partition
13 loft (over)

3 Children's washroom and WC, simple and practical.

2

3

building seem homogeneous, encouraging the children to move freely from space to space.

There are two conventional activity areas, one at either end. The southern end is a music space and adjoining it is a small paddling pool sunk into the floor. A staircase leads up to a loft which overlooks the space. It is an area which is clearly meant for children, and it can be used in any way as long as activities in the music room are not disrupted. In the northern activity space there is a sand pit built into the floor and beside it a small hearth, a remnant from the former domestic building. A staircase leads up to another loft space which has been furnished and decorated like an old-fashioned sitting room with a sofa and full-size chairs, along with a double bed. When the sand pit is not in use it can be covered over, and the space becomes a dressing-up area with floor-to-ceiling mirrors. A range of different costumes is provided, hanging on child-height rails. It becomes possible for the children to play in ways that are usually restricted to outdoor areas.

All the spaces in this pleasant environment appear uncluttered and simple. The interior could almost pass as a fashionable clothes shop – never hectic or noisy, almost minimalist in feel. The architect states that the rooms and the way in which they are considered is of primary importance, since they are expressions in their own right, as important as any form of expression; just as one would not expect to see an unhappy teacher every morning, the same logic applies to the environment:

5 Main activity area with steps leading up to the children's loft.

6 Sketch of the former row of artisan's cottages prior to conversion.

for that reason we must make something of them [the spaces], to ensure that they don't seem accidental or a matter of indifference. Aesthetic considerations are discussed before any purchase of furniture or equipment: quality of design, material and colour are taken into account . . . In short, we try to maintain a high level of awareness in our activities with the children, and to our surroundings, both indoors and out.[9]

Although the intention was to create a homely atmosphere, this is an extremely elegant and comfortable interior, which works in tandem with the garden. The simplicity of the light floor set against the heaviness of the external walls provides a strangely harmonious balance between old and new. This project shows that an imaginative response to the curriculum needs of young kindergarten children can create good kindergarten spaces.

4 Architect's sketch of curriculum play activities inside the kindergarten: sand pit, fireplace and loft – elements of the domestic environment.

5

4

6

Scuola dell' Infanzia e Asilo-nido Cantalamessa, Bologna

Architect: Stefano Magagni, Architects' Dept, City of Bologna.

Client: City of Bologna Child Care Services.

Occupancy: 156 pre-school children in the following groups: 36 babies and toddlers up to the age of three, divided in four groups; 75 full-day children aged three to six; 20 part-time three- to six-year-olds; 25 places in a two-hour 'drop-in' centre.

Construction cost: £1.05 million.

Construction: the kindergarten is a conversion of an old palazzo. The new single storey baby unit is a concrete frame structure with brick infill panels and a flat asphalt roof.

Completed: October 1993.

Kindergarten classrooms: 310m^2. Storage:15m^2. Total area: 550m^2, 7m^2 per child.

Attic 'drop-in' centre activity areas: 190m^2. Storage: none. Total area: 225m^2.

Baby centre activity areas: 272m^2. Storage: none. Total area: 450m^2, 16m^2 per child. Garden area: approximately 1 acre.

Parking: none.

A dilapidated Palladian style palazzo on the outskirts of the city of Bologna was donated to Child Care Services and the site is in the process of being transformed into a children's world, which is already providing care and education of the highest environmental quality. The architects, in consultation with educationalists, psychologists and other experts, established a structure that was intended to serve a wide range of different needs.

A kindergarten for full-time children aged three to six is accommodated on the raised ground floor and first floor of the refurbished palazzo. On the attic level, with its own separate entrance, there is a 'drop-in' centre where mothers who perhaps do not require full-time care for their children can come for a couple of hours a day, to establish contact with other parents and acquaint their youngsters with the social world. In the basement there is a service area with a kitchen and staff facilities. The baby unit (for children up to three) is located in a completely new building connected to the palazzo at the ground floor by a glazed corridor. It was felt that the particular needs and the significant scale difference between babies and four- and five-year-olds justified the new structure.

The palazzo accommodation is organized around the thick structural walls which divide the building. On the ground floor there is a generous entrance with parents' noticeboards. A new glass staircase faces this, with a small office to its left. The classrooms are either side of this lobby space; both have lavatories

1. The Palazzo kindergarten, with blinds drawn against the midday sun.

1

Scuola dell' Infanzia e Asilo-nido Cantalamessa, Bologna

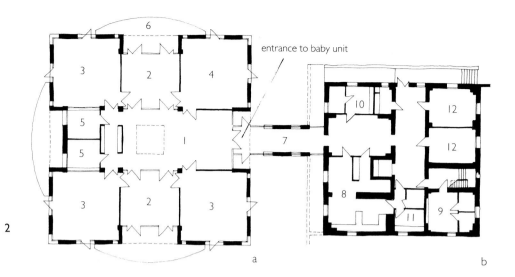

2

entrance to baby unit

a

b

2 Ground-floor plan.
Key:
1 atrium
2 art room
3 activity spaces
4 dormitory
5 washrooms/WC
6 garden terrace
7 glazed link
8 kitchen
9 store
10 staff area
11 WC
a the baby unit
b palazzo service level

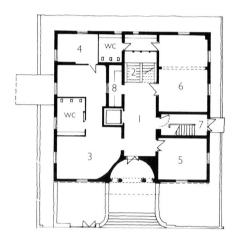

3

3 Raised ground-floor of palazzo.
Plan of kindergarten.
Key:
1 entrance with lift
2 main staircase
3 classroom one with WC block
4 quiet area
5 art studio
6 classroom two with WC

7 staircase up to 'drop-in' centre
8 office

4 Entrance elevation of baby unit.

5 The garden entrance, linked to the basement level of the Palazzo.

4

5

which are ingeniously slotted in around the existing structure. The remaining space on this floor is a single 'atelier' room which can be used by any one of the three groups. This organization is effectively repeated on the first floor, with a classroom and a group activity room which can be used as a music and movement space. Although ceilings are high, they have acoustic finishes that nullify reverberation; suspended down-lighters effectively reduce the scale when the lights are used on dull days but the relatively large windows and bright reflective wall surfaces in blues and ochres reduce the need for this. Specially made furniture which is wholly related to the scale of young children creates an elegant matrix which enables the children to relate themselves within the large spaces. The uncluttered environment is maintained by ensuring that all materials are stored in coordinated movable cupboards which are accessible to the children.

The drop-in centre in the attic is served by a lift and has its own staircase so that part-time children can enter either through the main entrance or from the side of the building. The attic is ideally suited to the scale of the children, with low laminated timber beams drooping down to their head height. It is designed to be as flexible as possible with four distinct self-contained rooms that can be used by different-sized groups.

The form of the new baby unit is deliberately low and horizontal, not only to relate to the scale of the children but also to act as an architectural foil to the height and bulk of the adjacent

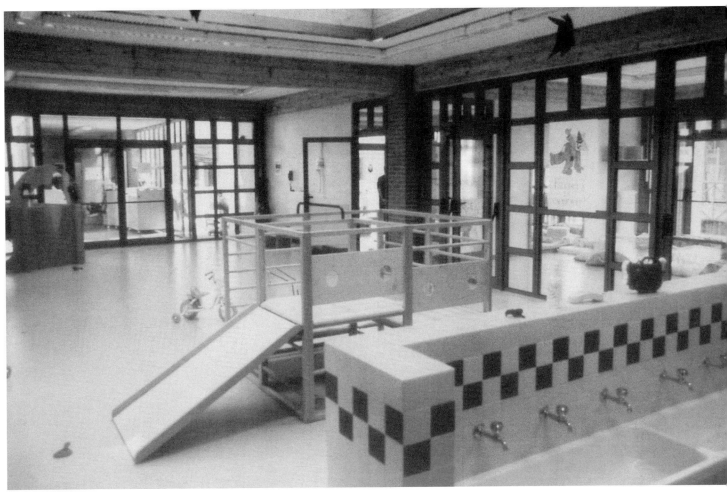

6

6 The baby unit's central atrium with washbasins in the foreground has a light, transparent quality. Note the faceted acoustic ceiling finish.

palazzo. The new unit is at basement level (almost as if it has been slid out from beneath), and the plan echoes the organization of the palazzo with a symmetrical quartic arrangement. The entrance is from the side, through a partly brick and partly gridded glazed entrance area. The unit is self-contained and inward-looking. The central communal space is naturally lit by a pyramid-shaped rooflight which is cooled by water trickling down from its apex; when the blue shading curtain is pulled across, the whole space is filled with a blue dappled light, soothing and fascinating. Around this central play space there are four identical enclosed rooms, which can be used either as sleeping or activity areas. Between them are two 'atelier' rooms intended for more messy craft-based activities. They are

glazed but shaded by being recessed further back behind the external wall.

The materials and colours are muted in the baby unit. The central space furthest from the entrance has an open wash space, and the whole atmosphere is homely with soft, plain curtains for all external windows. Although the building is divided into separate rooms, internal glazed panels, particularly those at the corners of the activity spaces, create privacy but also allow long diagonal vistas both in and out. The young child's perception of the world is a safe but unrestricted one in this pleasing environment.

Special significance: its programme is expertly organized to provide a range of different types of child care within a single site.

Neugereut Kindergarten, Stuttgart

Architect: Behnisch and Partner, Stuttgart, with project architect Christian Kandzia.

Client: Protestant Church of Stuttgart–Neugereut.

Occupancy: 60 pre-school children in two groups (today 56).

Construction cost: DM 432 000.

Construction: steel and timber frame with laminated timber beams and steel joints, with a flat projecting asphalt roof.

Completed: July 1977.

Classrooms: 136m^2. Storage: 9m^2 (plus 7.5m^2 added later as part of hall). Total area: 136m^2. Garden area: not known.

Parking: spaces for two cars.

Do we remember the layout of the flat or house where we spent our childhood? – We would have to think back for a while. But we do recall the worn sandstone steps, the flaking rendering on the bottom of the wall, the colourful glazing in the front door, the striking of a clock, the sound of a door closing, the smell of warm wood, the rain on our hands, the feel of sand beneath our feet . . .[10]

This romantic summary of Günther Behnisch's thoughts and preoccupations alludes to his own personal memories of senses heightened to the play of materials and nature as a young child. He is perhaps implying that as adults we lose this awareness. This building entwines itself around its natural setting, dissolving the boundaries between inside and outside, manifesting these sensory concerns through a series of child-orientated details to make it much more than merely romantic. Although small compared to the size of many contemporary German 'Kitas', it is perhaps a reminder of the modest ideals of the early kinder-

1 Plan.
Key :
1 covered external terrace
2 communal hall
3 activity area/class base
4 group room
5 materials store
6 head teacher's office
7 toilet/washroom

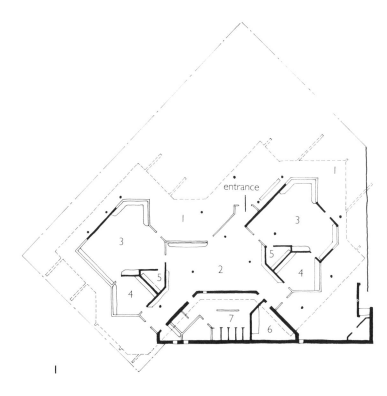

2 View of play-den roof. Note the structural and textural pattern making.

2

3 Group room. The natural materials and textures, with complementary furniture, provide a harmonious, warm evironment.

4 External terrace with projecting structure provides an 'inside–outside' quality, which is amplified by the lush and varied planting.

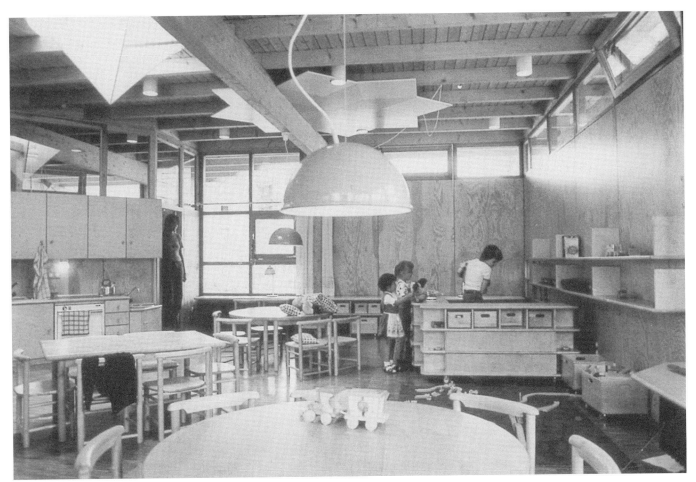

3

garten builders of the 1970s who provided domestic-scale spaces in an unassuming lightweight architectural form.

Located in a suburban area and surrounded by a mixture of high- and low-rise residential buildings, the challenge for the architects here was to create something special from a very low budget on a somewhat leftover triangular site. Although constructed some years ago (in a similar manner to the Reggio Emilia Diane kindergarten), the value in seeing this project now is to appreciate its mature form. It has a well-tended garden which has integrated itself naturally into the structure of the building as the architect intended, a well-maintained building

4

5. Timber fixing details.

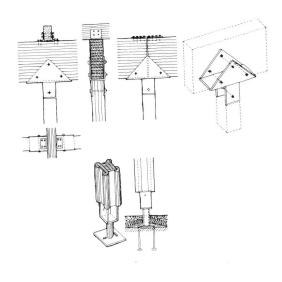

fabric and, most importantly, a sophisticated, liberal pedagogic system applied with commitment, professionalism and a profound understanding of the importance of the environment to pre-school kindergarten children.

The configuration of the building relates strongly to its site and construction. The geometric play of an orthogonal form set against the 45° angles of the site boundaries ensures that the internal spaces are full of interesting corners. The whole is unified by a single main structural system of laminated timber beams at 4-metre spacings, which sail over the spatial gymnastics of the plan. The entrance hall is designed as a transition space between inside and outside. Group spaces within the building are made by slightly above child-height partitions that allow adult views throughout yet maintain privacy for the children. The external walls provide sheltered niches and corners; with details such as transparent rainwater pipes and trickling water pools set into the terraces close to the activity areas (rather than being remote decorative features), a close connection to the natural elements is maintained, and the architecture is almost instantly comprehensible to the children.

5

References and notes

1. Day, Christopher (1995), *Caravan*, no. 2, April 1995, p. 20.
2. Behnisch, G. (1994), 'Kindergarten in Luginsland', Behnisch and Partner, October 1994.
3. Morris-Nunn, Robert (1994), 'Building Magical Realism', paper presented at the Royal Institute of Australian Architects' bi-annual conference, Hobart.
4. Skinner, P. *et al.* (1988), 'Bungawitta Children's Centre', *Architecture Australia*, July 1988, p. 44.
5. Scogin, Mack (1994), 'Children in Motion', *Architecture*, July 1994, p. 58.
6. Dietson, Deborah K. *et al.* (1989), 'Prefab pre-school', *Architectural Record*, June 1989.
7. Blundell Jones, P. *et al.* (1991), 'Kindergarten Contrasts', *Architectural Review – Schooling*, September 1991.
8. Malaguzzi, L. *et al.* (1987), *The Hundred Languages of Childhood, op. cit.*
9. Davidson, L. *et al.* (1991), *Children's House*, Educational Workshop, Viborg College of Education for Pre-school and Child Care Teachers.
10. Architekten Behnisch & Partner, *Arbeiten aus den Jahren 1952–1987*, exhibition catalogue, Stuttgart, München PT, p. 60.

Illustration acknowledgements

The author and publishers would like to thank the following individuals and organizations for permission to reproduce material. We have made every effort to contact and acknowledge copyright holders, although multiple changes of publisher have sometimes made this difficult. If any errors have been made we would be happy to correct them at a later printing.

Numbers appearing in **bold** refer to colour illustrations, which appear between pages 114 and 115.

Individuals and organizations

Peter Bareham: 2.29, 2.30
François Bertin: 4.1, 4.16
Tom Bonner: 4.45
British Architectural Library, RIBA, London: back cover
Courtesy of The Frank Lloyd Wright Foundation, Spring Green, Wisconsin: 2.25
Copyright © The Frank Lloyd Wright Foundation: 2.23, 2.27
The Froebel Educational Institute, London: 4.25
High/Scope Press, Ypsilanti, Michigan: 4.26
Christian Kandzia: 4.6; p. 209, Figs 2, 3, 4
Waltraud Krase: p. 179, Fig. 2; p. 168, Fig. 8
Le Corbusier/Le Jeanneret, copyright © DACS 1996: 2.34
Lewisham Local Studies and Archives: 1.1
Kenneth MacDonald: 3.10
Mitchell Library, Glasgow: 4.24
Kim Müller: front cover; **21, 22**; p. 190, Fig. 4
New Lanark Conservation Trust: 2.12
The Museum of Modern Art, New York: Ozenfant, *Fugue*, 1925, pencil, 18 x 24; Gift of the Artist: 2.19
Karin Nepilly: **3, 4** p. 147, Fig. 7
Henning H. Nielsen, Kompan A/S:
Royal Commission on the Ancient and Historical Monuments of Scotland, copyright ©: 2.17, 2.18

Ulrich Schwarz: pp. 192–3, Figs 2, 3
Ullstein Bilderdienst publishers, Berlin, copyright ©: 2.22
Victoria and Albert Museum, London: 2.28
Kris Weishaar: 4.28
William Lescaze Papers, Syracuse University Library, Department of Special Collections: 2.1, 2.2

Publications

Aus Zwei Mach Drei, a pamphlet published by Frankfurt City Architects Department: 4.35
'A Week in a Belgian Nursery School' in Tricia David (ed.) *Educational Provision for Our Youngest Children – A European Perspective* (1993), London, Paul Chapman Publishing Ltd., copyright © 1993: 1.7
Diana Hop, a brochure published by Scuola Comunale dell' Infanzia Diana, Reggio Emila, September 1990: 1.10
Progressive Architecture, July 1961, and the Estate of Frederick Kiesler, courtesy Jason McCoy Inc., New York: 3.8
Berg, Marjanna (1987) *Spatial Aspects of Social Organization – A Study of Building for Daycare*, Gothenburg, Chalmers University of Technology: 1.5
Saint, Andrew (1987) *Towards a Social Architecture*, New Haven, Connecticut, Yale University Press: 2.13
Herausgeber, *Moderne Schweizer Architektur* (1942), Basel, Verlag Karl Werner: 2.4, 2.9, 2.10, 2.11
Myles Wright, H. and Gardner-Medwin, R. (1938) *The Design of Nursery and Elementary Schools*, London, The Architectural Press: 2.7, 2.14, 2.20
Winkler, Klaus *Archigrad 1 – Planning and Building on the 50th Parallel*, Franfurt, Verlag AFW: 3.4

All other illustrations were provided by the author or the featured architectural practice.

Index

Index

Index